AN INSTITUTIONAL INVESTOR PUBLICATION

SIMULATION, OPTIMIZATION and EXPERT SYSTEMS

Dimitris N. Chorafas

PROBUS PUBLISHING COMPANY
Chicago, Illinois

This publication is designed to provide accurate and authoritative information in regard to the subject matter covered. It is sold with the understanding that the publisher is not engaged in rendering legal, accounting or other professional service.

Library of Congress Cataloging in Publication Data Available

ISBN 1-55738-231-X

Printed in the United States of America

BB

2 3 4 5 6 7 8 9 0

Contents

Foreword

Brian R. Bruce
Vice President, Asset Management
State Street Bank & Trust
Boston, Massachusetts

Dimitris Chorafas has written a very timely book. Technology is exploding upon the investment community. How does an average investor or investment professional understand this bewildering onslaught of new ideas? Enter Dimitris Chorafas. In a clear, simple, easy-to-understand manner, he has broken up this mass of information into smaller logical pieces and explained each one fully.

This book's topics, however, are not simple. Artificial intelligence, expert systems, and fiber optic networks are among the leading-edge topics covered in this volume. Despite the complexity of topics, the writing style is clear and easy to understand. Points are made simply in the text and the book's style is extremely easy to read.

The breadth of coverage of technology in this book is excellent. In-depth hardware topics like supercomputers, databases, and networks are covered. The software that works in conjunction with the hardware to process information is also analyzed, in addition to software uses in investment management, trading, and securities processing. Coverage is also given to important software modeling techniques like optimization and simulation. Finally, Chorafas looks at how that particular hardware and software enhances the ability of firms to compete.

All in all, this is a wonderfully complete book for those who want and need to keep abreast of the rapid technological advancements in the securities industry.

Brian R. Bruce

Foreword

Sam B. Gibb
Director of Technology
County NatWest
London, England

Securities trading is evolving as a reaction to the continued volatility in the financial markets. Like every evolutionary process only those who are equipped to adapt will survive. Through the 1990s investment banks and securities houses can no longer afford to be merely international. Worldwide competition demands they globally address their clients' needs—wherever, whenever. In the global marketplace the sun never sets. For an organization to be successful, it must master new and effective technologies. As the 21st Century approaches, it is not enough to look upon information technology (IT) to provide a competitive advantage; an integral business and IT infrastructure is what will provide the ability to adapt and survive the evolution.

Every investment bank and securities house expects business to become more competitive, competition to be fought
globally, and, as a result, margins to drop. For IT to support
the business in meeting this challenge it has to be effective.
Often the quantitative nature of new business can raise the
profile of technology from a facilitating medium to a powerful product generator in its own right. Technology can take
advantage in the growth of electronic delivery of market
information and in the development of intelligent analytical
application engineering to bestow its own competitive advantage.

These developments in IT, decreasing costs and increasing
capabilities, are changing the face of the securities business.
However, in order to take advantage, it is vital to build on a
sound technical infrastructure. The platform must provide a
cost-effective, high-performance systems architecture to underpin the future. A technical infrastructure will be effective
only if it can put the right information into the right hands
at the right time. If developing the infrastructure worthy of
being the backbone of the business appears a daunting task,
fear not, it is! But you're certainly not alone. Hopefully the
content of this book, with chapters covering topics spanning
the spectrum of issues, will provide you with some of the
insight and guidance needed.

The key to overall success in the 1990s and beyond will be:

1. Using information technology and communica-
    tions to good effect.

2. Having the right people in the right place at the
    right time.

It is people who use the information infrastructure; therefore, human skills need to be a priority. The right people
attract clients, and clients bring business. More and more, the
demands of the market place will require specialists with

in-depth understanding of their products and their markets across the globe. This will be supported by their general technology skills to ensure effective use of the supporting computer and communications power available to them. Specialist software engineers will be needed to manage and develop the technology within this fast moving environment. Flexible and creative minds combined with a high degree of motivation will be essential to seek out opportunities and create competitive advantage. Success will depend on a strong and focused management which has the ability to integrate both business and IT skills into a responsive, dynamic and competitive team.

Sam B. Gibb

Foreword

Morihiro Matsumoto
Deputy General Manager
Yamaichi Securities
Tokyo, Japan

Information and the analysis of information play a vital role in the securities markets. Based on all available information, an investor analyzes and evaluates the expected returns and assets and decides to invest in or withdraw from particular securities accordingly. In the same manner, a person who needs to raise funds for equipment and facilities, or for any other reason, analyzes sources of funds such as securities markets and banks around the globe.

Based on careful analysis of all available information, this manager will finance with securities if they appear in his analysis to best match the financial requirements. Fund managers, fund raisers, and other participants in the financial market try ardently to gather and analyze relevant information before deciding how to best fulfill their needs.

It is important to recognize that, when someone decides as a result of analysis to participate in the securities market, a security is only a tool or a means of applying that analysis. That is to say, the securities market as a whole provides its participants with tools to optimally utilize the information they have acquired and the analyses they have performed.

The above discussion raises two questions regarding securities houses: "What is the role of information in securities houses?" and "What is the source of revenues for the securities houses?"

The answers to both questions rest on the fact that information is the product sold by securities houses. Securities, in this sense, are only tools for selling information.

Some feel that the marginal value of information as a product has fallen due to the easy and instantaneous accessibility of large amounts of data from various media and vendors. This may be true for raw or roughly processed data; however, high quality analysis of raw data has further increased in value. The quality of data analysis differentiates suppliers of analyzed information and creates competitive advantage for the suppliers of high quality analysis.

As the economies of major countries and their financial markets become more sophisticated, securities houses need to provide information analysis services of higher quality in all financial areas. Furthermore, higher fees from better products enable them to increase profitability and enhance efficiency. Accordingly, the ability to produce first class analysis is a vital requirement for survival for securities houses in the globally competitive business environment.

Almost twenty years have passed since modern financial technology was first applied to the fields of proprietary trading and asset management. Roughly speaking, by uncovering the factors causing security price fluctuations, and measuring the sensitivity of each security to these factors, financial technology has allowed funds such as indexed funds to be systematically managed. More generally, financial technology has enabled managers to more accurately control risks and returns by controlling exposure to these factors, or to design around specific what-if scenarios.

Until recently, few financial technologies were available for active fund management, as the "efficient market hypothesis" which prevailed among the theorists implied that future moves could not be accurately forecasted. Nagging worries about the validity of this hypothesis remained, though, as certain experts seemed to be able to beat the market. Passive management, exemplified by indexed fund management, did not satisfy the needs of many fund managers. They were not content to leave the return on their investment up to exogenous unpredictable factors, such as the behavior of the whole market or of interest rates.

For this reason, there has been increasing pressure to develop new financial technologies to address active management of funds. Expert systems, using fuzzy logic and neural networks, have been employed to attempt to refine investment moves. From these efforts, tactical asset allocation techniques have emerged which challenge the random walk theory.

Financial technology has begun to spread in all asset management and trading areas of the securities market. The use of financial technology in these areas may obviate the need for experts, the loss of whom might otherwise substantially disrupt the business of the firm.

Computers have become increasingly important in the implementation of financial data analysis. In addition, securities houses need to maintain massive amounts of information about their current and potential clients. Furthermore, the importance of management information systems for internal communication and prompt strategic decision making has intensified.

As a result of these changes in the business environment, today's securities firms require advanced computer technology to collect investment data and create high quality information services, to maintain databases about clients and potential clients, and to collect, analyze and communicate strategic management information throughout the organization. For efficiency, processing and data bases should be distributed. Considering the huge cost of such a global network, it needs to be flexible for easy enlargement and modification, rather than simply stuck on the existing mainframe-oriented computer system. Finally, the system should be easy to use so that it can be easily propagated.

In short, for a securities house to survive amidst global competition, it must aggressively implement what I call "Financial Science," which is the integration of financial technology and computer science. Having superior Financial Science will allow a firm to provide more sophisticated information products and to expand the volume of assets managed.

When these information business lines are combined with outstanding business judgments and strategies resulting from internal use of Financial Science, an excellent company will result, and it will establish an indisputable position in this fast changing industry.

Morihiro Matsumoto

Preface

Securities traders are paid for results, not for time spent at a desk—and they make most of their money in bonuses, not in wages. Hence, they need all the assistance they can get from computers, communications, and mathematical models. Also, alert traders, as well as forex dealers and investment advisors, know that strategies formulated today will help to determine who dominates the markets tomorrow. That is why interactive computational finance is becoming an essential element in the competitive arena of Wall Street.

This book has been written not only for securities professionals who want to work with state-of-the-art technology, but also for managers who understand that in order to get a competitive edge in the market, investment banks and brokerage houses must take sophisticated approaches that utilize supercomputers, expert systems, distributed databases, imaging, interactive workstations, visualization, and intelligent networks.

In the foremost financial markets of the world, particularly New York, London, and Tokyo, computers, communications, and artificial intelligence are seen not only as tools for gaining an edge in the market and holding it, but also as a means for attracting brainpower. Know-how and leadership within the organization are more crucial than ever to investment bankers, whose clients tend to retain them only as long as they offer a superior quality of service. Chapter 1 of this book gives some pertinent examples of this technological revolution on Wall Street.

Chapter 2 brings under perspective European examples, explaining how the winds of change affect the financial industry in England and Switzerland. Chapter 3 demonstrates the way Japanese financial institutions have risen to the challenge.

Trading today requires a significant amount of financial and market research. Chapter 5 supports the thesis that quantitative approaches can be effective in gaining leadership in the financial markets, specifically in money management. This argument is documented with a number of practical examples.

Quantitative approaches are further explained in Chapter 6, which focuses on the analysis of investments and relationships; and in Chapter 7, in which the process of simulation and optimization in securities decisions is presented in a comprehensive, down-to-earth manner. The text is written for non-mathematicians.

Chapter 8 discusses the services a modern technological infrastructure should provide to investment banks and securities houses and reviews the current status of some financial organizations in this domain. High technology is a precondition for success in securitization and other financial products—but are we taking advantage of it?

More and more, financial products are being judged by the quality of their technological content.

Using practical examples from the United States and Japan, Chapter 8 explains how expert systems can offer a first-class service in trust management, and why today the use of knowledge engineering is a "must."

What is modern portfolio theory? Can we benefit from quantitative approaches to investing? Is there a place for qualitative solutions to asset management? Chapter 9 not only answers these questions, but also discusses market volatility, the fundamentals of the capital assets pricing model, and the alpha, beta, gamma, delta, and tau functions.

The subject of Chapter 10 is the polyvalent approach of computer-based trading. Practical examples are given of developing and implementing a trading system; then, the theoretical bases behind these constructs—systematic and specific risk, indexing, program trading, and portfolio insurance—are explained. The chapter concludes with a discussion of whether stock markets are efficient or inefficient.

Chapters 11, 12, and 13 focus on the three main areas of high technology today: intelligent networks, distributed databases, and supercomputers. Each chapter's topic is supplemented with practical examples.

I want to thank everyone who contributed to this book, especially Heinrich Steinmann and Kurt Wolf of the Union Bank of Switzerland, Sam B. Gibb, County Nat West; Hansruedi Wolfensberger and Dr. Peter Jackson, UBS Phillip and Drew; Edward Dunne, UBS Securities in New York; Dr. Gilbert Lichter, CEDEL; Colin Crook and Kenneth A. Hines, Jr., Citibank; DuWayne J. Peterson, Merrill Lynch; Fred M. Katz, Goldman Sachs; Thomas Cranfield, Manufacturers Hanover Trust; Dr. Gabriel Jakobson, GTE Laboratories; Haruyuhi Okuda, Mitsubishi Bank; Takeshi Shinohara, Nomura Securities; Eiichi Ueda, Mitsui Bank; Mitsuru Fuji, Nikko Securities; Shojiro Ono, Sanyo Securities; Marihiro Matsumoto, Yamaichi Securities; Dr. Josef Fritz, Oesterreichische Laenderbank; Dr. Peter M. Bennett, International Stock Exchange; Mike Flinder, Lloyds Bank; John Timlin, Allied Irish Bank; and Frank Shanley and Bernard Enright, Riada Securities.

Special thanks to Eva-Maria Binder for the artwork, typing, and index. Also to Probus Publishing Company for encouragement and support.

Dimitris N. Chorafas
Valmer and Vitznau

Chapter 1

Wall Street's High-Technology Revolution

Chapter 1

Wall Street's High-Technology Revolution

1. Introduction

The typical scientist may rebel at the idea that he or she should be a salesperson. But in financial institutions, even the best technical people will become liabilities if they do not make the effort to talk frequently and persuasively with marketers in their own organization. R and D (research and development) people must also learn how to function in a tight timetable. In banking, particularly in the securities industry, institutions that do not move fast may see competitors go to market with products similar to those sitting in their own laboratories.

In a dynamic financial industry new product development has become a prerequisite to profits, and product research is now part of the mainstream. Wall Street's "rocket scientists" are the number-crunchers and logicians who make up banks' and securities firms' R and D laboratories. They simulate bond market movements, plot interest rate trends, calculate option against spread (OAS), and estimate the best market timing. Some of their other specialties may include inventing new generations of securities backed up by almost any kind of debt; developing instrumental forex schemes in order to benefit from currency differences in financial markets; mapping out computerized trading strategies that fuel wild gyrations in stock prices; and devising complex hedging formulas for pension funds and other institutional investors.

In research and development, speed is the key to success. Says Morihiro Matsumoto, director of Strategic Product Development at Yamaichi Securities, "It is really tough for our competitors to catch up with us. We did a lot in the last three years and keep on moving very fast."

Communication between departments is especially critical in the service industries, and securities houses are advised to establish interdisciplinary teams to move products quickly from lab to market. Developers of financial services must be able to discuss the products on which they are working with the "front desk" (the salespeople); thus, securities houses and other financial institutions employing rocket scientists are teaching them to ask questions, listen for cues, be empathetic, and work toward consensus. Such techniques may sound obvious to salespeople, but to those whose training is mostly technical, they may not come naturally.

While rocket scientists must map the market into the computer, in many investment decisions the key issue is representation. Technicians therefore need a good understanding not only of economics and market fundamentals, but also of the viewpoint of the end user—for whom the new information systems are being built.

2. The Role of Research and Development in Financial Institutions

Research and development are key words at Morgan Stanley. Its management believes that in the coming years the largest market will be in packaging banking services for a diverse clientele, but with a touch of personalization for each client. This undertaking requires not only sensitivity in marketing, but also considerable technological assistance, applied within the framework of both relationship banking and transaction banking.

Relationship banking, in which corporations direct all their business to specific investment firms, has been common for years. Recently, however, it has been supplemented, and in some cases superseded, by transaction banking. That is, as a range of new financial products has been introduced, the ability to perform financial transactions quickly has become crucial to keeping a firm's business.

In the new style of banking, three factors stand out:

1. A firm hand is needed to assure the bank's dependability in innovative products and services.

2. Alternatives must be examined and tested in any financial market, at any time and from the viewpoint of different financial products.

3. Speed is essential, since a deal often has to be done before a competitor can offer a better one.

Thus, trading has become the profit center in many investment banks, with the trader's approach replacing the more traditional one of the corporate advisor who represented firms exclusively.

Efficient transaction banking requires considerable research, which, in many cases, has to be done in real time assisted by intelligent networks, distributed databases, supercomputers, and knowledge engineering. As a senior executive of a major securities house comments, "Heavy duty R and D is becoming a hallmark of modern banking."

Product and market research should be implemented with the help of proper expertise and the best equipment technology makes available. The supports to be developed on the software and hardware side are—

1. artificial intelligence constructs;

2. fourth- and fifth-generation languages;

3. knowledge banks;

4. distributed databases;

5. database management systems (DBMS);

6. knowledge bank management systems (KBMS);

7. teleprocessing routines (TP) and real-time software;

8. operating systems (OS);

9. supercomputers;

10. powerful workstations;

11. local-area networks (LAN);

12. wide-area networks.

This infrastructure will be animated by small teams of highly trained, dedicated researchers who focus on a specific project without a hierarchy of bureaucrats to impede them. The teams operate in much the same way that commando units operated during World War II.

"Securities companies need the best brains as well as the most advanced technology they can get," says Morihiro Matsumoto. "It is not only the planning of the product, but also the timely execution which is instrumental in bringing results."

A system view of the support provided to the trade at Yamaichi Securities is shown in Figure 1–1. Everything is studied in detail, from the design of the financial service to its production, distribution, and certification. Technology is used to reduce costs and increase personal productivity as well as to enhance the decision capability of each trader.

In the way that the Bank of America restructured its operations by creating a research department, responsibility for the R and D effort must be shared by the technology and marketing divisions. In the case of the Bank of America, the R and D organization reports to both BASE (Bank of America Systems Engineering, the computers and communications division); and the line department (Commercial, Forex, or Treasury) that needs the R and D project.

R and D in banking requires the use of the best analytical and conceptual minds available in the organization.[1] It also calls for integrative perspectives regarding the work to be done. "You cannot divide trading, execution, and control from R and D activities," says Dr. Nunzio A. Tartaglia, former managing director of Morgan Stanley's Advanced Development Group (ASG). His division, he emphasized, is a research laboratory similar to those at Bell.

The goal of an R and D effort in the financial industry is to implement automated analytical trading, with an emphasis on risk management. This involves doing basic research activities; undertaking projects that focus on command, execution and control; and developing the newest technological infrastructure of the investment bank—its algorithms and heuristics.

**Figure 1–1   A Professional's Workstation Must Be
                  Networked and Supported Through
                  Powerful Tools**

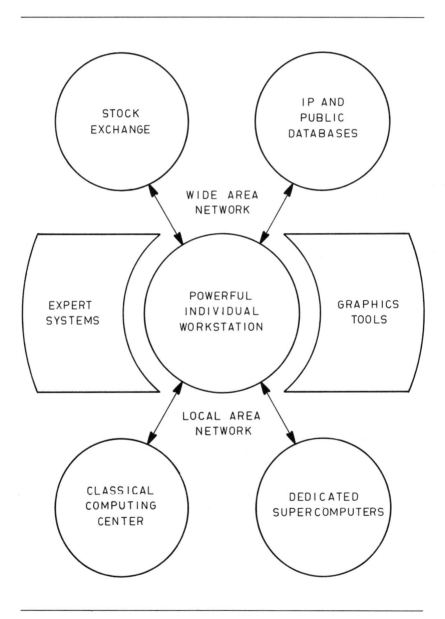

Today, major financial institutions are keen on developing advanced systems focused on investment analysis and able to package new financial products that give them a competitive edge. This thrust toward developing new products has had the result that the American market is experiencing soaring sales of mini-supercomputers, with annual shipments growing by 25 percent, while mainframe shipments are growing by only 5 percent.[2]

Another major trend is identified by statistics on specialists needed in the American market. ACM reports that "AI experts are in short supply, as companies are intensifying their search for experienced software professionals who can design and develop artificial intelligence systems."[3]

To become more competitive, American companies are now willing to pay starting salaries of from thirty-five to almost forty thousand dollars per year for college graduates with some AI experience. Corporate demand for AI skills is expected to grow 25 percent per year throughout this decade—and securities firms consider themselves fortunate if they have a team of rocket scientists with the skills necessary to develop new financial products and to control risk. Financial organizations that have an established R and D function give the following reasons for this initiative:

1.   The complexity and size of funds has increased to the point that they can no longer be managed using classical methods.

In the past, profile analysis typically involved questionnaires that could be put to investors by relatively unskilled salespeople. Today, the acquisition of high-net-worth individuals as clients requires the creation of a sophisticated financial profile, which in turn needs expert systems assistance. It is no longer a case of providing a simple, routine plan.

2. A surplus of information is presently available
    and needs to be properly filtered.

Information from public and private databases must be
carefully analyzed in order to create individualized evaluation
schemes. Trying to do that through classical computer procedures is difficult. Fine-grain filtering requires both accurate
theories and an impressive array of tools. (See Chapter 9 for
a discussion of Yamaichi's Integrative Stock System.)

3. Performance against competition is a matter of
    both top brains and infrastructure.

Competitiveness in the market has increased to the point
that superior performance has to be documented. For example, the appeal of Mutual Funds decreases quickly if their
performance is not clearly better than that of other investments.

4. It is necessary to establish the magnitude of
    market inefficiencies.

There are several methods available that mathematically
evaluate market performance. They also monitor market fluctuations and gauge their possible impact on the bank's portfolio, that is, they determine how market inefficiencies will
influence customers' and the bank's holdings.

5. It is important to identify and explain market
    movements from the perspective of individual
    securities as well as to create new marketable
    products.

Each bank's goals are those of improving the total rate of
return on invested capital (the bank's own as well as that of

its customers) and coming up with new, appealing products. Analytical approaches help in managing the risks of securities positions, singularly and from a portfolio viewpoint.

The development and marketing of new types of securities requires intensive cross-section market analysis as well as option valuation based on the trader's premise that "Something will happen if..." Such experimentation calls for large-scale computing power able to sort out alternatives, evaluate hypotheses, estimate risk, and test possible market moves.

All four functions call for heuristics and for stochastic calculus to be done in real time so as to forecast the range of possible choices/odds. Heuristics involves possibilities rather than probabilities and helps provide qualitative, not just quantitative, results. The theory is available, but current computers, even the larger mainframes, do not have the needed power—only supercomputers can do this job.

6. Optimization theory can determine an optimal set of assets and associated premises, including mortgages and options.

One of the most promising uses for AI and supercomputers is in securitization of complex deals by having a solid basis for real-time experimentation. This is important to securities houses, not only because it is a new and lucrative product line, but also because of the amount of institutional assets locked up in mortgages.[4]

7. Pension funds and other institutional investors have become too big and too knowledgeable for banks to apply classical approaches in handling their accounts.

In America and in Japan, pension funds are growing an estimated 30 to 40 percent per year. In Japan they represent nearly 50 percent of the business done by securities firms—and they are demanding in their requirements.

If a securities house cannot match the best its competitors can offer, then it generally cannot keep a client. There is a great push toward becoming wizards in portfolio analysis and risk evaluation. Unless an investment company wants to lose half of its market, it has to move forward in this domain.

Raising money from clients is becoming an increasingly complex affair that calls for considerable know-how and experimentation.

To grow, a financial institution needs to steadily increase its performance, say both Tartaglia and Matsumoto. This is a dictum every banker should learn to appreciate. In the 1990s, survival demands the ability to identify important trends, forecast coming events, and manage daily business efficiently. At Yamaichi Securities and Morgan Stanley this means utilizing portfolio theory and supercomputers.

3. Morgan Stanely: A Case Study in Leadership

This case study focuses on the Morgan Stanley investment bank and is based on a personal meeting with one of the chief architects of Wall Street's high-technology revolution. This meeting provided a good opportunity to discuss some of the prevailing concepts in analytical approaches to investment banking and securities trading.

Morgan Stanley is organized into Profit Centers. In foreign operations, for example, profitability rests on currencies, and futures. In this domain, as in others, emphasis is placed on analytical techniques and on supercomputers, with the aim of improving profitability. "You have to be able to get real-time prices," says the managing director of the R and D unit. "You trade in a successful way when nobody can deal with you on a tick-by-tick basis, because they have neither the organization nor the computer power to match your own."

Morgan Stanley's strategy is one of gaining a competitive edge by using analytical proprietary trading and other applications using the best available mathematical tools and supercomputers to facilitate Wall Street dealmaking, risk management, and Forex operations.

The investment bank's R and D laboratory has a dual role—to provide analytical support and to help create new products. A focal point is trading, with projects including any and all instruments in any and all markets.

In this investment bank, as in a growing number of American and Japanese securities houses, management is careful not to enforce old, obsolete concepts associated with classical data processing; they know that such an action would antagonize traders and salespeople and impair teamwork. The best salespeople will not rearrange their work styles just to accommodate EDPiers. EDPiers are there to serve, not to inhibit, productive bankers and dealers. This is a good example of strategic vision.

"You cannot seperate trading, execution, and control from R and D activities," says the managing director of the research lab at Morgan Stanley. Figure 1–2 shows an approach that has been taken to automated analytical trading. The cornerstones of this approach are—

1. research and development;

2. command, execution, control;

3. technology, algorithms, and heuristics.

The corporate goal is to obtain an edge in all three areas by providing real-time supercomputer-based support. One application for example, is the analysis of a large portfolio, either a customer's or the bank's own account. Such analysis becomes computationally intensive when a portfolio contains securities with an option component, such as mortgage-backed securities.

Supercomputers are able to give traders direct access to complex models that otherwise cannot be run during the day. When compared with classical mainframes, supercomputers'

Figure 1–2   Component Parts of an Automated Analytical Trading System

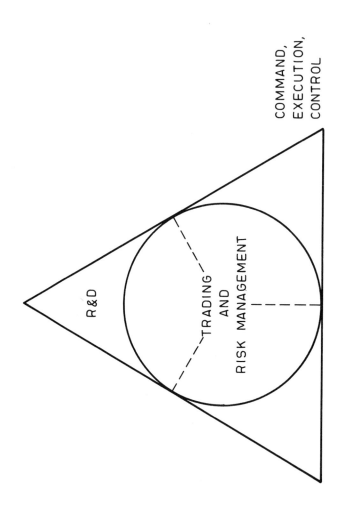

processing speed is impressive. How well this speed is utilized depends, however, on how one runs the application; hence, the need for R and D work.

Research also focuses on the benefits and risks involved in a contrarian approach—which has to be executed at very high speed and exceeds the limitations of classical data processing (DP).

At Morgan Stanley, computers and communications are seen as a competitive weapon, able to help in simplifying some of the complexity of the modern financial world. Supercomputers and AI not only permit sophisticated problem solving, but also allow major corporations, banks, and investment houses to move enormous sums of money around the world or between markets in seconds through their networks.

Such solutions come none too soon. The volatility of national economies—and of the international economy—has greatly added to financial complexity. Financial markets have witnessed wild fluctuations compounding executives' and professionals' need for forecasting, monitoring, and control.

In the future, there will be multiple services in trading, including complex operations in the futures market and a whole range of portfolio-handling tools. The efficient management of transactions is no longer enough by itself. The whole market must be mapped into the computer.

This whole-market orientation is fundamental to the use of supercomputers and analytical techniques at Morgan Stanley. New procedures are easily connected to solve diverse problems.

One capability of modern financial technology is that of taking a whole portfolio and turning it around. (Only supercomputers can do this job). This technology also has the capacity to do global-risk management, that is, to track positions, pinpoint opportunities, evaluate risks, develop hedging strategies, and do cross-market arbitrage.

The analytical models that lead to optimization, which is based on identifying critical factors in trading and pricing securities, consume a large amount of cycles and require very large databases. Hence, they can be developed efficiently only by using supercomputers and AI.

4. The Integration of Front Desk and Back Office

There was a time when the operations at a securities house front desk and back office were considered distinct from each other—the first addressing itself to dealing and trading, the second to administrative duties. But twenty-four-hour banking operations and, more recently, after-hours networks have radically changed this picture.

After-hours crossing networks not only support twenty-four-hour banking, but also lead to increased business. The more investment banks use their international strength to turn themselves into an international trading network, the more the need for a full integration between back office and front desk becomes apparent.

In fact, by using after-hours networks, banks could bypass clearing houses by interconnecting their own networks. CHIPS and CHAPS[5] may become obsolete unless they restructure and provide value-added services such as portfolio management and analytical advice for money managers, corporate treasurers, and so on. Classical DP work cannot provide these types of services. Intelligent networks, distributed databases, imaging and expert systems are necessary to ensure that one package will have a competitive edge, significant market visibility, the full automation of document handling, and a profit-making ability. In other words, there is a coming front desk—-back office merger through the use of technology.

The key question is whether a securities company can afford not to feature an integrated front desk—-back office functionality, particularly if its major competitors are taking that route.

This is not a matter to be left to the discretion of DP operations. It is a vital decision to be made by a company's executive board, which should set goals in accordance with this decision. The wait-and-see attitude taken by some DP departments is not only irrelevant but can be destructive.

The effective integration of front desk and back office is a research subject—and R and D is a major part of the cost of staying in business. This has been true in the manufacturing industry for the last thirty years, and today it is a valid concept in banking.

Necessary support includes a good back-office information system able to make data available on-line in a very short time, thus integrating in real time back-office information with front-desk dealing. (The term real time was coined in the 1960s to differentiate between batch operations, whose output took a long time to reach the end user, and on-line information stored in the machine.) On-line access compresses to a few seconds the time necessary to obtain and/or manipulate data in computer memory. Real time has for some time been implemented at the front-desk level, (i.e., for current accounts and savings), but back offices have remained largely batch.

In many financial institutions, this combined real-time and batch approach has been a disaster, yet few have taken steps to change it. One exception is Dai-Ichi Kangyo, which since 1987 has had no batch operations. Still, for any financial institution whose goal is globalization, real time, while necessary, is not enough.

The new keyterm is real space, that is, mapping at subsecond speed and into one operation whatever is happening around the world. Global databases run by supercomputers and communicating through intelligent networks can do this job—but the development of real space calls for rocket scientists and expert systems.

In the 1990s, efficient banking will require full on-line integration. At Morgan Stanley and Salomon Brothers, this translates into push-button buy and sell, with visualization and selection by cursor on the dealer's workstation, featuring a simultaneous back-office update.

This is not just a matter of eliminating paperwork. For a number of years, particularly since the late 1970s, leading banks have decreased their use of paper as a way of cutting down on delays, costs, and mistakes. But the integration of front desk and back office is a much larger step.

To prosper in the 1990s, institutions must take a strategic view of information-system roles and perspectives, focusing their approaches on state-of-the-art technologies. Supercomputers and analytical methodologies are two tools on which the foremost securities houses will base their future. Another is worldwide networking all the way to the workstation (WS) level.

Networking and parallel processing are the wave of the future. The challenge is to analyze tasks and program them to take advantage of a high-technology environment. It will take years to learn how to use supercomputers in an effective manner in connection to artificial intelligence, and late starters may not be able to catch up.

With rule-based expert systems under control and widely implemented, new ongoing projects will focus on how to apply neural networks for tasks such as examining patterns of prices to find global inefficiencies. Other projects will utilize possibility theory (fuzzy sets); still others, pattern recognition.

At the networked WS level of implementation, attention is being paid to visualization and to creating an ergonomic environment, with color, sound, lighting, and reflections on the trading desk. The drive is to get an edge in every way possible, with user-friendly technology and analytical approaches at center stage.

Such an emphasis on analytical proprietary trading did not come about by accident. "The traders demand more and more services," says Dr. Tartaglia. "So we pay attention to long-term implications and we do so worldwide. Our goal is flexibility and the ability to add value without locking ourselves into a certain product."

In a networking sense, Morgan Stanley particularly stresses the issue of down time. System design centers on how to create backup in a fully efficient manner without interruptions to the on-line banking solutions that have been developed.

Workstations and computer servers are built with a high level of reliability in mind. Systems architects, knowing that greater performance, improved functionality, state-of-the-art hardware, sophisticated software, and worldwide networking can increase the chances of system failure, have given added attention to avoiding problems in design.

5. Restructuring and Reorientation at Merrill Lynch

The theme of this chapter is the arrival of the Knowledge Age, which started with the free flow of information—precisely what has created the current network of far-flung global relationships among financial institutions and other industries. In our knowledge-based society, information is a key resource and building block for every type of organization.

Within a couple of decades, the share of the First World's work force engaged in manufacturing will be no more than 5 to 10 percent. Knowledge workers will take their place, the ranks of middle managers will thin, and the work force will become more mobile. To get prepared for such changes, businesses must learn to manage large numbers of specialists in much the same way a conductor leads an orchestra, advises Dr. Peter Drucker.[6]

Investment houses that have developed financial systems enriched by artificial intelligence, have discovered that the interaction between knowledge-based structures and trading specialists increases specialists' skills considerably. As Figure 1–3 shows, the reasoning methods imbedded in artificial intelligence and in decision-support systems (DSS) have in common facts and rules established through knowledge intake; hence, the expert systems that by now are widely used in the financial industry.[7]

Figure 1–3   Expert Systems Are the Common Ground of Decision Support and Artificial Intelligence

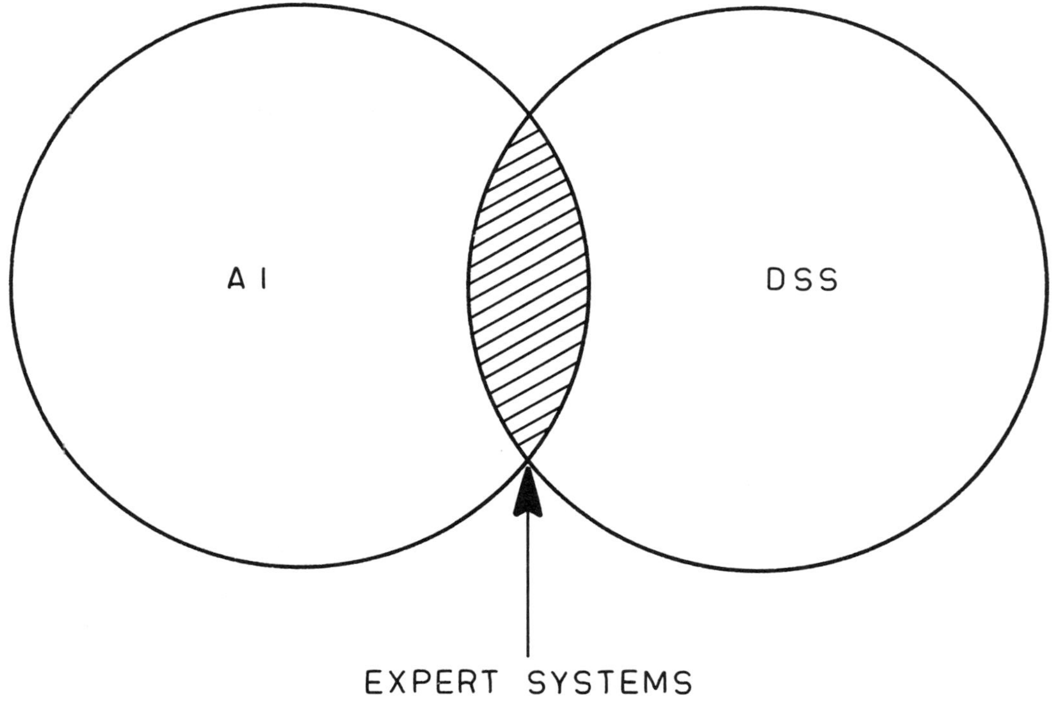

AI

DSS

EXPERT SYSTEMS

An artificial intelligence culture cannot be developed overnight. It takes time and effort to master this field, which involves not only expert systems but also computer vision, pattern recognition, robotics, language understanding, and language translation. The implementation of AI comes in successive layers.

The lower layer is decision support systems, in which the end user suggests situations and wants "what if" answers.[6] Computer software helps in evaluating the answers. The middle layer is expert systems. In these, the computer-aided intelligent construct suggests and evaluates situations, giving the proper advice and then justifying it. The upper layer consists of more sophisticated applications in AI support. This system identifies relevant cases, establishes patterns, evaluates situations, and constructs documented solutions.

Full-blown artificial intelligence implementations, enriched with learning capabilities, are further off. But work on expert systems is leading up to them, just as able DSS applications have been instrumental in the development of expert systems.

Figure 1–4 shows an expert-systems application composed of eight modules built piecemeal, with each module put in operation as soon as it is ready and tested. It includes a human window for agile man-machine communications, a market analyzer, money-exchange functions, a module dedicated to ECU (European Currency Unit)–type transactions, and commodity and options modules as well as one able to present an integrative picture. Another vital AI component that has recently been added focuses on pricing and commissions.

As far as trading assistants are concerned, the distinction between pattern-oriented and rule-based systems is critical. Rule-based constructs work best when the possible outcome(s) is (are) known and a programmer can chain backwards from that known result—such as the conditions under which a bank would grant credit or make a certain investment.

**Figure 1–4   A Modular Expert System
                 Implementation in Securities**

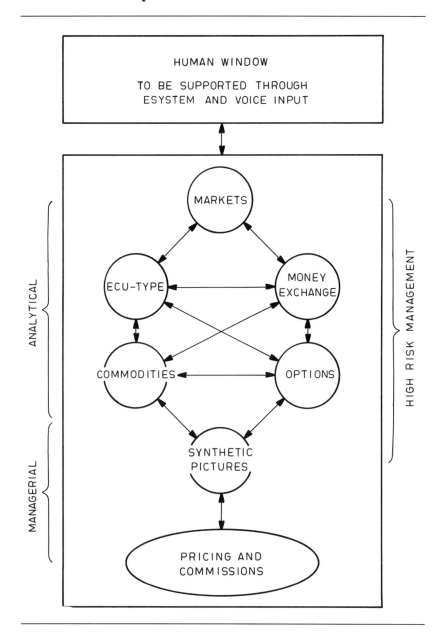

But in many instances neither the procedure nor the outcome is known; this is the case with different underwriting patterns. The results are unknown and must be reestablished for each underwriting deal. To do so, requires using AI tools; furthermore, generating a pattern is much easier if the operator is assisted by supercomputers.

In pattern-recognition situations it is not possible to anticipate what the pattern is going to be in a classical sense, especially if the number of variables involved is large and the variables interlinked. The AI construct can help in projecting a pattern that can be used at least tentatively, and can continue to evaluate patterns as the market situation unfolds.

Pattern-recognition models, neural networks, and fuzzy sets are part of the second-generation wave of AI implementations in financial institutions; therefore, many are still at the research-and-development level. But a wealth of other relatively simple (as well as some fairly complex) rule-based expert systems have been producing first-class results for years.

Merrill Lynch is one firm that has profited from extensive use of the new technology. Says DuWayne J. Peterson, executive vice-president of Operations:

"At Merrill Lynch we have some superb expert systems helping us to handle securities and link to the market....One of the expert systems projects will be automating the interface as customers call in, asking questions on the client's problems, trying to figure out what is the problem, and possibly provide the solution to the problem—or otherwise channel it to the appropriate executive....Image processing and pattern recognition are important enabling technologies in a banking environment, if we wish to control costs and bend the curve of employment."

To face further system challenges as market perspectives develop, Peterson has established for his financial institution a two-tier architecture (1) putting maximum power at the WS level, and (2) implementing a network of database machines.

Figure 1–5   A Communications-Based Software and Hardware Integration

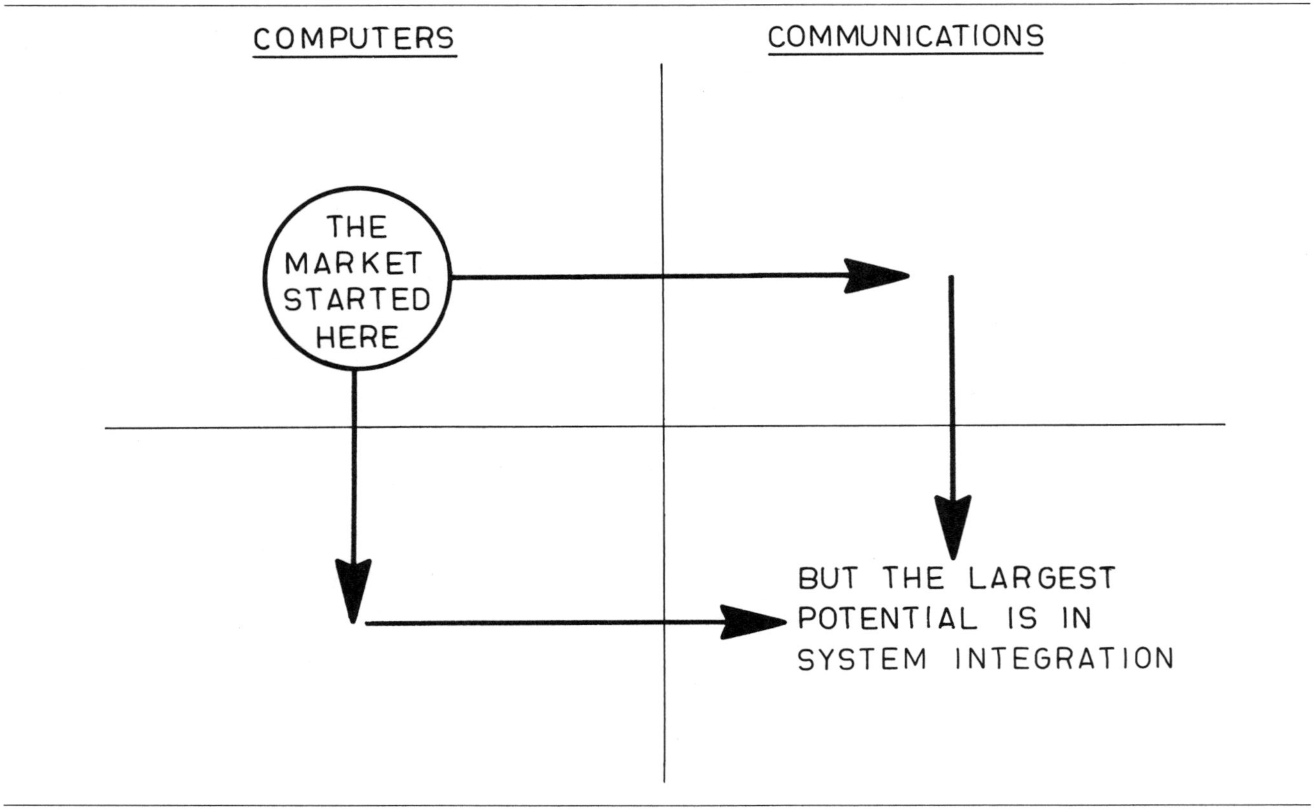

COMPUTERS

COMMUNICATIONS

THE MARKET STARTED HERE

BUT THE LARGEST POTENTIAL IS IN SYSTEM INTEGRATION

An ingenious network structure has been designed using a peer-to-peer architecture, supported through teleports. It permits greater transparency, better integration, and faster response. To appreciate the impact of such an effort, one might note that Merrill Lynch addresses itself to two large markets worldwide.

The Consumer Markets division services individual investors and small businesses—and sales are mainly in stocks, bonds, mutual funds, and insurance. This division employs some twelve thousand financial consultants (brokers), who work through five hundred offices in the U.S. alone and handle five million in accounts. It also represents $250 billion in customer assets—or an average of $50,000 per customer.

The Capital Markets division sells to governments, mutual funds, pension funds, and other institutional investors. It manages roughly ten thousand big-account clients whose interest lies mainly in global trading.

Internally, the risk-management system monitors every trader's activities, inventory, and limits. Internationally, the new telecommunications network covers every aspect of operations. "In the past we had focused on many branches," says DuWayne Peterson. "Now we create competency centers. The more routine business can be done through telecommunications and workstations."

This system was not developed overnight. An article in *Business Week* details how the restructuring of Merrill Lynch back office and information technology operations was started and now continues in synergy with the new strategy of William A. Schreyer, chief executive officer: "His game plan is simple. Use Merrill's huge retail operations to sell the new securities generated by a beefed-up investment-banking operation. Says Schreyer, 'We are not just stockbrokers anymore.' "[9]

With Schreyer's strategy and Peterson's emphasis on high technology and the integration of computers as well as back office operations, Merrill Lynch is now the market leader in underwriting preferred and common stocks, initial public offerings, and debt instruments.

6. Do's and Don'ts in a Networked Organization

While high technology is usually associated with expert systems, it also drives intelligent networks, that is, enterprise-wide communications systems based on artificial intelligence. AI is also an important component of systems integration.

Thirty-five years ago, computers were used by financial institutions mainly at the hardware (HW) level, as shown in Figure 1–5. During the following three decades the emphasis shifted to software (SW) and to the communications domain. In the last five years, however, system integration has stolen the limelight, and this will continue to be the case well into the 1990s.[10]

Integrative approaches to systems solutions, network-level support, natural language understanding, real-time language translations, automatic load balancing, intelligent diagnostics, self-healing, and other AI-enriched facilities will be increasingly critical for companies operating in competitive environments.

With one networked WS per desk, another at home, and a third portable—and with the growing range as well as density of personal communications networks (PCN)—comes a revolution that companies must join in order to remain competitive. Personal communications networks blurs the boundaries between wire-bound and wireless networks, leading to fully networked organizations.[11] This is a major transition.

Through the concept of the personal number, which a user may keep for life, PCN could trigger the most fundamental change in communications since the invention of the telephone.

- ◆ Communications will become subscriber-oriented rather than being based on terminal or network termination points.

- ◆ Wireless rather than wired connections will dominate.

- ◆ People will communicate as individuals—not just as disembodied voices.

- ◆ One instrument, the personal telephone, will be used at home, in the office, or on the move.

- ◆ In its completed version, this personal telephone will be a fully networked portable PC, but pocket varieties will also be developed.

Not many data-processing organizations have planned for this PCN revolution. As a result, when it comes (perhaps by the mid-1990s), it could make obsolete—practically overnight—billions of dollars of computer software and hardware made for a static environment.

In turning itself into a networked organization, no company can afford to look for off-the-shelf solutions. What is now happening in computers and communications requires a thorough reappraisal of policies, and companies such as Citibank, with its development of Network 2000, and Weyenhauser, with advanced telecommunications technology in its manufacturing processes, are doing just that. When we talk about the new wave of automation, by definition we talk about custom solutions, whether the tools that we are using are electronic tellers (ET), computer-aided design (CAD), computer-aided manufacturing (CAM), robotics, computer-integrated manufacturing (CIM) and generally flexible systems.

These ongoing advances will impact on a wide range of business concerns, including cost, quality, flexibility, delivery, speed, and design. For example, a recent study of CIM systems in twenty U.S. companies showed that they had reduced by more than 50 percent the amount of labor required to perform certain jobs, and reduced total product costs by as much as 75 percent.

In banking, the counterpart to CIM is flexible automation, which has had a significant impact on cost, delivery, and service. Unfortunately, many DP managers are not taking advantage of the new tools available to them. For years, they have used new equipment much in the way a people sometimes use a new car; that is, they enjoy the faster, smoother ride and go on with life as before.

With the new technology, this can mean disaster. Banks and securities houses must realize that acquiring an advanced technology system is similar to replacing an old car with a helicopter. Managers who fail to understand and prepare for the capabilities of the new systems will become part of the problem rather than part of the solution.

In the interests of avoiding this scenario, here is a list of do's and don'ts for both the strategic and the technical aspects of running a business in transition.

DO's, STRATEGIC

1. Plan for the next five, ten, fifteen, or twenty years. But organize the system starting at the top, not at the bottom.

2. When doing long-term planning, set goals and try to ensure that they are met.

3. Expand company resources to meet goals if necessary.

4. Monitor employees and reward those who work to help the company meet its goals.

5. Maintain ongoing training programs. Knowhow develops very quickly, and can be just as quickly lost.

6. Promote people on the basis of merit, not seniority.

DO's, TECHNICAL

1. Emphasize the importance of intelligent networks and global databases.

2. Convert all applications to real time and real space.

3. Employ new-generation languages, such as 5GL and 4GL, but reuse software.

4. Make the transition to AI and to supercomputers.

5. Use rapid prototyping for all new programs.

6. Do DP/WP at the WS level. Use mainframes only for central databases or, better yet, employ database computers.

DON'Ts, STRATEGIC

1. Don't live in the past.

2. Don't think short-term.

3. Don't assume that plans have been executed without monitoring results.

4. Don't assume that employees will retain know-how without constant hands-on experience.

5. Don't start at the bottom of the organization; you will have nowhere to go.

6. Don't plan on the basis of available human and financial resources rather than expanding resources to meet goals.

DON'Ts, TECHNICAL

1. Don't install equipment (HW, SW) without studying and understanding what the resulting environment will be.

2. Don't continue to develop batch programs or any other type of non-interactive routine.

3. Don't use old and relatively inefficient languages such as Cobol and Fortran.

4. Don't delay in integrating DP and AI;

5. Don't use mainframes for DP, or use too many OS and incompatible DBMS.

6. Don't confuse end users with heterogeneous presentation formats and protocols.

The new technologies can greatly enhance the potential of a business organization. In manufacturing, automated machine tools can produce parts to more exacting specifications than can the most skilled human machinist. In banking, new perspectives in communications can greatly improve the relationship between a financial institution and its clients.

However, these technologies also require a quantum leap in attention, precision, and integration. Therefore, their implementation requires new skills, such as an integrative imagination and a passion for detail, on the part of managers. These characteristics will in the future distinguish the good manager from the bad.

Endnotes

1. For a discussion of analytical and conceptual approaches to problem solving, see D.N. Chorafas, *Membership to the Board of Directors* (London: Macmillan, 1988).

2. From a report issued by Electronic Trend Publications of Saratoga, Ca.

3. Communications of the ACM (December 1989).

4. In America, this represents about 50 percent of the assets of financial institutions.

5. The clearing houses for international payments respectively in New York and London.

6. One of the fathers of modern American management theory.

7. See also D.N. Chorafas and H. Steinmann, *Expert Systems in Banking* (London: Macmillan, 1991).

8. A good example is spreadsheets, which constitute the first popular and truly packaged DSS application. Another example is simulation (see Chap. 4).

9. *Business Week,* 17 July, 1989.

10. See also D.N. Chorafas, *System Architecture and System Integration* (New York: McGraw-Hill, 1989).

11. See Chapter 11.

Chapter 2

The Winds of Change in England and Switzerland

Chapter 2

The Winds of Change in England and Switzerland

1. Introduction

In the course of my 1991 research, one remark consistently made by a number of banks and securities houses in America, England, continental Europe, and Japan summarizes and represents the conclusion reached by financial institutions of the First World: "Pity the business which falls in love with the Status Quo."[1]

In London, the National Westminster Bank expanded on this issue by emphasizing, "Today the financial industry has a technology we would not have dreamed of ten years ago, and yet people take 300 percent more time to do a data processing job." This connection between Information Technology (IT) and the development of the financial business is

not surprising: the latter depends on the former for its infrastructure.

A modern brokerage house can operate in a profitable
manner only when it is able to provide added value to its basic
investment product line. Successful financial products are
market-oriented, technology-based and increasingly focus on

1. Institutions

2. Corporations

3. High Net Worth Individuals

4. Municipalities and Governments

The support to be provided to financial products will emphasize client, market and function, as for instance is the case
with

◆ Asset management services, for all four client
   populations

◆ High technology assistance to help maintain the
   cutting edge of competitiveness

Making money for its clients is a key element in the
maintenance of the institutional business. Hence, throughout the First World, leading investment bankers who target
the development of superior expertise in growth-oriented
business sectors require an increasing amount of support in
terms of computers, communications and mathematical
modeling.

In the 1990s, the foremost securities firms see themselves
as major players in the debt trading business. They also aim
to leverage their transactional expertise into the higher-mar-
gin, fee-related sectors where information technology provides the competitive edge.

Brokerage firms in England and in continental Europe have now begun to understand what investment banks in Japan and in America began appreciating in the mid-1980s: *the biggest issue is one of cultural change.* Three queries management poses to itself are as follows:

◆ Which is the culture in which we will work in the 1990s?

◆ How can we influence the market through technological leadership?

◆ Will we be able to survive in a fiercely competitive environment if we fall behind?

In the new corporate culture, an investment bank has to develop must be able to motivate its own people as well as its clients. How is *our* company rating in comparison to its competition?

Competition today is worldwide, hence our firm should be able to hold its own in a global sense, not just locally. And it is not surprising that the most proactive investment banks can be found among the smallest but very dynamic institutions. At Lazard Brothers, for example, simulation and expert systems are strategic tools in studying, optimizing and answering customer requirements.

2. European Financial Institutions Face the Technology Challenge

There is a wind of change sweeping the European financial business at this moment, and this clearly affects information technology in banking. The impact is particularly visible in three areas: networks, databases, and end user computing.

As is to be expected, some banks and securities houses are faring better than others in the race to streamline and integrate their computers and communications systems. By far the better off are those which have addressed (though not necessarily solved) their *integration* problems through tough, sound architectural choices and the implementation of knowledge engineering.[2]

In several cases, because of a kind of hype and inactivity which has settled into banking, financial institutions find themselves obliged to take draconian measures for reasons of cultural changes. In England these consist of literally chopping off the top echelons of data processing organizations.

Executives with longstanding positions are retired at 50 years of age, their jobs becoming redundant overnight. The reins of information technology are given to the younger generation, which is expected to lead the bank into the new technological landscape of the 1990s.

There is another strategic change to be accounted for, apart the introduction of new technology and new people. British banks and securities houses are currently reorganizing along client lines and product lines. This contrasts to the former organizational structure which was largely built along functional and accounting lines. The reasons for this major restructuring are as follows:

1. The longstanding functional organizational scheme has become too bureaucratic.

2. A business organization along customer and product lines is much more effective in improving customer relationships.

As will be appreciated, such restructuring can have a significant aftermath. Its impact is felt all the way from policies reached at the Board level to the information technology landscape and its choices; and, most importantly, it affects the bottom line.

No doubt, the transition is not without problems. On its way to restructuring customer relationships, County NatWest found two salient issues:

1. Data in itself not unique. Today it exists in double and triple copies through the organization.

2. The topology of usage is not really deterministic. It is stochastic, with plenty of *ad hoc* queries being asked by users.

Consequently, Sam Gibb the new executive in charge of Technology at County NatWest, is restructuring operations in a way that will streamline databasing and provide the needed support for *ad hoc* queries—including those of an analytical type. In a securities trading and asset management environment, *ad hoc* queries addressing the global database become increasingly crucial to competitiveness in the marketplace.

The lesson learned from England and America is that if we are not careful on these matters, one day (in the not too distant future) we will find banks in the same position a well-known financial institution found itself in recently—having fifteen incompatible databases even though it uses one vendor, IBM. A recent study undertaken by this bank has unearthed twenty-seven incompatible lending systems as well. This is what happens when complacency filters in.

Since not only financial institutions but also the vendors of information technology equipment and software have been careless in watching their product line, banks and securities houses find themselves today with huge incompatibilities. This happens even if they have strictly observed single sourcing principles—today, the dominent wish is to implement a multivendor policy as well as to streamline and control heterogeneity.

The goal of multisourcing has led to new corporate policies which aim at greater cost effectiveness through *open systems*. "We steer the bank towards vendor independence," was the message of the majority of British banks.

Many financial institutions have discovered that the cost of supporting a rampant heterogeneity is tremendous—even if they are hooked up to single sourcing. One of the comments most frequently heard in this research has been: "We want to get out of the closed, monolithic vendor relationship."

It comes, therefore, as no surprise that many studies are recently oriented towards open systems. Virtually homogeneous databases are seen as an ideal ground for such implementation. At the same time, cross-database integration helps identify glaring weaknesses in current customer- and product-oriented practices.

One British study, to which reference was made during the research, established that in many commercial and investment banks there is not even *the concept of a customer*. There exists just the concept of an account number, and the same customer has different account numbers which do not integrate easily. Therefore, the point was made that prior to talking of database integration, we need to rethink the *customer relation*—particularly so in the corporate world.

These are issues which will dominate work in information technology during the 1990s and will command the associated investments, not only in technology but also in organization. Solutions will not come easily. They will require many imaginative new departures and an open mentality on behalf of information technologists. They will also require object-oriented approaches and a good deal of the type of work today typically done in leading financial institutions by "rocket scientists."

3. Working Meetings with British Banks and Investment Firms

Many of the problems which dominate the landscape of American, Japanese, and continental European banks were found to prevail with British financial institutions. Some of the foremost banks and investment houses provide excellent examples.

Back in the 1970s, the National Westminster Bank evaluated GEIS[3] and other publically offered networks. It finally decided that DSS[4] should be developed in-house on in-house mainframes. Originally, this was thought to be an integrative approach realized by means of an information center capability—but was quite soon superceded by the spread of end user developments on PCs.

In the majority of British financial institutions, as well as in practically all First World countries, many users programmed their own applications and set their own database standards, placing an extra burden on central operations. "Only now," a cognizant British investment banker was to suggest, "our people are beginning to understand the difference between a data access goal to be implemented on a distributed basis and the failures into which centralization can lead an institution's information technology policies."

Delays in vendor software and associated support have contributed to this downgrading of the centralized solution: "The situation became critical as more and more executives and professionals in the bank asked for database-wide access and integrative information capabilities."

Failures by IT in ably addressing these subjects ensured that today, in a growing number of financial institutions, there are applications where

◆ End users have to do manual jobs because they don't have global access to databases due to their heterogeneity.

◆ It is increasingly urgent that something be done on this account, and financial institutions find that this "something" cannot be a sort of global schema, as some vendors suggest.

The result has not been positive. "The global schema will not work," said both the National Westminster and County NatWest executives. "You spend time and money, and finally end up with no usable approach." Both financial institutions emphasized that this is not just a technical problem. It is an organizational and business problem.

The technical problem cannot be solved, however, without providing a sound solution to the organizational and business problems—which help define the priorities.

As an example, the Group Data Architecture Unit (GDAU) at one of the British banks has had six to eight people working for three years creating a data definition and logical data model. This project focused on two applications—one with DB2, the other with Link/Unisys—concerning major corporate customers. But as both management and specialists found out, it is not even possible "to define customers the same way"—especially large customers and partnerships. As a result of linguistic discrepencies regarding the two database management systems, the project ended up with profiles which were totally different from one system to another—hardly a usable result.

In their effort to rationalize the end points, other banks too tried the global schema road and got nowhere. One said that in the early Eighties it undertook a bank-wide model with centralized database ideas in mind, but as the years progressed, the problems mounted. At the end, nothing came out of it and it was abandoned.

Like so many other projects in America, Japan, and continental Europe which started on the wrong premises without consideration of the technical fundamentals, this one went ahead just for the sake of it. When it failed, management ordered a thorough auditing which found that several database-oriented projects were half-baked from the start:

◆ Their concept was not particularly coherent.

◆ The software which they used was wanting.

◆ The hardware could not support an ambitious undertaking.

Failures should be opportunities for learning, and at the foremost banks the decision was made to be pragmatic in the future, with emphasis being placed on end user wants rather than the whims of the data processors.

Systems solutions in the 1990s should begin with the query, "What do the users like?" "That's the whole idea of MIS and of ad hoc analytical queries," said a responsible executive of a financial institution, adding that "For fast response, we need parallel handling of data."

4. Exposure Management at County NatWest

Like all financial institutions which face the challenges of the 1990s, *global risk management* is at the top of the agenda at County NatWest. As is the case with Japanese and other leading banks, this is one of the projects which attracts a great deal of management attention.

Of course, exposure management exists, but it is all historical. "By the time the problem comes, you are not able to control it," a cognizant executive has commented. This is generally the problem throughout the banking industry— with *limits* which are typically sectorial. Besides that, the current emphasis on the transaction level is towards the functional department and the account number rather than on the *client*, as it should be.

Therefore, a new approach is required, and, like all the foremost investment banks in the world today, County Nat-West is in the middle of a cultural change occurring through the transition from an accounting-based to a customer-based system.

A key element in this process is classification.[5] The proper classification can reveal *patterns* and therefore help in making the financial organization (and its management) customer-oriented rather than accounting-based. It can also assist in assuring that an integrative approach brings into perspective client-related risks and prevailing trends in risk-taking.

This great leap forward led to a conceptual approach towards database mining,[6] bringing major system changes across the board. "We give people new integrative jobs—but we must also give them specific tools permitting them to handle their new jobs," suggested Sam Gibb. Hence the search is now underway for both integrative and analytical solutions.

The able handling of new departures from the beaten path of information technology largely rests on a coordinate system like the one shown in Figure 2–1.

1. First comes the *choice of method* which will permit the new orientation.

2. This is followed by the selection of the appropriate *shell and language,* with object-oriented solution having the upper hand.

3. Then *cross-database* approaches must be provided, independent of the specific DBMS under which the local applications run.

Within this coordinate system, new technologies are at the top of the list of priorities. For equities, for example, the bank considers optical disks to hold online information for long historical references. Not only hard numbers but also soft information such as,

◆   The integration of *news* releases

◆   Evaluations of why changes in prices happened

Figure 2–1   A Frame of Reference for New Departures in Information Technology

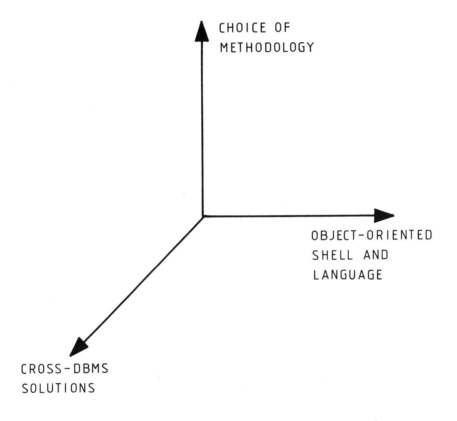

◆   Experimentation on ranges of variation

One of the problems being tackled is how to take tic-by-tic text and data, as it comes off the wire, and hold it for five years—but in an easily retrievable sense. The goal is to integrate this type of information, making it available to *ad hoc* analytical queries.

"Registering what has happened in the market is not enough," it was remarked during a meeting; "we have to filter the data and integrate the news items."

The Japanese are doing precisely that through *fuzzy engineering*,[7] and they are successful in this process. A solution developed by the Laboratory of International Fuzzy Engineering (LIFE), in Yokohama, uses fuzzy sets to interpret news items and integrate their deductions with the results of a neural network which predicts yen/dollar exchange rates.[8]

Would the County NatWest executive consider using fuzzy engineering in his operations? "Yes, I come from the oil industry where we used it for correlating characteristics and the examination of local/global phenomena."

Another key question regarding British investment banking—and for that matter all brokers world-wide—is what to do with aging applications. The reply has been: "We cannot take the risk of converting whole systems, even if they have reached the end of their effective life." This is a very sound approach.

In banking and the securities industry today, most of the existing systems are heterogeneous, and they are aging. Conversion sometimes needs to be done—and can be done—selectively by one department or for one application, but not by the bank as a whole.

One of the reasons for the current heterogeneity exhibited by the majority of financial institutions is the fact that information technology solutions often started as a UK-only system, but then expanded world-wide—for instance, to cover the business contracted with transnational corporations and for global risk management.

This problem is global. Every major financial institution looks for the opportunity to serve multinational clients and bring worldwide risk under control— doing so across different functional operations and incompatible computer platforms.

This of course implies changes, which must be properly planned. "We cannot replace them globally, but we have to do the integrative work," clear-eyed executives suggest. Correctly, within the NatWest group nobody focuses on massive conversions, but some departments, like Treasury and Capital Markets, look for solutions which may involve software replacements. *Selectivity* is the keyword in this job, with the criteria being *competitiveness* and *return on investment*.

But software is not the only issue which selectively needs to change. Today, in British banks there is a wave of large personnel changes, as identified during the 1991 research meetings. This wave is mounting and many people consider it to be irreversible.

National Westminster, Barclays, Midland and their investment banking arms, as well as asset management subsidiaries, take concrete steps eliminating so-called "redundant DP positions." They say they do not eliminate people but jobs; in reality, however, they release aging employees in order to renew their human resources.

The renewal of human resources is a "must," but physical age should not be the overriding criterion. It is logical age— that is, *state of mind*, which should decide whom to keep and whom to let go. Still, the policy is good; without it, people will never get moving.

5. European Stock Exchanges Tried to Modernize through Networking

The drive towards the modernization of services to make them more appealing and cost effective is not limited to commercial and investment banks. It also includes the Stock Exchanges.

Since 1990, the Federation of Stock Exchanges of the European Community (FSEEC) has taken the initiative to develop a pan-European information network. Known as Price Information Project Europe (PIPE), this initiative has been funded by the twelve European bourses that make up the FSEEC. In its original scope, PIPE aimed to include:

◆ Updates on transactions taking place in any of the FSEEC members;

◆ Prices from European and non-European exchanges;

◆ Company news and the outcome of research projects; and

◆ Quotes regarding Forex and bond prices.

Subscribers were to be given the option of receiving the information directly or through established information providers. The emphasis was on a continuous data feed.

This effort got connected to the virtual integration of the European exchanges, and, not surprisingly, it became a highly political matter. Frequent meetings took place among the heads of the exchanges during which there seemed to be much disagreement. The split was created around two poles:

◆ England and Germany wanted the foremost criteria to be performance and service, with deregulation being the rule.

◆ The so-called Club Med, composed of France, Italy and Spain, pressed for a regulated solution—which by any modern standard is anachronistic, even more so when it comes to networked exchanges.

This is all very unfortunate, but it also reveald deep splits which exist within the Common Market, as well as the myopic way of approaching the issues which lie further ahead, and their aftermaths. That is how the European computer and semiconductor industries have gone down the drain—and how Europe has lost its leadership.

Seen in a pragmatic sense, the need for cross-exchange solutions is both actual and historical. Since 1985, London's International Stock Exchange (ISE) has been trading blocks of about 700 international stocks through its screen-based trading system, but settlement procedures are governed by each company's home market and that country's currency. Besides, much of the paperwork at ISE itself is not yet weeded out. Since transnational companies today master a large and growing chunk of the First World's gross domestic product (GDP), cross-bourse solutions are a foremost functional requirement. Some 185 American companies presently list their shares in London, while 70 trade in Tokyo.

◆ These stocks change hands as they do in New York.

◆ With prices rising and falling as market conditions warrant.

Much of the trading of U.S. stocks in London is program trading, because disclosure is minimal and so are costs. The ISE competition has consistently beaten the New York Stock Exchange's (NYSE) transaction charges.

But, competition among First World bourses is becoming global, leading to price cutting which further intensifies the race to capture trade business:

◆ NYSE's new after-hours system for program trading does provide an alternative to engaging in such trades in London.

◆ NYSE is also imposing no transaction charges and non-disclosure price and volume information on individual stocks.

In spite of this, not only London's ISE but also the private order-matching systems such as the Crossing Network, Instinet and Posit are expected to keep their market appeal— provided they come up with new, imaginative moves.

As a result of these trends, many people look at the establishment of global networks as intelligence-enriched distribution channels. Current support is only phase one of a venture which would eventually extend to the development of new trade execution services together with the creation of back office interfaces.

In this sense, the first goals of PIPE (renamed *Euroquote*), came to be viewed as a testing ground for further cooperation among Europe's bourses. If this first common effort were a success, then more detailed discussions were likely to follow on the thornier topics of the harmonization of European settlement dates and development of a central European clearing house.

Other future goals have been the creation of a common listing of top European equities and the eventual emergence of a pan-European trading system. But in July 1991, with the Stock Exchanges of London and Frankfurt having already abandoned the project, PIPE/Euroquote crashed—and this is a telling experience.

6. The Unable Were Asked by the Unwilling to Do the Unnecessary

On July 5, 1991, shareholders voted unanimously to fold the limping and wanting Euroquote project and its pan-European share price and information system plans. This is an experience which should be kept in the annals of international IT projects as a first class example which should not be repeated.

Over a period of about three years, PIPE/Euroquote over-spent on consultants and meetings, but little was done about establishing clear goals and reaching working agreements. Finally, the EC stock exchanges—that is the shareholders—came to realize that

◆ Their successively more messy approach was po-litically confused and technically wanting, and

◆ The creation of a thirteenth database would have added to the problems, rather than solving them.

This thirteenth database was projected by the consultants over and above the twelve other databases of the main stock exchanges (one per nation) in the EC. It was to serve as an interface and switching center. The concept was ill-defined, with more weaknesses than strengths.

But the thirteenth database was not the only soft spot. From the start, the whole plan lacked focus as well as the necessary underlying will to get results. It takes more than some initially good intentions to get a big project going.

After Euroquote's crash, the Federation of Stock Exchanges in Brussels suggested that it would continue studying the possibility of pan-European trading and settlement systems. However, the hard fact of life is that not only time and money was lost, but also this thirteenth database experience left deep scars—which are there for everyone to see.

The tombstone was put on PIPE/Euroquote in spite of all the money lavishly spent on it or, more precisely, because of the silly expenditures which were made. With the project killed by its shareholders, all the budget and effort spent for nearly three years has been thrown out of the window. Finally, in July 1991, the shareholders realized that: "The PIPE/Euroquote project lacked focus."

◆ To whom the blame for the indecisions?

◆ The retrograde concepts embedded into this project?

◆ The irrational horse-trading?

◆ The unwillingness to leave the beaten path?

There are lessons to be learned from the mistakes which led to this failure, and we should be taking notice. By playing the intermediary between twelve independent databases, one per major EC stock exchange, the thirteenth database of PIPE/Euroquote became the prescription for failure, while there was a crying need for highly imaginative work to be done.

Here, in a nutshell, is the list of ten technical problems and two major political issues (No. 1 and No. 12) which hit and grounded the project *after* the technical study was done by renouned consultants and the stock exchanges' own personnel.

1. Only one stock exchange per country was included in the study—hence twelve out of about thirty—which led the others to stonewalling.

2. No decision was made on whether to broadcast the updates only to the twelve—or to all subscribers to the EC exchanges (about 3,000.)

3. Due to complexity, not all 2,200 quotations of London's ISE were to be mapped—and the same is true of the other EC exchanges.

4. No decision was reached on compensation in buying and selling securities—even those featured in more than one exchange.

5. Fuzzy notions dominated the possible handling of ECU quotes; the only sure thing was disagreement.

6. No settlement procedures were being projected, or even considered.

7. No inkling existed on how long transactions should be managed, versus the better known short transactions.

8. Neither input nor broadcast to the PIPE/Euroquote network was error-protected.

9. No system decision was reached on primary image, integrity, and synchronization of databases.

10. No system solution existed regarding ad hoc queries, such as channel sorting.

11. Disagreements abounded regarding budgets, costs, services, and fees.

12. The division of turf created profound disagreements—pitting England and Germany against Clud Med (France, Italy and Spain).

Lessons learned from the Common Market's stock exchanges should be welcome. They help everyone who wants to take notice, thus saving time, money, troubles and misfortunes. Our goal should be that of maintaining a leadership position, cutting new ground in applications rather than making life difficult for ourselves and others. But is anybody listening?

7. Globalization Calls for an End to the Paper Age

Many stock markets today, like Tokyo's and the American NASD,[9] settle their shares electronically and, therefore, at low cost. Though paper certificates usually exist, ownership is simply transferred in a central, computerized register. This is not yet the case in London's International Stock Exchange, where settlement is still paper-based.

Manual handling involves both much greater risk and outrageous costs. It also makes the use of analytical approaches practically impossible. Back-office automation has been delayed for years as stockbrokers, banks, custodians, listed companies and registrars failed to agree (until recently) on the shape that Taurus, the proposed automated-settlement system, should take and what it should cost.

Furthermore, both networking and the able management of distributed databases should be given great attention. The same is true of knowledge engineering and analytical approaches, as the shares of the world's 500 largest companies are now globally tradable commodities.

If the proper infrastructure of computers, communications, algorithms and heuristics is put in place, the International Stock Exchange (ISE) in London can well be a beneficiary of internationalization. Foreign equities account for a quarter of all transactions reported to the ISE, and the ISE trades represent half of all *global-equity turnover*—that is, turnover in foreign shares away from their domestic exchange.

As the international business in equities grows, particularly in connection with transnational corporations, it is necessary to tackle structural challenges with a clear vision and mandate. Otherwise, globalization remains an empty word, costs mount, profitability melts, and competitiveness is lost.

This problem seems to be particularly crucial at London's International Stock Exchange; it is by far the most important exchange in Europe, accounting for nearly double the market capitalization of its immediate competitor, Frankfurt (as shown in Table 2–1), and for about 35 percent of the capitalization of all twelve Common Market Exchanges.[10]

Another challenging issue arises from the fact that the Common Market economies plan to integrate. It regards the ability to invest across stock exchanges, which is today a daunting job. Any practitioner would assert that assembling a portfolio of European stocks is difficult, as investors have to cope with multiple currencies, a number of custodians, and different settlement procedures.

Appreciating these challenges, the major stock exchanges are teaming up to simplify and promote *Euro-investing*. The aim is to create a single European equities market. The first step is the creation of a *Eurolist*, a pool of up to 300 of the continent's most vital stocks as measured by market capitalization. They will be traded on exchanges throughout the EEC, denominated in each bourse's local currency.

To a large measure, such a Eurolist will be a marketing tool, encouraging investors to think "European" instead of focusing on national, hence local, exchanges and firms. Major investors and money managers will thus be able to appoint one European custodian to take delivery of the securities, instead of using a different one in each country.

Such a concentration of accounts and of power has already taken place in commercial banking, where transnational corporations have dramatically reduced—by roughly 70 percent—the number of financial institutions with which they deal. Not surprisingly, the beneficiaries of such concentrations are those banks which lead both in technology and in customer handling.

There are, however, prerequisites to be met if the all-European stock market is to succeed. First and foremost, the different laws, compliance procedures, and settlement practices by EC country will need to be harmonized:

Table 2–1   Stock Markets of the European
               Economic Community*

Country	Market Capitalization (Billions of U.S. Dollars)
1. Britain	$694
2. Germany	354
3. France	340
4. Italy	171
5. The Netherlands	133
6. Spain	123
7. Belgium	76
8. Denmark	39
9. Ireland	12
10. Portugal	10
11. Luxembourg	10
12. Greece	6
Total	$1.968

* Data: Federation of Stock Exchanges in the European Community; Business Week, July 4, 1990. This data is rounded to the nearest billion dollars.

- ◆ In London, settlements take 10 to 20 days, which is planned to be cut to three days by 1992.

- ◆ The Germans settle in two days which is three days faster than in America.

While technology can provide a common link, the biggest single factor to the success of the single stock market depends on how well the competing stock exchanges cooperate. The incentive for cooperation is there, but what about the political will?

8. A New Era in Swiss Brokerage

A computers and communications revolution is transforming Switzerland's seven regional stock exchanges, as the country is moving towards a nationwide, electronic trading system. As Europe's stock exchanges are in transition, Switzerland offers a good case study on integration.

In October 1989, brokerage banks approved a far-reaching project which set up a Swiss Electronic Exchange at an initial cost of SF 35 million ($27 million). By the end of 1990, trading in straight (bullet) bonds took place on computer screens, with dealers sitting at their desks in banks throughout the country. Gradually, the system expanded to include all bonds. Share trading will follow.

As in practically all other countries, Swiss securities have been classically traded on the stock exchange floor with brokers shouting buy and sell orders around a ring. This open-outcry system created a tense atmosphere as traders competed.

But markets change. The globalization of financial markets necessitated altering the old ways. And, as the preceding sections suggest, there has been demand also to increase efficiency and international market share—both being driving forces.

In 1987, Swiss exchanges took one of the most radical steps into databasing and networking when they built the first fully-automated futures and options exchange: the Swiss Options and Financial Futures Exchange (SOFFEX). Opened in 1988, this was the world's first fully electronic exchange from trading to clearing.

The SOFFEX effort began shortly after the 1987 stock market crash—at a time when investors were wary about stocks, let alone new experiments. Yet today it is hard to imagine the Swiss equity market without its services.

Subsequently, Switzerland exported the exchange's technology, and in January 1990, the Deutsche Terminbörse (DTB) began operating in Frankfurt using SOFFEX software. For Switzerland and Germany, both of which were criticized in the past for having unimaginative equity markets, the electronic exchanges are symbols of innovative times and sweeping changes in the whole market.

Switzerland is a good example of exchange innovation and networking because, as stated earlier, the country had seven stock exchanges operating the pit system. Now, the shares they trade form the basis for SOFFEX options, available on individual blue-chip Swiss stocks and on the Swiss Market Index (SMI).

Over its short lifespan, SOFFEX has grown more rapidly than its initiators anticipated. In 1989, its first full year of operation, the total number of traded contracts reached 6,139,730, with an average daily volume of 24,757. The capitalization of traded contracts was SF 73 billion ($56 billion).

By making the main exchange electronic as well, Swiss brokers believe that they can better tackle problems which have threatened to reduce Switzerland's importance as a stock trading center. But, able solutions to *organizational* problems are just as vital.

Current criticisms include inadequate turnover and low liquidity, largely caused by the fragmented state of a market where regional exchanges divide up trading. This may well happen with the integration of the twelve ECM stock exchanges through networking, and the lesson should not be overlooked.

It is largely local pride and financial impact which prevent the selection of one Swiss site to concentrate volume on a single stock exchange floor. Among the approaches suggested to overcome this obstacle is a networked system with no regional base, but able to integrate turnover to form a truly national exchange.[11]

As we saw in preceding sections, this is also the best answer to globalization—an important issue as some 300 Swiss and 230 foreign shares, belonging to fifteen different countries, are traded on Swiss stock exchanges. There are, as well, 1,500 Swiss and 900 foreign bonds. Such figures do not include pre-bourse stocks and private placements.

Like everybody else, the Swiss are concerned by globalization. In the last couple of years, blue-chip Swiss shares have increasingly traded in London. This raised fears that in the long term Switzerland could lose its present position, and technology seems to be the answer to maintaining a cutting edge.

For this as well as efficiency reasons, many institutional investors would like a speedier introduction of new instruments. Swiss Volksbank pension fund manager Martin Burri points out that there is a rapidly growing need for more risk management tools as the wealth in pension funds mounts.

◆ Today, the sum held in funds has reached SF 320 billion ($246 billion).

◆ This has produced an annual investment need of
  SF 32 billion ($24.6 billion).[12]

Domestic investors, particularly the larger ones, have a
significant say in Switzerland because, unlike its great rival
the Deutsche Mark bond-market, the Swiss market is dominated by domestic investors. Banks and insurance companies
have traditionally been big investors in bonds, and, as else-
where, the largest new block of money is coming from pension funds.

In 1985 pension became compulsory. By 1995, the assets
that Swiss pension funds own are expected to exceed the
country's Gross Domestic Product (GDP). Already the pension funds' assets amount to around SF 280 billion ($215
billion). A large chunk of this money will have to go into
financial instruments enhancing operations in the stock market.

9. Rule by the Securities Market

The drive is on to modernize stock exchanges, networking
them throughout the Common Market, creating customer
databases and focusing on the efficiency of member firms.
This has much to do with the fact that today (as well as in the
future) the stock market, rather than the Reserve bank, is (and
will be) the most influential controller of the economy.

Ambitious First World banks, as well as financially mighty
institutional investors, depend on the stock market for a
source of fresh capital and the maintenance of their independence. The economic importance of the financial industry
used to rest on the ability to turn cash into credit. Over long
decades, banks had money left with them either as savings or
as payments. They used it to make loans and kept the loans
they made.

This practice, however, made them vulnerable if the loans in reference defaulted, given that most banks were highly leveraged: their loans were usually around *twenty times* the value of their capital base.

Designed to protect the security of the payments system, the new rules from the Bank of International Settlements (BIS) oblige banks to reconsider their ability to make loans and, most particularly, to start marketing them.[13]

The BIS rules require banks to

1.   Back the assets they keep on their balance sheets.

2.   Protect their off-balance sheet items such as interest rate and foreign exchange swaps.

Protection takes the form of a fixed amount of capital above a certain minimum. This, in turn, tends to prevent banks from taking more risks than they can cope with.

The amount of capital needed to back an asset varies according to the presumed riskiness or volatility of the asset. Home mortgages, for instance, are reckoned by the BIS to be half as risky as other types of loans, whether they are collateralized or not.

This emphasis on the market mechanism is further promoted by the fact that while institutional investors remain the big players, alert middle-to-higher net worth individuals show encouraging signs of beginning to understand what value for money is all about. British, American and European high-net-worth individuals excel in this respect. Until recently, the usual practice was to surrender meekly to the traditional attitude of the banks, and for their part, banks thought that somehow they were doing customers a favor by offering them accounts.

However, the agile, open-eyed consumer today has awakened to the fact that he is essentially making an interest-free loan to the bank when he opens a checking account. The attractions of long-term savings plans is promoted by the different governments (for instance France and Germany), but there is more than that:

♦ A growing awareness of the potential rewards and risks of mutual fund investment have seen a rising awareness about alternatives.

♦ Several high-net-worth investors have now become proficient enough to manage their own financial property.

All this has significant aftermath. The question has often been asked, "What kind of activity has really been created underneath the overall growth in the financial industry?" The answer is *immense activity,* as statistics help document. In *securities transactions,* during the 1980s,

♦ Shares traded annually have gone up more than six-fold.

♦ Corporate bond volume, options volume, futures volumes have all grown at high rates.

♦ Debt has become the key financial instrument, because debt is easier to trade globally than equity.

Money management has become a big industry. In America by the end of the 1980s, there were 460 money market funds versus 36 such funds ten years earlier, as well as over 1,000 different mutual funds versus 390 in the late 1970s.

In America as well as in Europe, the securities business boomed, but the insurance industry has not been standing still either. In the United States, consumers purchased $1.2 trillion worth of life insurance per year by the end of the 1980s versus only $290 billion ten years earlier. And in the banking industry, cleared checks and interbank payments totaled $87 to $92 trillion at the end of the 1970s.

Such statistics are even more impressive if we account for the fact that by the end of the 1980s, American financial institutions had installed about 60,000 automated teller machines (ATMs), a business growing at 30 percent annually (there were only 6,000 ATMs ten years earlier). Measured by transactions, their usage has been growing at almost 50 percent a year.

All this adds up to a lot of financial activity, and proportionally growth figures are similar throughout the First World. There has been a very tough competition to control territory and markets. One does not need to be a mathematician to figure out that financial activity has gone up faster than gross revenues and productivity combined. The challenge is there to be met.

Endnotes

1. To avoid repeating concepts which go against the status quo but have already been treated in Chapter 1, this chapter places emphasis on another vital domain to investment banking: *networking*. Correspondingly, Chapter 3 will focus on distributed databases.

2. See also D.N. Chorafas and H. Steinmann, *Expert Systems in Banking* (London: Macmillan, and New York: New York University Press, 1991).

3. General Electric Information systems, an information network.

4. Decision Support Systems.

5. See also Chapters 13 to 15 in D.N. Chorafas, *Handbook of DBMS and Distributed Relational Databases* (New York: TAB Books/McGraw-Hill, 1989).

6. Discussed in Chapter 3.

7. Fuzzy sets contrast to crisp queries which can take a yes-or-no, 0-or-1 answer. "Maybe," "more," "less," "about right," "not enough" are keywords in fuzzy engineering, expressing qualitative rather than quantitative values. They are also representative of the way professionals and managers think.

8. This solution is currently in operation at Yamaichi Securities among other Japanese institutions.

9. National Association of Securities Dealers, particularly addressing the former over-the-counter market.

10. Statistics as of mid-1990.

11. Transnational in the case of the EEC.

12. *Swiss Business*, July/August 1990.

13. See also D.N. Chorafas: *Bank Profitability* (London: Butterworths, 1989).

Chapter 3

The Japanese Market Rises to the Challenge

Chapter 3

The Japanese Market Rises to the Challenge

1. Introduction

Article 65 of the Japanese constitution stipulates that commercial banking and securities business should be conducted by separate companies. Such a rule naturally delimits the environment of a financial institution.

Yet, just as has happened in America,[1] since the deregulation of interest rates, there has been a rapid transformation, and money market certificates of over a half-million Yen have been liberalized. With this, competition in the Japanese financial market is becoming more tense.

For the time being, there is a fuzzy border between the business of banks and securities companies—with a review underway by regulating authorities. Since by now business conducted by commercial and investment banks overlaps, many people expect that Article 65 will be repealed.

This liklihood is taken into account by practically all medium-term plans of Japanese financial institutions. In a sim-

ilar manner, measures are taken that deal with the introduction of stiffer capital ratio requirements by the Bank for
International Settlements.

In examining the landscape of the Japanese financial industry as a whole, we should appreciate that it is more fragmented
than that in many other countries. This landscape is divided
into government and private institutions:

◆ *Government* financial institutions include 2
  banks, 10 finance corporations, 1 public corporation, 1 trust fund bureau, and the current ac-
  count/savings operations of 23,986 port offices.

◆ *Ordinary (commercial) banks* subdivided into 12
  city banks, 64 regional banks, 66 member banks
  of the Second Association of Regional Banks,[2]
  and 82 foreign banks.

◆ *Financial institutions for long-term credit:* 1 foreign
  exchange bank, 3 long-term credit banks, 7 trust
  banks, and 9 foreign trust banks.

◆ *Financial institutions for small businesses:* 2 Sogo
  (mutual) banks, 47 labor banks, 454 Shinkin
  banks (credit associations), 414 credit corporative
  banks, and 1 Shoko Chukin (Central Cooperative) bank for Commerce and Industry.

◆ *A Norinchukin Bank (Central Cooperative for Agricul-
  ture and Forestry),* on which depend 47 credit
  federations of agricultural cooperatives, 35 credit
  federations of fishery cooperatives, and 3,745
  agricultural cooperatives.

◆ *Insurance companies,* of which 26 are oriented
  to life insurance and 23 to property/casualty
  insurance.

◆ *11 private housing finance companies.*

◆ *6 Tanshi (call loans) firms.*

◆ *271 securities brokers*, and

◆ *3 securities finance companies.*

Nomura Securities, one of the 271 securities brokers, is the largest of its kind in the world. In 1988, Sanyo Securities (partly controlled by Nomura) opened a new trading floor in central Tokyo, which is believed to the largest such facility in the world. The huge hall, built at a cost of Yen 8.9 billion ($64 million), can hold up to 800 dealers buying and selling stocks, bonds and foreign currencies. Yet, Sanyo is only the seventh largest Japanese broker!

Among the Japanese securities houses are some of the most advanced in the global use of computers, communications, knowledge engineering, and simulators. In Chapter 1, Morgan Stanley was named as one of the best examples in America, and in Chapter 2, a similar ranking was given to County NatWest in Britain; there are many "best examples" in Japan.

This financial and technological might stands behind Japanese direct investments in America and in Europe, feeding with a steady money line the expansion of the multinationals. Investments made outside the country of origin—whether American, Japanese or European—are made for one of two major reasons:

1. Cheaper resources such as labor, capital and raw materials.

2. Access to the more lucrative markets of the 1990s and of the 21st Century.

Japan's investments in America and Europe are of the second type. By cutting transportation costs, avoiding the strong yen, leaping trade barriers, and adjusting product designs to local tastes, firms seek to expand their share of the booming First World market. In doing so, Japanese firms bring with them their most valuable assets: high technology and management methods.

2. Emphasis on Technology by the Bank of Japan

The Ministry of International Trade and Industry (MITI) provides macroeconomic guidelines to Japanese manufacturing and merchandizing companies. Through its Institute for Monetary and Economic Studies, the Bank of Japan plays a similar role in the financial industry:

◆ It monitors developments affecting financial institutions, and

◆ Guides the hand of these institutions in fields ranging from economics to technology.

As the 1991 meetings in Tokyo helped clarify, the Institute for Financial and Monetary Affairs is essentially the Research Division of the Bank of Japan. Among the projects to which the Institute addresses itself are the following:

1. Global System for Forex Transactions

Its goal is to examine, among other issues, those connected to cross-database access—including currency, country and credit. The project introduces a global concept which will, most likely, be popular in both Japanese and international banking during the 1990s.

2. The Study of Fuzzy Engineering, Implementation, as well as for Neural Networks

This study began in early 1991 with Forex as a target area (along with other cross-DBMS applications). The Japanese properly appreciate that differences in database management systems (DBMS) are only one aspect of the whole problem, and the emphasis is on the use of high technology to support complex financial transactions.

3. The Integration of Electronic Funds Transfer (EFT) within the Banking System

There seems to be a joint project between the Bank of Japan and Hitachi focusing on bank interconnection through novel approaches to networking and database management. In its work on this new generation of EFT, Hitachi benefits by finding itself at an advanced stage of developing an object-oriented multimedia DBMS known as Mandrill.

4. Creation of a Financial Database for Balance Sheet and Profit and Loss

The Bank of Japan follows the line of reasoning that generic database solutions require a careful study of transactional processing, the distributed database structure itself and management information system (MIS) perspectives. Such an approach encompasses both the overall concept and the possible constraints due to the heterogeneity of solutions which took place in the past.

The example of the Institute for Monetary and Economic Studies is unique. No reserve bank of the First World has so participated in helping financial institutions face the challenge of mastering future technology.[3] In all this effort, emphasis is placed on a system approach which considers both the policies and the technology necessary for migration towards the efficient use of newer technologies—as well as the need for Front desk/Back office integration.

With reference to the studies which it is conducting, the Bank of Japan emphasizes the growing importance of MIS and the need for online analytical queries. Both are cornerstones of competitiveness of financial institutions in the 1990s. While *ad hoc* analytical queries make the migration process towards a virtually homogeneous environment, they are thought to be an integral part of able solutions for this decade and beyond.

3. The Key Role of Financial Databases

After thirty-five years of computer usage, the foremost American, European, and Japanese financial institutions appreciate that their databases have become very significant corporate resources with a great deal of information which must be exploited in an able manner. Through knowledge engineering, simulation, and supercomputers, the more advanced financial institutions engage in *pattern recognition* for

◆ Customer profiles,

◆ Market trends, and

◆ Product penetration.

Through a process known as *database mining*,[4] they interactively extract from their database a significant amount of information which helps in accurately focusing on customers, markets and products—both orienting future actions and fine-tuning existing plans.

Such solutions are rich in knowledge-engineering applications as well as tools. Many go beyond expert system implementation, using advanced classification schemes and pattern recognition—as well as fuzzy engineering and neural networks.

In Japan, advanced database mining applications are typically done on-line through telecommunications interfaces and database sharing, an approach which has been initiated by the Dai-Ichi Kangyo Bank. The Fuji Bank provides another excellent example of on-line implementation of analytical queries.

However, the Bank of Japan seems to be concerned by the fact that many other financial institutions still rely on the outdated magnetic tape connectivity between the transactional database and MIS—working largely in a batch mode. (This, incidently, is no different than retrograde practices by financial institutions both in America and throughout Europe.)

"To work memory-to-memory, banks need to solve the problem of database heterogeneity," said the responsible executive of the Institute for Monetary and Economic Studies, adding that, "A pure data transfer process is easy, but cross-database access in a distributed environment is complex because of the overriding heterogeneity."

On-line MIS applications, the Bank of Japan insists, must be fed with *live data* from the transactional system—considering both *short transactions* and *long transactions*.

In a way similar to that prevalent in America and Europe, this problem is aggravated by the heterogeneity of equipment. Many financial institutions use Fujitsu machines for transaction handling, Hitachi computers for MIS and IBM for international operations—making an effective communication database-to-database difficult.

Therefore, a recent study by the Bank of Japan underlines the need to focus on virtual database homogeneity. The more advanced financial institutions, this study says, understand this problem. Further, they appreciate that for effective management control the following steps must be taken:

♦ MIS must expand its functionality into the area of analysis through algorithms and heuristics;

♦ The transactional system must become more tightly connected to MIS; and

♦ On-line solutions should dominate the financial industries' landscape.

In fact, the Bank of Japan study underlines that both transaction processing and MIS should be endowed with faster and more effective on-line solutions than currently available. This points the way towards *intelligent networks* interconnecting with *distributed deductive databases.*

The guideline is that development work must pay great attention to *ad hoc,* on-line analytical queries while accounting for the fact that some of the current applications run on old technology. Emphasis must also be placed on system integration requirements.

An excellent effort along this line has been undertaken by Nippon Telegraph and Telephone (NTT) with the *Multivendor Integration Architecture* (MIA). The object of MIA is the establishment of software platform specifications which permit

♦ An open networking environment

♦ Cross-system software portability

♦ Heterogeneous database interconnection, and

♦ The support of uniform human interfaces.

MIA Version 1 reaches the first two of these objectives and is already operating. Version 2, scheduled for completion in early 1993, addresses itself to the other two goals.

Clear-eyed Japanese bankers realize that able solutions to this problem are very important. The analysis done by the

Institute for Monetary and Economic Studies further suggests that truly on-line information systems solutions necessarily involve system migration, which is itself dependent on both

- ◆ The type of current DBMS, and
- ◆ The new database solutions being projected.

This study aptly documents that management-oriented and bank-to-client on-line communications can be more effective through distributed information systems, with transparent interfaces to applications. This requires very rich *data dictionaries* and object-oriented approaches.

The Bank of Japan also believes that those financial institutions which strengthen their transactional system are on the right track. One of its reports says that some Japanese banks (not identified) use supercomputers, as they find them more economical than mainframes, in facing growing transactional traffic.

It is also acknowledged that virtual database integration of heterogeneous files will have a great impact on computer power requirements. Virtual integration procedures act as cycle sponges in terms of computer power and further call under perspective supercomputer usage.

4. Solutions Adopted by Leading Japanese Financial Institutions

Meetings held with some of the Japanese City Banks[5] have yielded significant results. The best of these meetings was with the Fuji Bank, Dai-Ichi Kangyo, the Sanwa Bank, and— among brokers—Yamaichi Securities. (We will explore many of the breakthroughs of Japanese securities houses, and most particularly Yamaichi, in subsequent chapters of this book.)

Like all leading financial institutions, the Fuji Bank is currently faced by an accute database restructuring problem precisely because of its success in MIS implementation. Fuji is one of the few international banks which has inline as much MIS files as transactional files, precisely 750 gigabytes for MIS and 750 gigabytes for transactional—a total of 1.5 terabytes on-line. This large database structure is split between IMS, DB2, XDM/RD and other DBMS, posing the problem of virtual integration.

A major current project is to provide Fuji Bank managers and professionals with *ad hoc* analytical query capabilities. The leading applications are detailed below.

Asset/Liability Management

This project is undertaken as a joint effort with Hitachi. (The same is true of a model which has been developed by Fuji's Capital Market group.) Other preoccupations are exemplified by an emphasis on project control with knowledge engineering-assisted queries for management usage.

Several Fuji Bank projects mate the best in new technology with object-oriented solutions. An example is the ongoing study on assets/liability management.

Pricing Models for Bonds and Options

Other advanced applications, too, rely heavily on mathematics. Pricing models are an example. There is as well a movement away from magnetic storage through extended optical disk usage. Optical media are employed with applications such as transaction handling, foreign credit, documentary reference to stock and bond portfolios and so on.

Transition in Information Technology Project

Management sees such transition as a vital step for survival in an increasingly competitive marketplace. Though its specific goals were not identified, this project involves forty of the best information technology specialists of Fuji Bank, and it is done in cooperation with Hitachi.

Some of the peak technology projects the Dai-Ichi Kangyo Bank currently has in progress include global risk control, asset/liability management, and global cost control. All three are approached through database integration perspectives.

Like other peak technology financial institutions, Dai-Ichi is looking for the best tools in computers, communications and knowledge engineering to implement database integration. One of the major preoccupations of the bank's management is the full redesign of the Information System for Headquarters. This was originally designed in 1973 and steadily improved—but has now reached the level where significant changes are required.

The first of the new generation MIS subsystems appeared in 1985 and involved expert systems. Today the MIS at Dai-Ichi has twelve subsystems (each fairly complex) which are fully operational, making database restructuring mandatory.

In a cross-database sense, *ad hoc* analytical queries have been made a management priority, promoted by

◆ Globalization

◆ Deregulation, and

◆ New financial products treated as commodities

To enhance competitiveness within this challenging environment, everything operates on-line, real-time. There is no more batching at Dai-Ichi; now, the emphasis is on *end user computing* in order to cut the huge backlog in applications programming[6] and accelerate development.

The twelve MIS subsystems are credited at Dai-Ichi Kangyo for having significantly improved management and professional productivity. At the same time, they have accelerated user demands for new applications. "The only way out is to train the end user to develop his own applications," said the responsible executive. Then he added: "But you can't do successfully end-user computing without database restructuring and virtual homogeneity."

Four major system components must now be integrated in a cross-database manner to support global on-line profit and loss perspectives:

◆ Branches

◆ Customers

◆ Products and

◆ Markets

Global cost control, for instance, will be carried all the way to P+L by branch and customer reference, with *ad hoc* analytical queries being examined interactively. The bank anticipates that this will require integrating hierarchical and relational DBMS as well as heterogeneous data structures. An object-oriented approach is contemplated.

5. The Way to an Improved Corporate Performance

Among the current priority projects at the Sumitomo Bank are global risk management, interest risk computing, and global cost control. Here again, top management's preoccupations are no different than those of other leading Japanese financial institutions with advanced applications executed on-line, including

◆ Loans exposure

◆ Risk calculation and

◆ Asset/liability management

To avoid discontinuity between transactional and MIS implementations, the Sanwa Bank has focused its attention on Fourth Generation On-line Systems (4GOLS) which use artificial intelligence. Another key project centers on the need for closing the gap between fourth generation intelligent networks and second generation DBMS, which are used mostly in the financial industry. In the opinion of American commercial, merchant, and investment banks, the best of the currently available relational DBMS—from IMS, IDS and DMS to DB2, RDB, Ingres, Oracle, Sybase and Informix—have been designed for short transactions, and they are very limited in handling *long transactions*.

Short transactions have dominated banking so far (for instance, connected to current accounts, savings, the buying and selling done on a one-shot basis). Simple queries are also a kind of short transaction typically executed through mainly non-intelligent terminals—for example, interogating the balance of an account for the last withdrawal or deposit or a certain position in a portfolio.

For portfolio management purposes which are akin to long transactions, the basis of the support requirements has changed. A long transaction addresses itself to complex operations where a buy-or-sell order by a client may involve multiple updates in heterogeneous databases. For example,

◆ The contents of a client portfolio,

◆ The client's current accounts in different currencies,

◆ Securities held with corresponding banks,

◆ Commitments made in different currencies,

◆ Transactions executed at different exchanges
   and so on.

Alternatively, a long transaction may involve a sequence of
short transactions, where one operation leads to another
throughout the network of a financial institution. Typically,
commitments are made at each node which bear on the
further execution of the client's business. Long transactions
can only be assisted through object-oriented approaches.

The Sanwa Bank also addresses itself to the task of interfac-
ing and integrating heterogeneous databases, including extensive use of optical disks. The latter is an ongoing project,
as the bank considers *imaging* the way to solve many of the
anticipated database problems.

For networking purposes, Sanwa has adopted an ISO/OSI-
based architecture for its database integration—an approach
which is becoming quite popular in Japan. This has been
pioneered by the MIA project of Nippon Telegraph and Telephone discussed earlier.

Compared to the database problems faced by the larger
financial institutions, those of the Tomin Bank, a regional
Japanese bank, are relatively simple. So far, the Tomin Bank
has upheld the principle of database integration by sticking
to IMS. However, management increasingly finds that IMS
cannot respond to the growing wave of *ad hoc* analytical query
requirements.

Tomin serves 1 million clients through a network of eighty-
two branches in the Tokyo area (plus one in New York) and
has 2,400 employees. Strict control of personnel costs is a

characteristic of Japanese banks—using technology to truly automate operations. Tomin has a first-class record on this account. Table 3–1 compares five banks in terms of assets and number of employees. The statistics bring into perspective the huge discrepencies in terms of assets managed by each employee.

Japanese financial institutions clearly lead in cost/effectiveness, and such statistics provide food for thought. But to maintain its lead, the Japanese financial industry wants to break out of the limits imposed by the old DBMS. This is the starting point of the search for greater effectiveness.

6. A Quick Look at Meetings with Computer Vendors

The meeting with Nippon Electric (NEC) focused on database management systems and the distinction between *relational* and object-oriented DBMS in terms of interconnection. Relational and *object-oriented* approaches both complement and contrast to one another.

According to studies done by Nippon Electric, object-oriented databases and their DBMS should run on distributed workstations and file servers, predominantly under Unix. Many other computer vendors also have commented that mainframes are inappropriate for object-based solutions. This approach will underpin future developments in Japan, impacting on the solutions being adopted by financial institutions.

Today, all three major Japanese computer vendors work on object-oriented database management systems and associated software:

- ◆ NEC's object-oriented DBMS is *Odin*
- ◆ Fujitsu's is *Jasmine* (on Sun)
- ◆ Hitachi's is *Mandrill*[7]

Table 3–1   A Critical Comparison of Personnel Requirements vs. Money Center Bank Size and Worth of Assets

Financial Institution	World Banking Classification	Assets*	People	Assets** Managed by Employee
Fuji	3	$363 B	14,380	$23.60 M
Citibank	24	$217 B	57,250	$ 3.79 M
Barclays	13	$189 B	116,500	$ 1.60 M
BoA	50	$111 B	47,650	$ 2.33 M
Tomin Bank	—	$ 15 B	2,400	$ 6.25 M

---

* In billions of dollars.

** In millions of dollars.

All three are in development and testing. Practical applications with distributed networked computer systems are projected for 1993.

One particular implementation looks at object-oriented solutions as a metalayer over relational and other DBMS in current use.[8] According to the NEC researchers, a further significant strength of the object-based approach is in document management—including multimedia databases.

The demonstration of NEC's Odin has left a favorable impression. The application was a library management system handling, as objects, books, authors, and borrowers of books.

Being in the computers and communications business, NEC is also working on voice implementation of object-oriented DBMS. This gives the user the possibility to define a voice class, providing methods for object manipulation.

Part of the meeting with DEC Japan was devoted to the description of a project currently underway in Japan, under MITI sponsorship, on the 6th Generation Computers (6GC). An international policy meeting was held to that effect mid-March 1991 in Tokyo, with full implementation of the 6GC concept due by early 1992.

In accordance with the way MITI has structured this project, work is currently conducted by three parallel working committees, each addressing one of the following subjects:

◆ A thorough analysis of brain functioning

◆ New computers and communications hardware and software (including photonics)

◆ Social impact of the new wave in computing and community intelligence

DEC Japan is also one of the players in MIA. Hence, the DEC meeting covered the MIA partners' view of current efforts towards global specifications and open vendor policy by NTT. The same reference on ongoing projects by DEC Japan is valid for MITI's new project on an Intelligent Manufacturing System.

A subsequent meeting with DEC focused on global databases and, most particularly, the applications taking place at Mitsubishi Bank, Sumitomo Bank, Nomura Securities, and Nikko Securities. The goal of their unified database structures is the construction of a total dealing system for Forex Treasury, Securities.

Another interesting project being done by DEC Japan, at Yamaichi Securities, concerns networked file servers through FDDI, operating in real-time and replacing current Hyperchannel links for interconnected databases.

Still another important project, at Wako Securities, focuses on a *market data filter* and a *securities database*. Both are subjects which, in the 1990s, will distinguish those investment banks which know how to keep up with future challenges from those which don't.

7. Projects for the Securities Industry by Japanese Computer Firms

During our meeting, Fujitsu presented an imaginative application of neural networks for Stock Market Prediction. It is one of the best applications of its type. The Fujitsu neural network has been implemented at Nikko Securities, but is also available for other brokers. The model is based on Tokyo Stock Exchange (TSE) data and involves six key factors affecting the prediction process:

1.   Stock vector curve.

2 Turnover.

3. Interest rate.

4. Forex rate.

5. Dow Jones.

6. TSE learning curve.

The six factors are presented as a *radar chart* in Figure 3–1. There is enough information available to feed this chart with a comprehensive description of market movements; time of the day is the seventh dimension in a real life implementation.

In terms of database interconnection, Fujitsu follows the guidelines established by the Los Angeles-based SQL Access Group, which involves thirty-one companies from the United States and Japan. For database interconnection in a distributed environment, work is also done on ISO/OSI Remote Data Access (RDA), SQL 2 and SQL 3.[9]

Hitachi, too, is following the RDA approach, with particular emphasis on solutions in a transactional environment. Ongoing studies use as protocols ISO/TP and ISO/CCR.

In the opinion of both Hitachi and Fujitsu, the current RDA work should lead by 1992-93 to an international decision on standardization—provided that the SQL Access Group can create a trans-database command infrastructure for heterogeneous distributed databases.

Since this premise is far from sure, both companies are working on parallel projects which involve artificial intelligence—hence *deductive databases*. They are also investing in object-oriented solutions as stated earlier.

**Figure 3–1   A Radar Chart Implementation by
                Japanese Investment Banks**

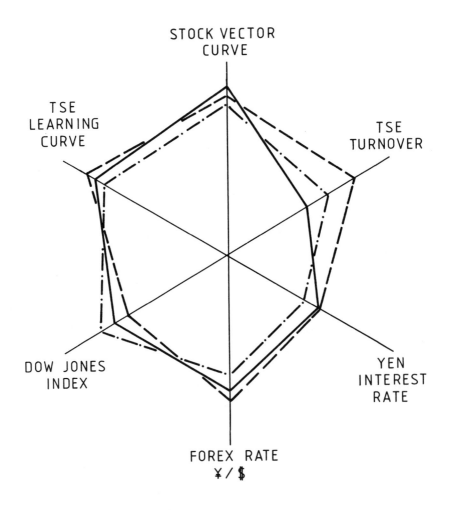

Toshiba specializes on workstations, and the same is true of the applications environment which it develops. Daiwa Securities and Yamaichi Securities have asked for a flexible, real-time stock-and-bond system of networked WS which can be customized.

In this as in similar projects, the goal is to support the trader's viewpoint by

◆ Providing real-time market information at the trader's workstation;

◆ Storing data for subsequent historical analysis through knowledge engineering; and

◆ Permitting self-actuated computing by the end user, as the need arises.

From a system viewpoint, this solution is currently in an advanced stage of development aiming at high performance, fast response time (0.3 seconds), data independence, and applications independence. The latter two are object-oriented requirements.

Knowledge engineering-enriched software assures that applications can be built and aborted by the user, and data can change dynamically while the application(s) continue to focus on the data flow. At the file server level, the goal is the ability to cope with

◆ Heavy traffic,

◆ Changing traffic patterns,

◆ Modular flexibility, and

◆ High reliability.

On the whole, the Toshiba Stock and Bond Trading application is imaginative and warrants a detailed study. The same is true of Integral 25 developed by Yamaichi Securities for stock and bond management.

In a way, the Toshiba and Yamaichi solutions complement one another but also have some overlap. Since Yamaichi will most likely be using the Toshiba trading solution, any serious study should definitely consider their integrative capability as well as the benefits each and both can provide to the user organization.

8. Standards Set by the Center for Financial Industry Information Systems (FISC)

Having completed a two-year study on behalf of the Japanese Ministry of Finance in connection to global risk management, FISC is currently focusing its activities on the following four areas, all of which have a database connection.

1.   Standards for a cross-vendor environment.

This concentrates on database integration. FISC works on concepts and standards but not on specific technical solutions; software development is not part of its mission.

2.   The implementation of risk management.

This is projected to take a cross-database approach, along the lines already approved by the Japanese Government on the basis of Report No. 13, which has been prepared by FISC on the Ministry's request.

3.   Security of personal information.

This, too, will be implemented cross-database; the specific strategy to be adopted will be based on the results of an ongoing study. To a large measure, the study favors the privacy protection standards of the European Community.

4.   The coming "Big Bang" in Japanese banking.

This FISC study is nearing completion, and the discussion which has taken place indicates that there will be a significant amount of political give-and-take prior to final decisions concerning the repeal of Article 65.

◊   ◊   ◊

One of the key issues to which FISC currently addresses its attention is the establishment of appropriate guidelines for security and the protection of personal data. These will influence substantially the practices and policies to be established and followed during the 1990s by the Japanese financial industry.

In light of such efforts, vital considerations in the construction and administration of a corporate database are the security/protection rules to be observed by financial institutions as well as computer and communications vendors. (This is the essence of the guidelines currently elaborated by FISC at the request of the Japanese Government.)

In relation to this research, a working group has studied Japanese financial institutions to elaborate basic principles on security and privacy to be adopted by the financial industry, including not only local banks but also foreign banks operating in Japan.

This study has followed the OECD directives of the 1980s which place emphasis on privacy, for example, from tax matters, providing the necessary protection of the contents of customer accounts. Similar guidelines have been issued by MITI for the manufacturing industry.

That Japan is following the lines of privacy protection as established by the European Community is significant inasmuch as America resists (and in some cases rejects) some of the European privacy rules. This is particularly true of those that restrict how computerized information such as personal medical or insurance records and airline reservation records, can be used by businesses and government agencies.

For instance, a new set of European proposals, currently studied by the Japanese, would prohibit a publisher from selling a list of subscribers to real estate developers unless the subscribers agreed to be included. Also, banks would be required to notify credit card holders before selling their names to mail-order houses.

Such legal restrictions do not exist in the United States, where companies have built huge databases of financial, medical, commercial, and other types of personal information that have become a critical part of the way they do business. America enacted privacy laws in 1974 to ensure that the Government did not invade personal privacy, but the law did not extend to the commercial sector. Japan seems to be moving along the European lines in protecting personal privacy from invaders.

Though the issue of personal privacy may seem distinct from the deregulation of the financial industry, in reality it relates to it. Rules must be established before the aftermath of deregulation leads to privacy invasion practices. It is, therefore, insightful that, regarding the forthcoming Japanese "Big Bang," a study is being conducted by FISC, on behalf of the government, on how to cope with the privacy aftermaths of deregulation.

No details were provided on this issue except that Article 65 will gradually drop, but the final decision on how the "Big Bang" will be implemented is not yet made. "The ways of implementation are being discussed, and they are in hot argument," said Mr. Hattori, the Executive Director of FISC.

It was also remarked that the Japanese government does not want to provoke complaints due to merits and demerits issued by the financial industry branch. Hence, deregulation will be tuned so as to distribute benefits rather than monopolize markets and products—but personal privacy will be protected.

Endnotes

1. The Glass-Steagall Act is at the origin of Article 65.

2. Former Sogo banks which changed their status to ordinary.

3. There is in Japan another institute co-sponsored by the financial industry and leading computers/communications vendors—FISC (discussed later).

4. To which brief reference has been made in Chapter 2. The term literally means mining the financial database for valuable information, such as customer profiles, demographic trends, hidden costs—which is transparent to the casual database user.

5. In Japan, City Banks are the main commercial banks.

6. Which, incidently, is presently experienced by every major bank of the First World.

7. A couple of Japanese universities are also developing object-oriented languages and DBMS. So does NTT Data, but is more secretive about its projects.

8. Hewlett-Packard has a similar project in Palo Alto distinguishing between object-oriented deductive database solutions through Pegasus, and local database management based on the IRIS object-based DBMS.

9. SQL2 addresses transaction processing requirements; SQL3, graphics and other interactive applications. Both are supersets of SQL1, the ANSI standard.

The Services a Technological Infrastructure Should Provide

Chapter **4**

The Services a Technological Infrastructure Should Provide

1. Introduction

Goldman Sachs & Co. investigated the massively parallel Connection Machine (CM-2)—the world's most powerful computer—for use in the mortgage-backed securities (MBS) market. Their researchers determined that massive parallelism cannot be exploited without *new mathematics,* a discipline now being used for economic modeling and trade analysis, to estimate accurately the prepayment characteristics of a mortgage pool, and to develop solutions for controlling risk in real time.

New mathematics, the domain of Wall Street's rocket scientists, consists of a combination of simulation studies and heuristics. *Simulation* refers to a working analogy that allows emulation of the behavior of financial systems. *Heuristics* is a conceptual, nonprocedural approach based on trial and error that makes it possible to study processes that involve vagueness and uncertainty—two qualities that are characteristic of the conditions prevailing in financial markets.

Much of the new mathematics comes under the cumulative name of artificial intelligence (AI). AI is both a concept and a set of advanced technological tools. These tools enable computers to understand and manipulate knowledge as well as information. AI allows users to perform many more tasks than they ever could with conventional approaches and techniques.

With artificial intelligence, knowledge is readily available at networked workstations, though some of the background work may be done on number-crunching supercomputers. The industrialization of knowledge transforms the work of investment bankers and securities experts from developing opinions that are often inconclusive to making factual and documented diagnoses of market situations. Experimentation makes possible the development of alternative hypotheses and assumptions and their weighting, including any relevant subjective judgements.

Complex financial models have to be executed in real time at subsecond speed, and this requires supercomputers. These parallel computers operate at billions of instructions per second. They are used as computational servers to augment the calculation power of existing data-processing installations.

Supercomputers are a new, highly cost-effective element in the solution matrix. The same is true of *intelligent networks,* which allow *distributed databases* to interconnect among themselves and with end users in a seamless manner. AI constructs at the nodes ensure that the system will make an optimal choice of routes, and also enable the speedy introduction of new services (See Figure 4–1).

Figure 4-1   Enterprise-Wide Communications Systems Enriched with Artificial Intelligence

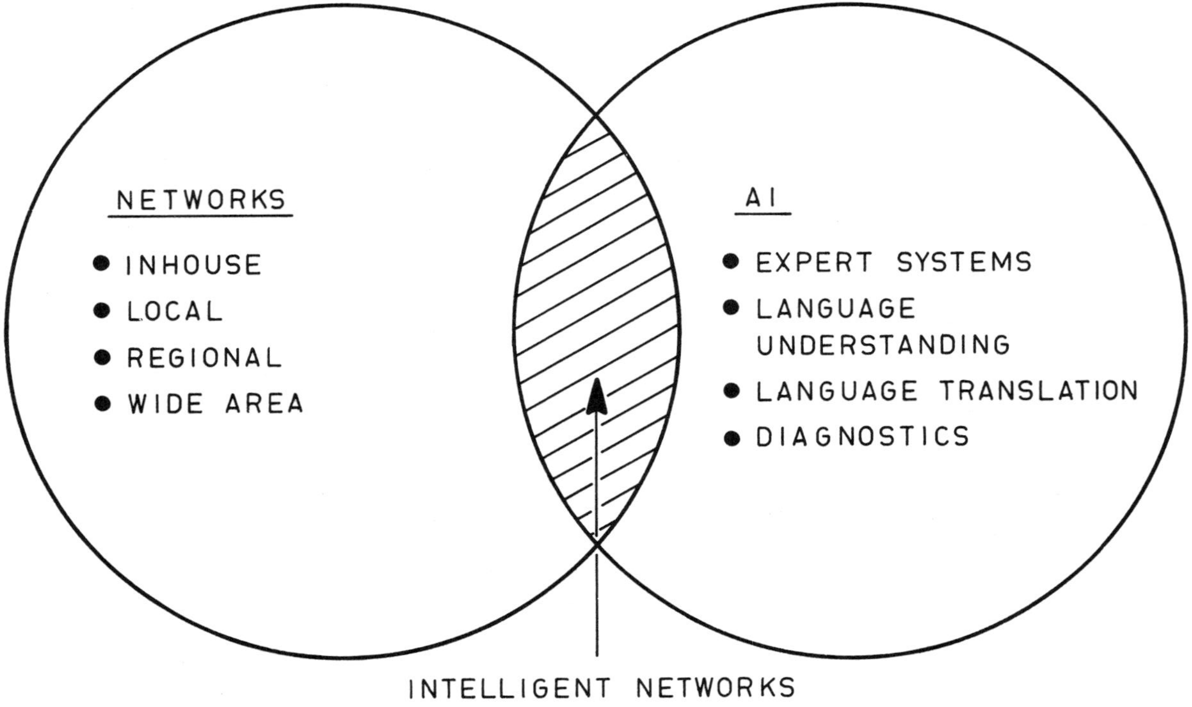

NETWORKS
- INHOUSE
- LOCAL
- REGIONAL
- WIDE AREA

AI
- EXPERT SYSTEMS
- LANGUAGE UNDERSTANDING
- LANGUAGE TRANSLATION
- DIAGNOSTICS

INTELLIGENT NETWORKS

2. The State of the Art in Banking Technology

Financial institutions, if they keep up with new banking technology, know that competition in personal communications networks, satellite bridges, and optical fiber highways results in a universal bypass that every knowledgeable firm can exploit. In the communications domain, fast-packet switching will soon make 64-kilobit-per-second (KBPS) transmission obsolete, with the future corporate network being a hybrid of public and private services.

- ◆ Bandwidth will become a commodity item, available on demand.

- ◆ The bandwidth unit of measurement will be megastreams and gigastreams.

- ◆ Fiber optics will be economical even for the local loop, while tariffs will fall steeply.

- ◆ Multimedia convergence will characterize networks, terminals, and applications.

Aware financial institutions recognize that inadequate network management has become a major impediment to profitability. The same is true of incompatible or incoherent databases, as well as a lack of the skills necessary to exploit text and data resources.

Very large databases must be managed efficiently. In larger financial institutions, such databases may exceed one trillion bytes[1] (terabytes) of storage available on-line and include the information the bank needs to carry on its business. This includes—internal data from corporate operations, such as accounting, transactions, financial products, production and distribution operations, personnel, marketing, and other pertinent information; external data from the environment, such as clients, markets, moneys, commercial and financial paper, competition (direct and indirect), interest rates, exchange rates, government regulations, status and trends in the economy, and other pertinent exogenous information.

The database of the financial institution can be managed by a Database Administrator (DBA) and his or her assistants with the aid of software such as a database management system (DBMS). This is a commercially available package that performs useful functions (such as file creation, access, update, maintenance, search, sort, security, protection, and report generation) over the data available in the database (see Figure 4–2).

Recent developments in software technology have made many DBMS packages user friendly. By using fourth- and fifth-generation languages, these packages provide considerable flexibility which can be further enhanced through AI. (To manage expert system rules as well as states and functions of the domain, knowledge-bank management systems (KBMS) are needed.)

Many financial institutions are now implementing database systems enriched through AI. This convergence of research in artificial intelligence and database management makes it possible to—

1. support efficient user interfaces and natural language for question/answering sessions;

2. endow databases with reasoning, planning, and justification capabilities;

3. permit effective specification, prototyping, testing, and debugging of complex database applications;

4. provide sophisticated tools to support the indexing, manipulation, and evolution of large databases;

Figure 4-2   End Users, Distributed Databases and Data Sources

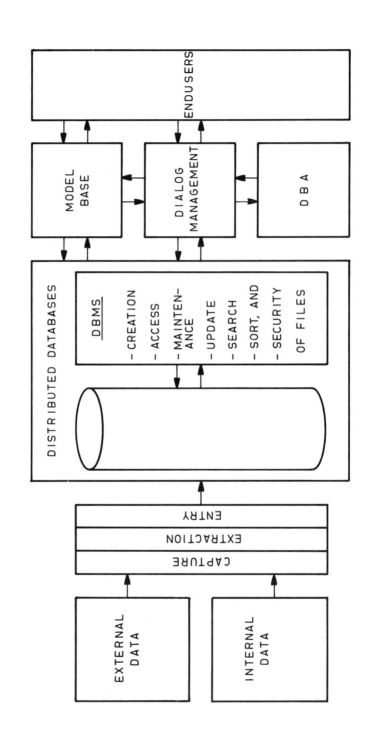

5.   integrate KBMS and DBMS functionality into
     new software and hardware environments.

According to a study done by Datapro, 57 percent of 1,729
American information-system executives polled have implemented electronic document processing and retrieval systems, or are considering doing so.[2] Electronic document
processing, also known as imaging, is based on optical disk
technology. It offers a high density of recording, cost effectiveness, and the ability to handle compound electronic
documents, thus automating paperwork that has long resisted
computer processing.

In terms of bits per gram, image-handling applications have
a density of recording 5 orders of magnitude (100,000 times)
greater than paper and 2 orders of magnitude (100 times)
greater than magnetic tape. In Babylonian times, cuneiform
recording held 10-2 (one hundredth) of a bit per gram; paper
records and books feature 10-3 per gram; microfilm, 10-5;
magnetic tape, 10-6; and optical discs, 10-8 per gram.

The difference between cuneiform and optical disc is 10
orders of magnitude (10,000,000,000 times) and recording on
paper stands mid-range. Yet, many financial institutions have
not yet benefited from what recording technology has made
available to them.

Another area where technological breakthroughs may be
advantageous is that of *human windows,* more commonly
known as man-machine interfaces. The dialogue component
should be efficient and user friendly; therefore, it should
include different types of hardware and software enriched
through AI, such as visualization through graphics terminals
and agile software interfaces. Since the majority of end users
in the financial industry are not computer experts, ease of
usage plays an important role in the acceptance and efficient
implementation of computers and communications systems.

Multimedia visualization is the eyepiece of the computer. Its effective application requires supercomputer power that can model and predict complex dynamic systems. Gary Demos said during the Frontiers 88 Symposium, "Graphics stresses a lot of general performance capabilities." Demos uses the Connection Machine in his work on animated graphics.

Visualization refers to turning numbers into images. It accelerates the discovery process and reduces time spent in problem conception and data analysis.

In comparing such supercomputer developments to the microscope and the telescope, Nobel laureate Kenneth G. Wilson once said that visualization is not yet perfected. But technology is now firmly headed in this direction, with immense architectural implications for financial systems to come.

3. Computers, Communications, and Human Resources

The research done by the author in 1989, 1990 and 1991, in America, Europe, and Japan indicates that high technology is being implemented by the major financial institutions, particularly in America and in Japan. Also, financial institutions that continue to make investments for "historical" or "cosmetic" reasons are discovering that the return on investment is dubious at best. The leaders in the financial industry are investing in supercomputers and intelligent networks, not in EDP.[3]

It is important to note, however, that a sound high-technology implementation starts on a selective basis. Some financial institutions, in simply buying more machinery and hiring more programmers, have ended up with more unsolved information than they could manage; they have also lost their flexibility in facing fast-developing market requirements.

In 1987, according to an article in *Business Week,* the Bank of New England fielded a staff of fifty to convert all its computers and software to a single standard—a monumental task not yet completed, and one that led to other problems. Information was sometimes lost because so many conversions were pushed through as fast as possible, and customer accounts got scrambled in the rush. "At BNE-North, which covered the Marrimack Valley in northern Massachusetts, where many of the real estate problems first surfaced, officers were unable to produce a loan-delinquency report for four crucial months at the end of 1988."[4]

Some financial companies try to correct past errors in their information-systems policy only to discover that this entails a lot of write offs. In January 1991, Merrill Lynch reported that, of the $470 million expenses it incurred in 1990, $125 million resulted from dismantling assets, largely an array of computer systems and software. This scrapping included some computer gear that had only recently been installed, according to Merrill Lynch chief financial officer Thomas H. Patrick.

Yet, a financial institution simply cannot afford to continue on the old, beaten path of conventional thinking. A leading American banker states, "When it comes to new technologies most data-processing specialists have a low threshold of psychological stress...That is why they reject outright supercomputers and AI. They are scared." Another executive says, "It amazes me that so many EDPiers are seized by inertia and act as if they can continue to cling to their jobs without having to exert themselves. We have lost precious time because of that inertia." The bottom line is that top management must take the initiative. There is a personnel problem to be solved in many financial institutions. Given the fast pace of competition and technology, many systems specialists' skills have become obsolete.

The same is true of bankers, traders, and back-office personnel. The securities house that will succeed in a high-technology market is the one that has traders, bankers, and accountants who are computer literate.

Whether a person is a mergers and acquisitions (M&A) expert, an investment banker, a securities analyst, a developer of new financial products, a trader or a systems specialist, the technology that he or she must cope with is changing so fast that it is easy to lose contact with the state of the art. One Japanese banker suggests that in the computers and communications profession, so-called experts are nothing more than apprentices: If they are wise, they realize that they must learn and relearn their trade every day.

Japanese banks, as a case in point, not only hire people who are keen to learn, but also provide a work ethic to ensure that their specialists become steadily more sophisticated.

4. Preparing for Supercomputer Usage

Currently, many Wall Street investment banks are moving their most computation-intensive applications to supercomputers. Among the tasks are packaging asset-backed securities, calculating derivative financial instruments (swaps, options), doing arbitrage in Forex, developing new financial products, computing options against spread, performing portfolio analysis, and focusing on risk management. These applications take hours on mainframes but can be run in seconds on supercomputers at a much lesser cost (see Chapter 13).

Any problem that requires billions of floating-point operations per second will run dramatically faster on supercomputers. There is only one problem with this new generation of machines—they do not presently have the input/output (I/O) capability of mainframes, maxis, and minis. Further, they are unable to run large database applications except through the use of a database server, for example, a networked backend machine. Networked servers, however, are a viable solution.

The competitive advantage of supercomputers is that they are enormously cost-effective when it comes to calculation (see Figure 7–3). As this news spreads among investment banks and brokerage firms, a growing number of current research projects are evaluating different software/hardware platforms to support computer-intensive applications. The aim of such projects is to assess the relative merits of various alternatives on a broad spectrum.

The acid test most banks have done centers on price versus performance. The next criterion has been response time, not only in number-crunching but also in queueing up queries. Computers should also be capable of effective parallelization of financial problems to further benefit from the new architectures.

The most advanced investment banks have already developed programming products able to exploit supercomputer power. Whether in the Forex or the securities domain, the goal is to provide the financial institution with avant-garde applications emphasizing high-power, low-cost technology—all of which translates into a competitive edge in the marketplace.

Among the applications that can profit from supercomputer usage are securitization (modeling and simulation), portfolio evaluation and optimization, forecasting (time series analysis and experimentation), arbitrage (pricing and calculation of margins), trading strategies (involving pattern recognition, filtering, and transformations), and real-space risk management—done worldwide on a real-time basis.[5]

Supercomputers have significant competitive advantages over classical mainframes. (During the 1980s there was an improvement in the MIPS performance of classical main-

Figure 4-3   Ratios in Cost/Effectiveness of Alternative Solutions

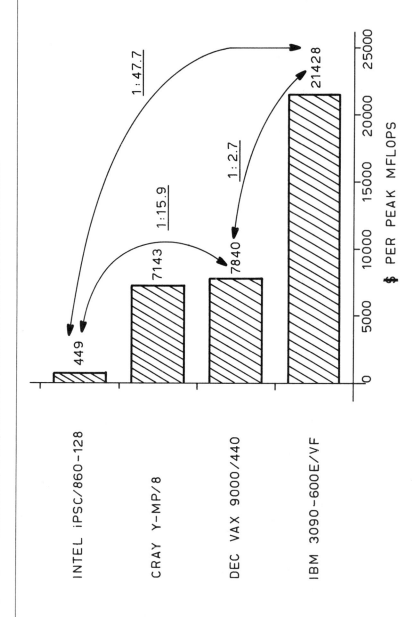

frames, which, nevertheless, today falls short of the power requirements of the financial industry.) Supercomputers can

1. improve analytics done within a specific time window,

2. enable the use of new quantitative and qualitative techniques in solving financial problems,

3. find solutions to problems that cannot be approached with current computer resources,

4. solve problems faster,

5. help to radically reduce costs.

Investment and merchant banks, securities houses, multinational commercial banks, investment management firms, pension funds, mutual funds, and even securities regulators and exchanges, can benefit from having supercomputers.

Through supercomputers, user organizations aim for greater capabilities and lesser costs (cost effectiveness). Supercomputers also enable the banking industry to face more efficiently the huge volume of exchange operations and other financial transactions, as well as the multiplicity of moneys being handled. (In terms of market valuation, the volume of securities outstanding has grown 500 percent since 1978).

Today, the ability to exploit parallel processing is constrained more by the tradition of sequential methodologies than by any other factor. However, given the increasing emphasis on parallel techniques, it is only a question of time before the new computer technologies mature and, with them, the AI implementations.

Some financial institutions are working on image processing and computer vision. They are also preparing for the time when massively parallel computers will feature a several-thousand-dollar price tag. Most likely, this time will come by the turn of the century.

Advances are steadily being made in supercomputer technology. In January 1990, Bell Telephone Laboratories announced that they had developed the first operating optical computer, which can reach speeds a thousand times faster than the most powerful conventional machines available today. More importantly, Bell researchers said that such optical systems will be able to handle information using methods that are beyond the reach of today's computers and be reconfigured to attack new kinds of problems.

Also notable is DARPA's[6] Touchstone project, which has been farmed out to two U.S. parallel computer manufacturers, Thinking Machines and Intel. This supercomputer will perform in teraops, that is, trillions of operations per second, or roughly a thousand times faster than the swiftest computer ever built.

According to the Defense Advanced Research Projects Agency, both Intel and Thinking Machines will build scaled-up models of the new generation of massively parallel computers. The machine that can do double-digit teraops will unleash computer capabilities that match the human brain in thinking power.

As computers become faster and more intelligent, their potential will be limited only by the skill of their operators. Hence, financial institutions should gear up now for the powerful equipment that will soon be available. Banks and securities houses should integrate supercomputing into new financial products, offer them to new markets, and provide user support at all system levels.

This involves workstation-to-supercomputer connectivity, cooperative processing, high-performance large-capacity file archival, visualization, and superfast data transfer (100 megabyte per second to 2 gigabyte per second).

It is not possible to build up a high-technology environment overnight, but if a firm's goals are clear, solving the high-technology problem is not difficult. The focus should be on simplicity and economy.

Simplicity means eliminating, as far as possible, superimposed systems structures with scientific-sounding terms and symbols that might confuse the nonspecialist who is its end user. *Economy* means waiving distinctions that involve no practical differences, keeping flexible and inventive, and providing information beyond what is normally necessary in daily operations, within the limits of available resources.

5. Financial Applications Enriched with Artificial Intelligence

A study done in 1988 by Peat Marwick indicates that many financial institutions are not profiting from technology, in spite spending large sums on computers and communications. Some, however (such as top American and Japanese firms), are profiting from technology in a big way, by having mastered the implementation of artificial intelligence.

Those banks that have clear marketing objectives, developed from collaboration between their commercial, specialist, and information-technology division, will be the first to bring new financial products to the market, to price them correctly, and to know how to sell them.

If a firm's marketing organization is in place and its products are good, the following domains are open to AI implementation:

1. foreign exchange

2. money markets

3. interest accruals

4. commercial lending

5. syndicated loans

6. arbitrage

7. mortgage-backed securities

8. different types of options

9. financial futures

10. dealer aids

11. securities trading

12. portfolio management

13. risk and exposure management

Assisted by expert systems, real-time calculation of exposure is an important area for any bank. Providing risk-management information is complicated by the current restricted (discrete island) coverage of business applications; it is, therefore, an area in which networks, supercomputers, and AI can provide the necessary breakthroughs.

Several investment banks are currently using expert systems to upgrade their fixed-income analytics as well as to assist in the productization of asset-backed securities.[7] One software program that has been written to run on a supercomputer analyzes 150 stocks, each with 15 options, for 500 different accounts, providing an instantaneous portfolio analysis.

For every one of these applications areas, the AI assistance will be (see Figure 4–4) multilayered.

◆ The top layer is the applications system, visible to the end user through the human window.

Figure 4–4   **A Layered Approach to Knowledge
Engineering Implementation**

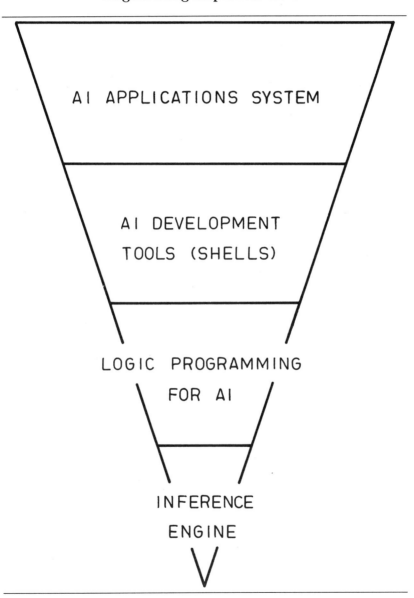

◆ Next comes one of the AI development tools, typically an expert system shell that functions as fifth-generation programming language.

◆ This shell should be written in C or C++ rather than a logic-programming language (Lisp or Pro-log).

◆ At the implementation stage, all three software layers will be integrated and processed through the inference engine.

While the technical details are not necessarily a concern of the end user, the policies that are adopted and followed can make a great difference to the bottom line. The reason for AI and for supercomputers in the financial industries is to improve profitability, and this has to be supported through appropriate strategies.

In 1985, the management of Yamaichi Securities decided, rather than putting the programs for option pricing, optimization of trades, and portfolio management on mainframes, to use powerful networked workstations with a supercomputer in the network acting as a server.

Today, expert systems are applied to both technical and fundamental analysis, pattern recognition, and the microeconomic and macroeconomic domains. These systems are applicable in trading environments as well as in econometric modeling. The Ninth Federal Reserve Bank, for example, is using a Cray supercomputer to make monthly projections of the U.S. national economy and to run models based on Bayesian Vector Autoregression (a forecasting technique).

"What we are doing would not be feasible on a conventional mainframe. The turnaround time would be prohibitively long," says a Fed executive.

The securities business has enormous volume and high risk and often a shortage of qualified local staffers. Hence, investment banks can use AI and supercomputers for pricing and yield analysis (non-linear programming), municipal bond bidding, financial futures hedging (goal programming), foreign-exchange basket optimization (non-linear programming), fixed-income and equity arbitrage (database mining), and for making improvements to trading practices.

In the area of foreign securities, expert systems can be useful for monitoring details such as commissions and price changes. Provisional dealing updates the clients' investment ledger and suspense position, but does not post to the nominal ledger until the deal is confirmed. In the event of capitalization, an expert system can add value. By knowing the client's profile it can provide advice regarding subscriptions.

Many bankers excel at handholding, but many have come to realize that to please sophisticated customers, they must tailor financial packages for investment reasons. For this reason, American banks now project that in the 1990s demand for qualified AI experts will increase by more than 25 percent per year.

The job of these experts is problem solving. A problem is, by definition, a matter involving uncertainty and requiring a solution. To solve it, it is necessary to develop a line of conduct to follow. Practically speaking, that is what a computer program does; conventional systems use algorithmic approaches which lead from variable input data to the output sought after in a definite, procedural way.

With expert systems we often use heuristic approaches to problem solving. These consist of making plausible and fallible guesses as to the best thing to do next.

Heuristics is not a monolithic field, nor is it only trial and error. It involves basic theories (e.g., possibility theory) and may incorporate

1. intuitive logic,

2. assumptions, robust or otherwise,

3.   processes operating sequentially or in parallel,

4.   the recognition of patterns,

5.   taxonomy and classification,

6.   logic constructs.

The interactions and interdependencies developed through possibilistic reasoning can be used for prediction as well as for the solution of complex financial problems that defy procedural approaches.

6. The Battle for Leadership in Securitization

Securitization is one of the most popular of the financial products now sweeping through the world's markets. It has increasingly displaced the traditional form of intermediation on which the Euromarkets and other financial markets were founded only a few decades ago. It has become a powerhouse of new financial instruments.

New financial instruments require new departures; they cannot be handled the same way that older banking products were. In other words, there must be a blending of financial expertise and technology that allows detailed experimentation on new instruments, concurrent pattern matching, distributed multiple-inheritance mechanisms, and object-oriented programming approaches.

These processes may sound quite technical, but they are fundamental to shaping products and services with market appeal. Simulation makes it possible to be competitive in compressed time. Pattern recognition is vital to controlling the risk in new financial applications.

Risk is the cost of uncertainty. When the potential outcome is either gain or neutral value, it is proper to speak not of risk but of opportunity. Generally, however, risk and opportunity are related. There is no significant gain without the ability to overcome adversity; this is one of the key tasks to which rocket scientists address themselves. New financial products are steadily being developed, in large part because of the efforts of rocket scientists, who work on supercomputers and use probabilistic and possibilistic mathematics (as nuclear scientists and aerospace industry engineers do). One such product is the evaluation of corporate and mortgage-backed securities under Option Against Spread (OAS) criteria. Today, when an investment bank sells a bond, its client often asks, "What's your OAS?"

Securitization, as well as the new wave of mergers, acquisitions, and debt financing, has created new forms of risk, which banks and securities houses need to control. Loans and investments should be calculated not on face value, but on the basis of Risk-Adjusted Return on Capital (RAROC). Some banks, for example Bankers Trust, have had a computer-based RAROC system in operation for several years, but the majority are only now starting to implement one.

For those beginning to implement a computer-based RAROC system, the infrastructure should include expert systems, intelligent networks, global databases, and supercomputers. Tasks to be undertaken will include acquiring skills and experience, developing an understanding of basic software and expert systems shells, proving the feasibility of new applications through prototyping, and providing communications links to existing applications leading into hybrid systems.

Here are some pointers for developing the type of technological environment that can serve the current needs of an investment bank:

1. End-user orientation should be on a par with the approaches taken by the most competitive investments banks.

End-user orientations must reflect the latest developments in computing. The capabilities of massively parallel machines are best put to use by thinking in parallel.

Also, new projects should utilize every advanced tool currently available that may be applicable to the bank's problems. Applications should incorporate prototyping and AI, as well as hypertext, in order to provide agile, comprehensive human windows.

2.   For a new architecture such as massively parallel processing, programs should be newly written, not converted from old, serial, non-robust routines.

A conversion to parallelization may be acceptable for benchmarking purposes, but if production routines are converted, the power of the parallel machines will be underutilized.

3.   New architectures have to be exploited in depth through becoming thoroughly acquainted not only with the relevant software and hardware but also with the application itself.

Information on the application itself has to be contributed by the end users who are the domain experts. Information on the basic software and hardware should be provided by the bank's own computer specialists, specifically those associated with the supercomputer project. In-house computer specialists should try to become even better acquainted with the machine than its vendor is.

Among the software that the system experts of the financial institution should master in connection to the supercomputer are links to all existing equipment (mainframes, maxis, minis, and PC), file I/O and concurrent file systems, internal memory management and shared virtual memory, mass storage and reliable disk arrays, and parallel graphics (including pixel planes). Systems experts must also be able to do performance analysis.

4. From the inception of the system, every application to be made should be highly interactive and use the functionality of networked workstations to full capacity.

This issue still does not seem to be fully understood by management and some computer specialists. Many of the latter, looking for the easy way out, still use mismatches. Only interactivity, not batch, can satisfy present and future end-user requirements.

5. Visualization should be the rule in designing and providing human/machine interfaces.

This principle has not yet been widely observed. Many PCs still work with obsolete 3270 protocol, not to mention the outdated nonintelligent terminals that still prevail in many institutions.

Furthermore, in many installations efficient links among hosts (particularly those running under a variety of operating systems) have not been established; nor is a homogeneous database management background present. Yet, there can be no successful application without first-class database management. Packaging mortgage-backed securities, for instance, requires intense number-crunching but also calls for steady interactive access to securities databases that are rich in content, protected in terms of access, and easily exploitable.

6. Efforts should focus on cost control and quality service.

Bank profit margins are very small. For many lenders, as well as securities houses, shrewd cost-cutting can make the difference between a profitable year and a bad one. Also, institutional investors have become very sophisticated, and bankers must learn to meet these investors' needs in order to survive.

Endnotes

1. Readers not versed in computer jargon may consider bytes as one character, whether a letter or a number.

2. "Datapro Reports on Document Imaging Systems" (A joint study, done by Datapro and the Association for Information and Image Management (AIIM)); Delran, N.J. 1989.

3. In the 1950s, EDP stood for "Electronic Data Processing." Today—investment bankers in New York suggest—it means "Emotionally Disturbed Persons."

4. *Business Week,* 5 February, 1990.

5. See D.N. Chorafas, *Risk Management in Financial Institutions,* (London and Boston: Butterworths, 1990).

6. Defence Advanced Projects Agency.

7. See also D.N. Chorafas and H. Steinmann, *Expert Systems in Banking* (London: Macmillan, 1990).

Chapter 5

Quantitative Approaches in Money Management

Chapter 5

Quantitative Approaches in Money Management

1. Introduction

Japanese money management institutions are actively using analytical software tools and have been practicing quantitative analysis for many years. The Big Four, Nomura, Daiwa, Nikko, and Yamaichi, all have quants (quantitative analysis) departments and some have teamed up with American firms to further enhance their know-how.

The Big Four are among seven Japanese investment firms and banks operating as primary dealers in the New York financial market. Nikko markets bonds models and so does Yamaichi Securities International. Thus, they have gained a foothold in the U.S. government securities market, the largest debt market in the world, as well as a position of strength from which to market their technology to institutional investors.

High-technology developments are coming fast in portfolio management (see Chapter 6). Nikko put in operation a complex, securities expert system that took three months to define in terms of specifications and six months to develop and test. Subsequently, it was integrated into its information systems operations. Similarly, an expert systems trader assistant grew from a training tool for dealers and still evolves, by incorporating a contrarian model.

To help with economic modeling, Nikko Securities found a partner in Barra, of Berkeley, California. They developed the Nikko/Barra Japanese Equity Risk Model. (Barra is an investment analysis and consulting firm.) Nikko's Niba is providing a Japanese equity service based on the CAPM theory. It was created as a joint project with Barra using data from the Nihon Keizai Shimbun—Japan's financial news and information company.

Nikko has also "Japanized" software it licensed from San Francisco's Wells Fargo Bank to manage index funds. "We think that good software is now in the U.S. in analytic systems and in money management software. So we are going to introduce U.S. software into Japan," says Yutaka Inoue, deputy general manager in the investment technology and research division of Nikko Securities.[1]

Nomura, one of the acknowledged leaders in modern portfolio theory and in quantitative approaches, is working on a competitive expert system based on quantitative investment theory. Yamaichi Securities has also done some impressive trading and portfolio models (see Chapter 9).

Japan's leaders in money management are systematically exploiting academic talent in structuring their computer-based investment models; each of the Big Four has separate investment research think tanks and information-technology subsidiaries. Whatever is developed is practical and is immediately put into production.

2. Research and Development in the Securities Business

Research and development of financial technology is a relatively new professional line. (This was discussed in Chapter 1 with reference to rocket scientists.) Talented R and D staff are developing numerous new systems based on advanced theories of economics and finance. They are also building prototypes of financial technology services that will provide back-up for financial products such as optimum stock and bond portfolios.

♦ Japanese equity models integrate transaction references into accounting standards, allowing institutional money managers to stipulate market capitalization conditions and screen for capital liquidity.

♦ These systems offer complex modern portfolio analysis in a user-friendly menu-driven package with color graphics.

♦ Advanced software tools help institutions build portfolios by comparing betas (amount of market risk) with alphas (company specific risk), a useful method for stock selection. (See Chapter 9 for a full discussion.)

Yamaichi has developed its stock system on a Sanyo PC 80, which it upgraded by inserting an Inmos (of Britain) accelerator board clocked at ten megafloating points per second (MFLOPS). This is many times faster than the speed of a normal PC, says Yamaichi's Morihiro Matsumoto.[2]

In Matsumoto's department at Yamaichi, portfolio managers and research analysts work together to develop portfolio models. Matsumoto's staff of research analysts has grown from seven to sixty in a couple of years' time as the success of the Integrative Stock System (ISS) has prompted the securities house to develop similar models for other trades.

ISS is a sophisticated yet convenient system. It uses central database resources, market data from information providers, and its own dedicated database on the personal computer network to perform a variety of operations that assure that no opportunity for successful investment is wasted.

ISS accesses international stockmarket reports and a range of information sources, each of which can be linked to any existing data-processing application. The market theory on which ISS is based combines capital asset pricing, arbitrage pricing, and other factors.

Many analytical models built for American investment houses have been designed around similar theories, but Yamaichi has attempted to refine them. "This is third-generation modern portfolio theory," says Tsutomo Fujita, portfolio manager with Yamaichi Capital Management in New York. Yamaichi's software determines stock prices by using three dimensional microfactors, macrofactors, and market factors.

The Japanese stockmarket is theme-driven.[3] Because Yamaichi's integrative stock system incorporates this concept, it is able to show which macroeconomic factor is influencing stock price movements by security, industry, and broad market.

Yamaichi researchers analyze about forty themes, but only six are available to institutional customers. The major themes currently influencing the Japanese stockmarket are—

1. capitalization,

2. domestic demand,

3. consumption,

4. export-oriented information,

5. cyclical industries,

6. information and communications perspectives.

Specific themes influence specific industries, and some-times certain companies within an industry. For example, Toyota is influenced by consumption, export, and domestic demand.

Theme-based computer models allow fund managers, who operate through on-line connection to databases, to experiment with and recompose the portfolio under their control. (Traders use these models to do similar evaluations.) Based on different scenarios regarding market trends, interest-rate goals, monetary-base factors, and Forex operations (variation in the price of Yen), portfolio managers estimate specific trends and execute interactively computer-assisted reevaluations. Upon request, the model with which they are working presents possible anomalies and lists for trading if the investment advisor decides that change is necessary.

Traders and investment advisors sometimes pose queries that need system intelligence to be answered; for example, "Can you give me the thirty stocks that will best take advantage of a rising interest rate?" Fuzzy sets, heuristics, and neural networks have been incorporated in order to respond to queries that involve vagueness and uncertainty.

For example, in its portfolio synopsis section, the typical intelligent stock system of Japanese brokers is able to compute the portfolio's exposure to each theme. It can also cross-list companies in different industrial classifications based on the percentage of each conglomerates' holdings in multiple-industry groups.

"Theme is more important in the Japanese market than P/E ratios," suggests Matsumoto. Average P/E ratios of 56 for Japanese stocks are four times the average P/E of 14 for U.S. stocks listed in the S&P 500. But, Japanese P/E ratios are not comparable to U.S. P/E ratios, and Nikko's model skips them altogether. Instead, it uses the ratio of value to price, defining value as a mixture of book value and cash flow.

A company and the equity invested in it are related. Company data can be evaluated through expert systems in terms of a number of crucial variables, as shown in Figure 5-1. Market strength, product appeal, cash flow, financial staying power, and other critical factors must be evaluated not only in an absolute manner but also relative to competitors' standing.

Portfolio managers know that a number of key variables must be examined prior to investment commitments. For instance, multinational companies, while popular stocks, are subject to fluctuations in value due to political upheavals, currency fluctuations, limits on the export of profits, and the risk of currency collapse in certain countries. Qualitative analysis models must therefore delineate objectively the risk profile of a Japanese equity portfolio to broad macroeconomic themes, and, at the same time, identify the risk characteristics of each stock or bond.

Some fund managers use these models (when it is possible) in a reactive sense. They look at their portfolio, and the dimensions identified by these models, and determine their weight for each industry. They examine the size of the company they bought and compare it to the market average. They do the same with product lines and market appeal—they also get an absolute sense of whether they are biased toward cheap companies or high-yielding companies.

In response to these challenges, the research and development sector of Yamaichi Securities has produced a whole family of economic models, simulators, and expert systems. Featured among them are the following financial technology systems:

Figure 5–1   Equity Can Be Expressed in a Multi-Dimentional Sense

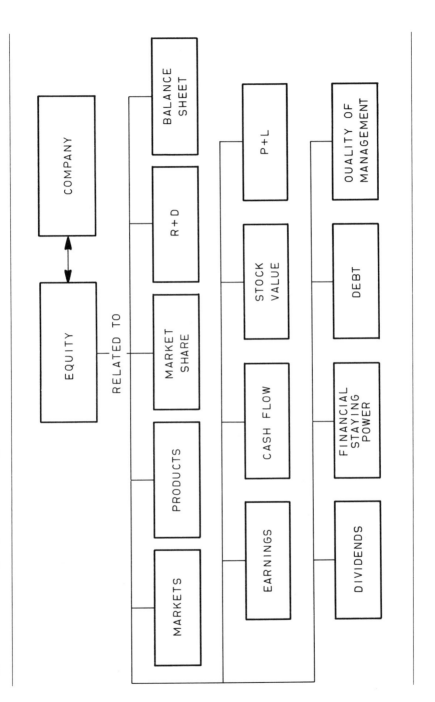

1. AES. Advanced Expert System based on fuzzy sets and neural networks. It focuses on trading and fund management.

2. IAS. Integrative Asset Allocation system. It handles stocks from thirteen countries and bonds from nine countries.[4]

3. IBS. Integrative Bond.[5]

4. ICS. Integrative Convertible Bond.

5. IDS. Integrative Data.

6. IES. Integrative Expert System.

7. IFS. Integrative Forex.

8. IIS. Integrative Index.

9. IMS. Integrative Money Market.

10. IOS. Integrative Options and Futures.

11. IPS. Integrative Position Management.

12. ISS. Integrative Stock. Its theoretical base is CAPMD (see Chapter 9).

13. ITS. Integrative Trading.

Based on some of these systems (which were co-developed by Yamaichi Securities and GAT), GAT has created a composite technology service to aid in asset management. This system is shown in Figure 5–2.

Integral 25 aggregates all of the above AI-enriched services and is capable of real-time trading. The securities house considers this a breakthrough in managing investments efficiently. Products such as Integral 25 are all within reach of any financial institution with a well-tuned R and D organization.

Figure 5-2   An AI-Enriched Composite Financial Technology Solution

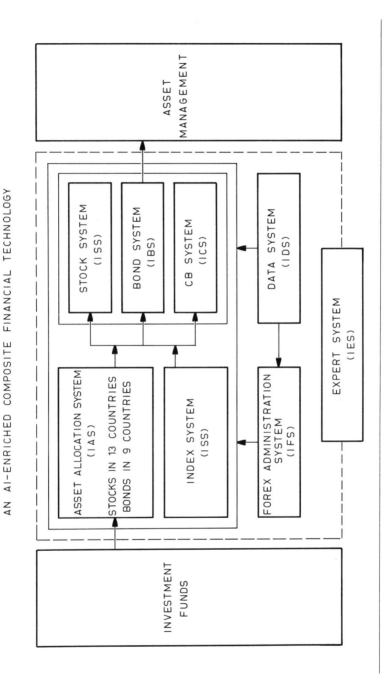

AN AI-ENRICHED COMPOSITE FINANCIAL TECHNOLOGY

INVESTMENT FUNDS

ASSET ALLOCATION SYSTEM
(IAS)
STOCKS IN 13 COUNTRIES
BONDS IN 9 COUNTRIES

INDEX SYSTEM
(ISS)

FOREX ADMINISTRATION SYSTEM
(IFS)

EXPERT SYSTEM
(IES)

STOCK SYSTEM
(ISS)

BOND SYSTEM
(IBS)

CB SYSTEM
(ICS)

DATA SYSTEM
(IDS)

ASSET MANAGEMENT

3. Pricing and Managing Corporate Bonds

Investment houses in New York, such as Morgan Stanley, Salomon Brothers, and Goldman Sachs, have developed powerful models to measure the yield and duration of securities. These take into account the chance that bonds might be called before maturity if interest rates change.

One approach in developing a market-oriented bond system is to focus not only on interest rates and bond prices but also on special features and volatility. This involves defining analogies, matching the current problem to an analogy, developing a model, turning the system, and putting it to use.

Bond models may be done for portfolio optimization and allocation of funds, as well as for trading. Allied Irish Bank has developed a decision support system that allocates a block of debt securities and/or shares among different pension funds. The point is to maximize returns consistent with each fund's varying rules.

National Westminster Bank has an expert system that handles gilts (government bonds) to assist its dealers. It rationalizes data obtained from information providers (using a rule-based framework to select issues and prices), then presents them in a comprehensive way to the bond broker's job.

The use of expert systems, simulators, and other quantitative approaches is particularly important with new issues, polyvalent portfolios, complex offerings, and voluminous trading propositions. Experimentation using mathematical models with option-adjusted spreads (OAS) has shown that the market often pays too much for bonds with call risk, as opposed to bullet bonds. When an investment bank makes an MBF offer to an institutional investor, the client typically asks, "What is your OAS?" Not surprisingly, the mortgage-backed market has taken eagerly to the mathematical models.

As rocket scientists have begun to calculate the probability of consumers repaying their mortgages, they have discovered that this varies according to where they live, the length of time their home loan has been outstanding, and the size of this loan. Researchers try to establish both whether loans in a pool will be repaid prior to maturity and what the repayment pattern will be. The latter helps in projecting the cash flow over the pool's life cycle.

Rocket scientists also chart how homeowners respond to changes in interest rates. If the researcher believes that one group of homeowners is likely to behave irrationally—for instance, by paying off low-interest rate mortgages—he passes on this finding to the traders who buy their mortgages.

Many traders in mortgage-backed securities, influenced by the methods of rocket scientists, have adopted an alternative to the cash-flow method of pricing that accounts for call risk in securities. While the corporate bond market has been generally slower to respond to the new wave of analysis, asset-backed financing (ABF) is now using these powerful mathematical tools.

The suspicion that many callable corporate bonds are overpriced, coupled with event risk, has lessened their appeal. As a result, corporations may have to pay higher yields than they now do for bonds having either call features or subject to possible takeover uncertainties.

Securities other than mortgage pools can also benefit from treatment with algorithms and heuristics. One example is that of hybrid products designed to protect clients. High-premium but low-quality convertible bonds and commodity-related bonds may be issued with common stock warrants—for example, one having four parts exchangeable into silver, one into gold, two linked to the price of oil, and another based on the volume of trading on the New York Stock Exchange.

The rocket scientist's ingenuity lies in establishing the right mix. Many of the references which have just been made are as valid for portfolio managers as they are for traders. Both pruning existing investments and making new ones are made easier by the mathematical approaches now being developed.

Yield to maturity, for example, is a promised rate of return that will be earned only under the assumption of a horizon date. Securities are bought to be sold. When an investor purchases a security, it is in hopes of earning a fair rate of return up to some terminal horizon date; at which time, the securities will be sold for cash.

Understanding the concept of a horizon date is critical in calculating portfolio yields, risks, and trading strategies. A corporate bond has three distinct components:

1. a Treasury-bond-like instrument that reflects interest rate risk

2. a credit component based on corporate or bankruptcy risk

3. an option contract reflecting call risk

Through research, securities analysts have found that an option's value can be isolated to provide an estimate of its worth and its effect on the price of the bond, if interest rates change.

It is common knowledge that when purchasing a corporate bond, a buyer acquires a stream of future cash flows through interest payments. Less well-known is the fact that he is selling a call option to the bond issuer. The latter has the option to call in the debt at a specified time and price.

If interest rates fall as the call date approaches, the option may be exercised as the issuer becomes increasingly likely to call a bond from investors. If interest rates rise, the option becomes out-of-the-money, since the issuer has no interest in refinancing the debt.

Investors are compensated, to a degree, for this call risk. The compensation they receive is, in effect, the premium on the option, usually figured out by rule of thumb. Now that investors are using quantitative tools such as options theory to calculate the call option, they may want their bankers to do so as well.

A New York University finance professor named Thomas Ho has applied what is called the Arbitrage Free-Rate Movement model to bond analysis. In collaboration with Yamaichi Securities, Ho's Global Advanced Technology (GAT) developed IBS.[6] Through it, it prices all interest-rate products, including interest options, mortgages, treasury bonds, and corporate bonds.

The model works under one theoretical infrastructure with modules dedicated to each variance. Some fifty American and Japanese institutions (mostly life insurance companies and money managers) are using this model. The integrative product system (IPS) is another model that has been built for hedging multi-currency portfolios.

Qualitative analyses made possible through heuristics and expert systems, as well as quantitative evaluations utilizing algorithmic approaches and simulators, can be instrumental in supporting valid investment decisions and in doing composite risk management. Figure 5–3 shows an integrative approach to handling a stock-and-bond portfolio. Each component part has a risk module, and these modules are integrated among themselves.

Forward-thinking investment banks and institutional investors are using such quantitative and qualitative approaches in fields like option analysis. Many bond buyers, unaware of the technology available, remain more concerned with high coupons for maximum current income than with options theory. But the use of options analysis is growing, and the market could be in the first stages of a major change.

This change should be accelerated by the availability of new financial instruments such as the swap options. This model is essentially a variation on an interest rate swap, in which

Figure 5-3   Experimentation Is the Cornerstone of Stock and Bond Portfolio Management

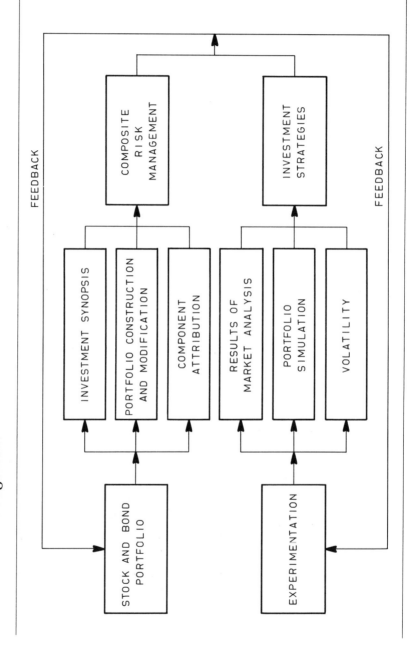

one party pays for the right to terminate the agreement early. Analysis should focus both on the fundamentals and on the purchaser's goals.

The key assumption underlying the swap option is the expected volatility of interest rates.[7]

An option's value is a function of interest rate volatility; thus, the higher the volatility, the more valuable the option. Whether interest rates rise or fall, the option is crucial, because it is essentially a choice. Once the value of a bond's option has been determined, it can be subtracted from the nominal yield to indicate the bond's effective return to the investor.

In an option-adjustment model, the spread typically refers to the bond's yield relative to comparable Treasury securities. With this model, it is more important to pick volatility assumptions that stand the market test than to predict interest rates correctly.

Most of the swap-option purchasers are banks and S and Ls looking for a hedge against rising interest rates. But there are also market-makers speculating on volatility. The latter are sharp market players willing to pay for the option.

Volatility measures are just as applicable to interest rates. Current studies show that in the 1980s investors have significantly underestimated the volatility of interest rates. In the late 1980s, the implied volatility for corporate and mortgage-backed bonds, as measured by their actual purchase prices, has averaged less than 12 percent; yet, during that time, actual volatility has averaged around 18 percent.

By underestimating volatility, investors undervalued the price at which they sold options to issuers when purchasing callable debt. GAT compared interest-rate options traded on the Chicago Board of Trade with embedded options on corporate bonds with one year of call protection left. It found that the options markets were paying 50 percent more than the corporate bond market was paying for the call value.

4. Risk Factors, Constraints, and Experimentation

Along with the issues of having a horizon date, the need for paying attention to callable bonds, and the wisdom of experimenting prior to making investment decisions, the concept of duration is an important one in developing investment strategies and policies.

Speculators use a bond's duration to estimate the percentage change in a bond's price for a given change in interest rates. This aids in finding a bond's present value at various interest rates. Investors use duration to minimize the extent to which they are exposed to interest-rate risk.

By selecting bonds with a duration equal to their horizon date, investors and speculators try to ensure that reinvestment rate and price risks associated with changing interest rates will offset each other. A rise in interest rates will cause losses due to bond price declines. However, if duration equals the expected selling date, payout at par will offset this risk.

Thus, if a certain amount of money will be needed at a given future date, interest-rate risk can be controlled by selecting bonds with an equivalent duration. Managers of pension funds, for example, study their cash-flow needs (i.e., they make sure funds will be available for both the retirement of their members and payments due on principal) and select bonds accordingly.

The income-cash flow-payments model is more complex than it may seem at first. This is because some income-making financial instruments, such as MBF, have a decay curve that is a function of many variables, for example, interest rate fluctuation and early repayment of mortgages.

Analytical studies done on supercomputers, using simulators as well as AI, make it possible to evaluate in advance the possible match or mis-match between interest and repayment of principal and cash flow requirement (e.g., for pensions). Two of the basic tools in these studies are Monte Carlo simulation and pattern recognition.

Since a single horizon date does not exist, and the concept of duration applies to both assets and liabilities, a portfolio manager needs to examine the timing and duration of cash needs (hence potential liabilities) and select bond investments with similar durations to minimize treasury-type risks.

Theoretically, if the liabilities of a mutual fund have an average duration of two years, bond investments with a duration of two years would minimize reinvestment and price risks. In reality, however, things do not work out with such regularity. We should therefore work out investment models that permit experimentation under different hypotheses for a sound portfolio allocation.

Constraints and filters play a major role in the models that investment managers create. Initial hypotheses, or recommendations, have to be scrutinized and accepted (or rejected) if they pass (or fail) one of many constraints. A model for fund managers may behave as follows:

1.   It will buy any asset that contributes to the value of the portfolio in terms of pricing, yield, and intrinsic value, unless there is a constraint to prevent it from doing so, such as, unacceptable level of risk.

2.   It will work to maximize the value of the portfolio in terms of the same factors, possibly by having a level of importance (weight) attached to each goal.

3.   It will avoid bypassing or breaking constraints while observing the general rules of portfolio construction.

This means that a search driven by multiple goal and constraint satisfaction should be carried out according to certain criteria. These could be, for example, choosing an initial configuration for the portfolio, determining how well it meets the conflicting goals and constraints, and trying to improve the match by exchanging assets chosen for others that better suit the user's goals until a local optimum is reached.

The searching technique must be general enough to allow new goals and constraints to be easily incorporated. A weight can be attached to each goal, and, additionally, an acceptable tolerance for achieving them may be specified.

Assisted by rocket scientists, a number of financial analysts have mathematically developed ties between duration and bond volatility. They have also developed several risk-related goal/constraint models, such as, price risk, marketability risk, default risk, call risk, and reinvestment rate risk.

In the price risk model, bond prices are inversely related to required rates of return. If these increase, bond prices fall and vice versa. Barring default or call, the only date at which a bond's price is certain is at maturity. Hence, price risk exists whenever an individual's horizon date and a bond's maturity differ.

Price risk affects the buyer. The corresponding risk for the issuer is that of marketability. In theory, the marketability of bonds is determined by how suited they are to the investor's possible needs for return on investment, as well as their immediate cash value. But, given the large number of actively traded bonds, marketability is relative to where the market stands at the moment of issue and the placement power of the underwriter.

Price and marketability risks can be plotted by using an operating-characteristics curve, as shown in Figure 5–4.[8] Anything that influences the distribution of realized horizon-date returns also affects these risk factors. This is also true for default risk, call risk, interest rate risk, and reinvestment rate risk.

Figure 5–4   An Operating-Characteristics Curve Can Be Implemented in Securities

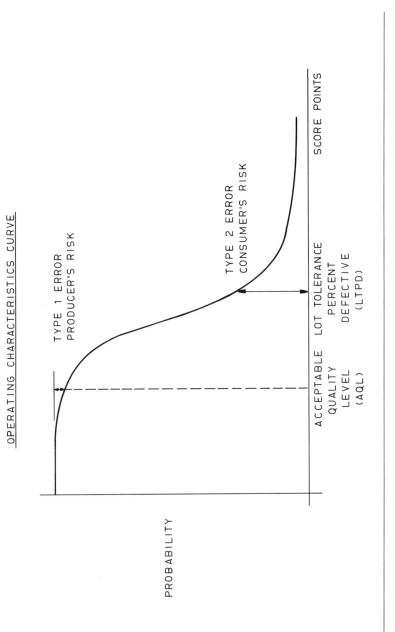

OPERATING CHARACTERISTICS CURVE

PROBABILITY

TYPE 1 ERROR
PRODUCER'S RISK

TYPE 2 ERROR
CONSUMER'S RISK

ACCEPTABLE
QUALITY
LEVEL
(AQL)

LOT TOLERANCE
PERCENT
DEFECTIVE
(LTPD)

SCORE POINTS

If the issuer of a bond is unable to make all coupon and principal payments as promised, realized yields may be much less than projected. The greater the uncertainty about default, the greater the discrepancy regarding the availability of realized returns at some horizon date.

Therefore, an acceptable level of default risk should be specified (often in terms of rating), and purchases limited to these quality grades or better—which is a clear enough constraint. However, since default risks on individual bonds are likely to change, a diversified portfolio should be held, by virtue of its composition, to be in itself another constraint.

Also, the possibility of call risk should be examined. If noncallable (bullet) bonds or callable bonds with a deferred call date beyond one's horizon date are available, they should be strong candidates for purchase. In addition, low-coupon issues, purchased at a discount, whose prices are not likely to rise enough to be subject to call are also viable candidates.

As section 3 has emphasized, attention should be paid to the fact that issuers often permit themselves to retire a bond issue prior to scheduled maturity. The result is that investors are uncertain if coupon and principal payments will be made as scheduled in the indenture agreement. Purchased at discount, callable coupon issues have another advantage. If the lottery turns up the investor's number, they are paid at par.

No matter what the type of investment is and how well the portfolio has been assembled, default and call risks cannot be eliminated; however, bond yields can and should be adjusted for the relative degree of each. By contrast, reinvestment rate and price risk can be virtually eliminated by selecting appropriate bond lives to compensate for uncertainty about future interest rates.

Reinvestment rate risk reflects the uncertainty about possible shifts in the yield curve and, therefore, about future returns from coupon reinvestment. As stated in the preceding paragraph, this is a special case of interest rate risk.

5. Bond Portfolio and Annuities

Bond portfolios with a weighted average duration about equal to the investor's expected horizon date will limit reinvestment and price risks caused by potential shifts in the yield curve. Different durations might be held which will average the desired duration as opposed to buying only bonds of one specific time horizon.

Periodically the portfolio should be rebalanced and restructured, always keeping in mind that this involves commissions and fees. As bonds approach maturity, it is necessary to consider replacements. For certain clients, such as those with a low-risk, steady-income strategy, it is necessary to hold bonds with carefully chosen dividend dates to maintain a continuous flow of income. For other clients who are sensitive to fluctuations of principal, it is important to avoid selling at a loss.

Some clients, although aware that certain investments may drop in value, have an irrational dislike of actually selling at a loss. Consequently, the fund manager may be inclined to hold onto debt or equity that really ought to be disposed of, in the hope that the stocks will eventually climb above the original purchase price.

Notice also that the impact of a change in interest rates works in opposite directions on reinvestment and price risks. With interest rate increases, reinvestment income increases whereas bond prices decline; a reduction in interest rates causes reinvestment income to decline while bond prices increase.

Since these two forces move in opposite directions, it is possible that the favorable impacts of one offset the unfavorable impacts of the other. However, while this is the concept behind strategies that are said to immunize a portfolio against interest rate risk, it is not the way to bet.

A better idea is to do computer-based experimentation after having constructed the necessary models. We must map the market into the computer, then feed in prices, interest rates, time horizons, applicable risks, goals, and constraints.

Mapping in this context does not require a strong structural similarity. Rather, pragmatic and semantic knowledge can be used to define factors and their attributes. Such attributes may be indexable, procedural, and inferrable:

1. The sector of an equity is indexable.

2. The fact that a bond or stock is not being followed closely is procedural.

3. Attributes resulting from rules for use of the asset are inferrable.

When developing experimental models, it is possible to include complex causal chains representing a reasoning trace from the analysis of an asset to the decision to deal. In this case, the inference will consist of inferring causal relations so long as attributes, constraints, and antecedents are satisfied.

The management of a portfolio is not an area in which novices or non-experts can thrive. While bonds are generally considered to be a more conservative and simpler investment vehicle than stocks, the great variety of fixed-income financial instruments available in today's market, as well as the complex cash-flow requirements faced by institutional investors, make cash management quite challenging. Thorough, back-to-the-fundamentals research, supplemented with the use of algorithms, heuristics, and supercomputers, can be instrumental in providing insight as well as foresight to portfolio managers—but, its absence is a major handicap.

Two of the reasons why financial instruments have become so complex are that different types of risk are increasingly embedded into them, and they are repackaged after being put on the market. Home loans are a good example:

1. A consumer wants to buy a house and takes out a mortgage from a Thrift.[9]

2. The Thrift may carry a million mortgages in its books. Periodically, it asks investment banks to make a bid for packaging them and selling them to the market.

3. Successfully selling securitized mortgages requires thorough financial and mathematical analysis.[10]

4. Securitized financial products are bought by institutional investors such as insurance companies.

5. An insurance company will purchase mortgage-backed financing instruments only after it has examined how well these instruments fit into its cash-flow obligations (e.g., as annuities).

6. These annuities are sold to consumers who in other times would have generated extra retirement income through having a savings account.

The classical savings account has lost its appeal for consumers (with the exception of low-net-worth individuals) who have previously lost savings to inflation and other factors. But only sophisticated investors understand MBF, ABF, and other complex financing media, or metrics like OAS. A majority of people tend to buy financial products such as annuities, because they seem more user-friendly.

The market is huge. Some three million Americans are now eighty-five and older, and seven million are projected to reach that age in just thirty years. In planning for a retirement that might stretch over three or four decades, consumers increasingly are turning to annuities which place funds with institutions (for example, insurance companies) that will provide a monthly income for life.

Since the Tax Reform Act of 1986, annuities have been one of the few investments left where interest accumulates untaxed until it is collected. Also, deferred annuities offer yields well above Treasuries and bank certificates of deposit (CD). Insurance companies capitalize on novel financial instruments by investment banks.

Originally designed for retirement, annuity plans today cover financial liabilities such as alimony payments or nursing home costs. Some insurers even offer the option of closing an annuity account with no penalty charge.

All these plans require complex computations that are invisible to investors. Financial institutions, however, must deal with this complexity in order to stay in the market. As new products are steadily revamped and made more sophisticated, the process of banking itself is being fundamentally altered.

6. Developing and Using an Options System

In November 1988, Nikko Securities put in operation the OTT[11] trading expert system. In its first version, it was used only for futures and options training; but, even at that level it was a sophisticated solution, rich in graphics and simulation. Subsequently, OTT was converted into a future-options-dealing support system, the unveiling of which was timed to coincide with the opening of Osaka futures market in June 1989.

Nikko has now developed an intelligent chart-analysis module enriched with knowledge-based constructs. It also has a Swap-CAD, which acts as an intelligent assistant to the design of new swap instruments. An impressive range of other

AI projects, some of which involve neural networks and fuzzy-set theory, should be added to these two instruments.

Nikko Securities is not alone in the emphasis it places on the use of artificial intelligence in futures and options. Option trading is a dynamic domain with many entrants, and logic programming seems well suited for handling some of its aspects. But let's start with the fundamentals.

Options are contracts whose value is contingent upon the value of underlying assets. One type of option, among the most common, is that of stocks.

A call option gives owners the right to buy a fixed number of shares at a fixed price until a certain date.

A put option gives owners the right to sell shares at a fixed price.

When we buy we exercise the option. The limiting date at or prior to which we must act (strike) is the option's maturity or expiration.

Option contracts are usually purchased in lots of 100 shares. Entities creating or issuing options are known as sellers or writers, and the holders or buyers of options are the purchasers.

In general, option trading involves complex combinations of an options package with shares, bonds, and commodities. For instance, a butterfly consists of buying two calls, one at a lower strike price and one at a higher strike price, and, at the same time, selling two calls at a middle strike price. While loss is limited if the price of the commodity moves by a large amount, a profit is made if the price stays around the middle strike price.

Complexity makes option trading a prime area for AI applications, more so as options play a central role in modern financial practice, in which sophisticated trading strategies are involved. A characteristic of options is that returns are contingent on future, uncertain market states with many possibilities for large portfolios. As a result, portfolio managers and, even more so, traders use heuristic and ad hoc techniques widely and base their theories on a number of assumptions.

The professional entrusted with decision making in this domain should be able to evaluate hypotheses and assumptions in real time as the market moves. Experimentation and valuation techniques, however, frequently involve significant numerical calculation and require appropriate computational models as well as supercomputer power.

This reference is valid for global market valuation and/or the larger portfolios. Investors, using personal computers and spreadsheets, typically seek "what-if" answers regarding the risks and returns and other constraints on limited option positions.

The management of large portfolios is much more demanding. A design framework for a complete option-analysis system must provide

1. a clear description,

2. facilities for symbolic analysis,

3. rule-based or heuristic approaches,

4. a range of simulators,

5. integrated numerical computation,

6. distributed database access.

Some projects use constraint-logic programming, a paradigm successful in both graphics and electrical engineering. This paradigm makes concise representation of complex problems feasible because

1. the constraints state properties directly in the discourse domain rather than coding these properties into predicates or lists;

2. such constraints can represent properties implicitly rather than having bindings to variables;

3. the logic-programming approach provides an overall rule-based framework to reason about constraints.

Interactive computational finance has much to do with constraints and boundaries. Constraint-solving paradigms are approached through knowledge representation, which allows the designing of systems over domains, such as, equality, graph isomorphism, and various forms of inequalities, associated with natural algebraic or logical operations.

Constrained domains are quite compatible with market operations. Other important approaches are volatility calculations and alpha, beta, gamma, theta, and, tau functions (see Chapter 9).

About twenty years ago, financial economists applied stochastic control theory to asset pricing and developed stochastic diffusion pricing (SDP) models. Academic literature contains single-factor and two-factor pricing models particularly written for bonds. One of the better known is the Cox-Ingersoll-Ross single-factor model (CIR paradigm). Such models express bond prices as a function of observed factors, parameters describing the probability transition functions of these factors, and market prices of risk.

Practical application of the CIR paradigm requires estimation of each of the parameters associated with the factors' transition densities and market-risk prices. Because of the resulting complexity, such estimations are not made for more than two factors.

Provided that it can be applied to a given situation, a CIR model can assure a sound economic underpinning permitting risk-management techniques based on changes in underlying economic variables rather than changes in yields. This model is also useful for direct pricing of callable bonds; for options and futures, however, it requires identification of parameters necessary to price the derivative—which is not always easy.

7. The Challenges of Marketing New Financial Products

Some of the quantitative approaches that we have discussed have been packaged and are offered as programming products in the market. As a word of caution to potential buyers, there are problems that may arise:

1. A financial institution that buys a packaged approach cannot develop in-house expertise; it must rely on a black box, (i.e., the software it bought from the vendor).

2. Because the software is not parametric, the buyer cannot—and in fact, should not—modify it to meet changing needs.

3. If a package is foreign-made, there is no assurance that package it will place emphasis on factors that local portfolio managers consider important.[12]

Perhaps the major problem confronting buyers of imported software is that laws regulating banking are not the same in all countries and can be subject to revision without much advance notice. During the last few years, for example, three new pieces of legislation in Britain—the Building Societies Act and Financial Services Act (1986), and the Banking Act (1987)—have drastically changed the framework of regulation for all British financial markets. This has, in turn, altered the focus of legislation on supervision of banks, building societies, securities houses, and other financial services.

Efforts are being made to assure a balance of supervision among all kinds of institutions, streamlining overlapping organizations, and creating a framework for progress toward international harmonization.

Within the constraints of law, financial institutions compete for new issue on equity and debt, participate in the configuration of public and private offerings, and package new products. Key decisions involve determining the value of and marketability of a new financial product, as well as its applicability to clients' needs, whether current or to be created.

Relevant information and computation requirements must be gathered and assessed. This could include historical data on similar products, current data on market drives and competitive prices, regulatory requirements, and other largely interactive applications.

Heuristics, calculation, and experimentation focus on the dynamics of a new financial product in an effort to determine its value and market appeal, as well as the potential size of the market given the specific attributes of the product and current demand for analogical offerings. It is a good idea to attempt to forecast the product's possible performance against competing products, its production and distribution costs, and its valuation.

To determine the clients for which a new product would be a viable financial alternative, a company must both track and analyze the market by segments. This is done through determining market response to various types of securities and evaluating market alternatives.

Quite often new financial instruments create a niche which, with time and a steady sales effort, grows into a wider market. Sometimes the new product displaces older ones, as happened with Eurobonds, that is, foreign bonds that supplemented the traditional issues of bonds in national currencies.

The first issue of a Eurobond was in 1957 for the Belgian oil company Petrofina. In 1963, in London, Siegmund Warburg organized a $15 million issue for the Italian auto trade. With a couple of more issues hitting the market and finding acceptance, banks decided these bonds were a profitable item and began actively selling them.

In the case of Eurobonds, even the market strata changed with time and with new offerings. Initially, most of the Eurobonds were sold to high-net-worth individuals who used them to avoid taxes, and much of the business, at first, centered in banks where Europeans and Latin-Americans could hold bearer bonds to make their wealth less visible.

In time, the Eurobond market became one of the First World's most exclusive clubs. The investors' profile changed, with the majority of borrowers of Eurobonds being corporations and institutions. It was not too difficult to obtain Eurocredits, and the market featured a variable interest rate.

Euroloans soon developed in size and became the responsibility not of a single bank but of a whole syndicate which shared the risk. In 1969 Minos Zombanakis, a Greek banker, manager of London's Manufacturers Hanover (an offspring of MHTC in New York and Rothschilds in London), was asked to raise an $80 million loan for Iran. Because the sum seemed huge, he decided to share it with other banks and put together the first Eurodollar syndicated loan.

In 1969, Guido Carli, the governor of the Bank of Italy, was facing a huge exodus of capital in one of the periodic Italian panics. He called on Zombanakis, who put together a $200 million Eurodollar loan supported by twenty-two banks. The interest rate was to be 0.75 percent above the prevailing London rate for Eurodollars, known as the Interbank rate, or Libor, with the provision that it would be revised every six months according to the fluctuations of Libor. This approach of revising the interest rate every six months, adding the extra margin, or spread, above Libor, soon became characteristic of Eurodollar loans, diminishing risks for banks but increasing the hazards for the borrower if rates moved upward.

The history of Eurobonds underscores the need to be aware of the market environment and its financial vagaries. Hence, new, successful financial products must be carefully designed using a valid methodology. Figure 5–5 shows one approach that could be taken prior to commitment to a new issue. A careful analysis using this line of thinking will

1. determine risk/reward,
2. identify potential clients,
3. establish the structure of the new issue,
4. estimate the potential market,
5. ensure that there is a technological infrastructure.

Sources of information will most likely be a central database of syndicated loans as well as legal, regulatory, pricing, and marketing data. Such information must be provided through an on-line interactive application.

It is important in new product development to identify emerging market segments, analyze interest rate relationships, monitor the market to see which product fits, and determine how to configure and price the new financial product. The product designer must do a financial analysis (i.e., entry cost and projected earnings) and legal investigations to establish, beyond a doubt, any possible liabilities.

It is also important to analyze the sales aspect, that is, developing and explaining new financial products, their characteristics, and the reasons that they fit into a certain portfolio. One good approach is that of educating customers by

Figure 5–5   Basic Functions of Product Development in Financial Institutions

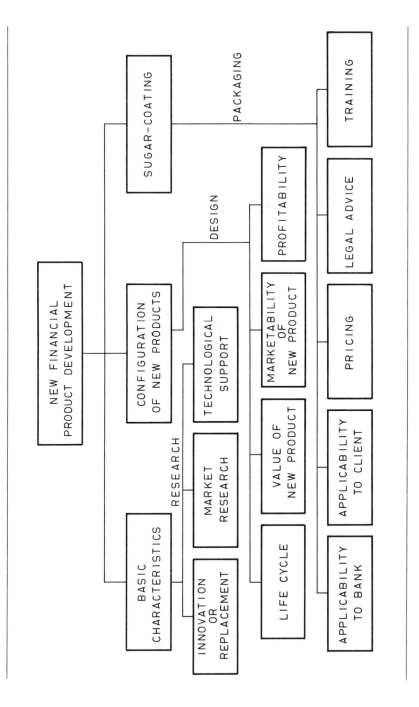

explaining how new products might suit the customers' investment or trading criteria.

Some key questions are, Which customers do we educate? Can we provide customers with direct link-up to information system operations? Can we explain to customers, in a comprehensive manner, the market exposure, trading limits, and expected performance of a new financial product?

To compete in today's market, it is necessary to supplement classical approaches to financial management with quantitative tools. Without strategic analysis and intelligent marketing, even the best new service will not sell.

Endnotes

1. *Wall Street Computer Review* (November 1988).

2. MFLOPS are a unit of measurement typically applied on large-scale computers. One should remember that the power advertised by the vendor is peak power, while sustained power in a given applications environment is another matter—usually a fraction of the vendor's peak power. Morihiro Matsumoto in this case is referring to sustained power (see Chapter 11).

3. A theme reflects Japanese government directives.

4. Denominated In U.S. dollars and yen.

5. Ibid.

6. Integrative Bond System.

7. Volatility is the quality of being changeable, transparent, and prone to evaporating rapidly. (See Chapter 7 for a discussion of market volatility.)

8. See also D.N. Chorafas, *Statistical Processes and Reliability Engineering* (Princeton, N.J.: D. Van Nostrand, 1960).

9. Building Society in the U.K.

10. See also D.N. Chorafas, *The Globalization of Money and Securities: The New Products, Players and Markets* (Chicago, IL: Probus Publishing Co., 1992).

11. Options Training and Trading.

12. These are not meant to be criticisms of all software packages. Commodity software for basic DP functions has many merits; however, advanced software must be personalized and rich in AI content.

Chapter **6**

The Analysis of Investments and of Relationships

Chapter 6

The Analysis of Investments and of Relationships

1. Introduction

One of the most promising uses for analytical tools is in the evaluation of investments and the management of large portfolios, either for a customer's or for a bank's own account. This work becomes computationally intensive when the portfolio contains securities with an option component, such as, mortgage-backed financing.

Supercomputers give traders direct access to complex models that otherwise cannot be run in a reasonable time (i.e., in subsecond speed or at least within a few seconds). Supercomputers' processing speed and cost-effectiveness when compared with that of classical mainframes, is impressive (see also Chapter 11).

When discussing investments, in particular the relationships between their various factors, it is advisable to use analytical reasoning and look for patterns. The raw data available must be refined through processing. Heuristics and algorithmic models become the mind's eye in understanding sophisticated investment situations.

2. Focusing on Financial Subjects through Research

Investment research must focus on both the benefits and risks of certain securities. The financial expert systems currently available allow general users to solve problems, whose solution previously required years of specialist experience. The processing of knowledge is not a new concept. What is new is the automation of the job.

It takes considerable research and effort to develop a knowledge-based system and even more to make it communicate intelligently with users. The knowledge-based system

1. is based on a completely different architecture than DP, yet has to interact with data processing programs in a hybrid setup;

2. often raises dinamic issues (queries) relative to the subject to which it addresses itself, instead of responding statically;

3. is able to adapt itself to its environment, modifying some of its rules, if learning features are included;

4. offers its user an opinion, then justifies it.

The justification of an expert system's opinion in investment consulting is enacted through rules, the development of these rules being the result of considerable research, done in co-operation with the domain expert. There is a degree of certainty to be attached to each rule—and this is often a matter of opinion based on an intelligent guess.

Also, the need for refinement is present all the time. Expert systems need a steady sustenance that should not be confused with maintenance. Updating the construct's knowledge bank is crucial to continuing implementation of the system.

Many important problems cannot be readily solved by conventional computing. Such problems involve decisions based on a complex interaction of a number of factors—and often involve symbolic processing.

This is why investment research is increasingly concerned with knowledge-based systems. As was discussed in previous chapters, these systems

1. are equipped with knowledge stored in rules or expressed in heuristics;

2. use flexible approaches when dealing with unanticipated paths and discontinuities;

3. are able to cope with ambiguities as well as vagueness and uncertainty, which are conditions that often characterize an investment environment.

Knowledge engineering, applied to investment analysis, has much in common with conventional financial research. Both include many criteria centering on financial standards and allow for evaluations based on performance results. These characteristics make knowledge engineering pertinent to banking operations; they make it possible to attach a rate to a given equity or debt instrument, or to evaluate historical precedents, such as, what bonds have already been issued, the rate that applied to them (and its rationale), and how successful these issues were in previous market offerings.

One expert system, which has been developed by the Mitsubishi Bank and the Mitsubishi Research Institute, features some six to seven thousand rules divided into five main modules, each with ample database support.

The first module is the P and L database of listed companies and its associated analyzer. The second is a database containing precedents (dating back fifteen years) of issued bonds and main underwriters and all parties involved in an issue.

The third module contains rules based on responses to underwriters' questionnaries of underwriting and bond selection. The fourth module focuses on proposal evaluation and the development of an underwriting offer, including market conditions and scheduling. This fourth module is also designed to enrich the historical database on underwriting cases and make charts. The fifth module allows management to do follow-up.

Significant segments of this AI construct are based on pattern recognition. Some modules allow specialists to add or delete selected clauses. While complex systems like this are today the exception rather than the rule, the concepts underlying them should characterize all analytical approaches in the investments domain.

3. Valuation through Knowledge-Based Systems

Until recently, financial analysts used earnings per share (EPS) as the fundamental guide to corporate value; now, they evaluate net-asset and book value per share as well as cash flow. It is generally recognized, especially among investors with a long-term approach, that high-net-asset value is a good basis, if not a guarantee, for sound long-term earnings growth.

In view of the risks associated with the stock market, the importance of price/book ratio as a criterion for the selection of stocks is growing. The same is true of taking an enlarged time horizon as a basis for valuation and of placing emphasis on a growing range of supporting factors, including intangibles.

Intangible assets like exploration rights, crews, and goodwill, may be hard to measure; but, allowing for fluctuations in the price of oil, the value of a prospective oil field and its reserves in the ground can be calculated. Future pumping volume is also (up to a point) predictable; a price range can also be assumed, which makes it possible to compute the most likely value.

The worth of oil reserves, as opposed to that of airlines, is only slightly complicated by labor and equipment obsolescence. Why, then would an oil company's stock sell at $12 if its reserves are worth $25 a share? The difference can be explained using the concept of a time horizon.

As the investment advisors and traders of Wall Street look years ahead, they see conservation, recessions, and technological advances working together to change the market's requirements for energy. When oil prices fall, the reserves of oil companies are hardly at a premium; but, a securities analyst who takes a longer perspective, for example, ten years, might find that the oil surplus has eroded, putting pressure once again on supplies. Hence, the different valuation between oil reserves and oil stocks.

A number of factors, some of which complement and some of which contradict each other, are involved in every investment situation; these often depend on the time horizon followed by the securities analyst. This brings into perspective the need to estimate trends and to determine the soundness of the rules that will be built into the system.

With securities analysis having many issues to follow at the same time, and the market being dynamic as well as global, AI constructs are useful assistants in doing financial appraisal. Expert systems have been built, for instance, by the National Westminster Bank to allow a reasonable degree of automation in doing financial analysis, sensitivity analysis, and project appraisal.

One of these systems will work in tandem with a spreadsheet, with the goal of distributing experience in financial evaluation to the branches that originated a given project.

Apart from these better-known applications,[1] expert systems have been developed and used by securities analysts to assist in their work on knowledge-based constructs. These constructs have made many DP programs all but obsolete.

The automation of the process of financial appraisal is a fundamental step in digesting masses of data and making sense of them. In well-thought-out solutions, an expert system accepts on-line input, filters as required, organizes the filtered data according to status, projects ahead, pinpoints potential problem areas, and presents the results in graphics.

In Wall-Street applications, knowledge-based systems use rules that may be subjective and empirical but are consistently employed by securities analysts in their evaluations and decisions. For example, if a company posts bad news one quarter, the chances are 35 to 40 percent that it will issue disappointing results the next quarter. The same holds true for positive results.

Those odds are good enough for financial analysts to recommend selling a stock, or shorting it, the first time it shows disappointing earnings—provided there is no other reason to hold on to it. Likewise, it is usually considered a good idea to buy a stock after an unexpectedly positive report.

Many market watchers subscribe to this empirical approach. "We tend to agree with the adage, 'There is no such thing as one earnings surprise,'" PaineWebber wrote in a report. And, since negative surprises tend to outnumber positive ones, when a company has a positive surprise, that new reality gets quickly reflected in client communications by the analysts.

When there is a negative surprise, it can take six months to filter through.

Therefore, securities analysts are optimists. There is always the hope that what happened one quarter was a fluke. But while the expert system bases itself on the securities analysts' subjective criteria, it has time and power on its side in evaluating large public and private databases while making use of rules such as, "A soft landing in the economy often leads to a crash landing in corporate profits."

4. Expert Systems for Logistics and Securities Investments

Almost all of the relatively simple algorithms that have so far been discussed can be enriched through AI. In fact, they are an ideal ground for the implementation of knowledge-based systems, providing qualification and documentation to the quantified expressions given by the formulas that have been reviewed.

One relevant domain is that of procurement, and this is written in a logistics management sense. An expert system called ESAS, which helps to elaborate an acquisition strategy that is a prerequisite for procurements, has been developed for the U.S. Army. It involves fourteen key criteria expressed as rules. Significantly, the ESAS implementation has demonstrated that many of the army's procurement practices do not follow the rules.

Why is this reference relevant? Because there are sometimes significant similarities between financial and military AI projects, and what is learned from one area can be applied to the other.

We have discussed the complex expert systems and databases structure used for underwriting by the Mitsubishi Bank. Along similar lines, the U.S. Army has developed a large logistics-oriented expert system called the Time project, which helps to determine crucial criteria in the test-and-evaluation phase of procurement.

Time's program-overview function allows management to determine probable costs, set schedules, and monitor performance in the areas of contract clauses, financial issues, technical developments, logistics, and administrative matters.

One financial institution has built an expert system for its loan department. This system consists of eight modules, shown in Figure 6–1. Some of these, such as Economic Indicators, are also used in other subsystems, but are called into play in the loan-evaluation process whenever medium to large commitments are contemplated.

Finding wide-ranging, cross-industry domains of application is another group of expert systems that relate to logistics planning and requirements simplification. Functions may include—scheduling advice; critical items evaluation; milestone representation; product selection; warranties; statement of the work to be done; program planning and control.

Many of the milestones in these references involve financial analyses, but the bottom line is administration and logistics. However, similar concepts (though not the same expert systems) apply to securities.

In terms of end results, the development of knowledge-based constructs is more rewarding when rules are available and are used to evaluate real world situations, as is the case with investments. For instance, the criteria for bond selection can be expressed in a few concise rules:

1. The high-rate taxpayer tends to select low-yield coupons.

2. The low-rate taxpayer tends to select high-yield coupons.

Figure 6–1   General Conceptual Representation of
Loan Evaluation Expert-System Modules

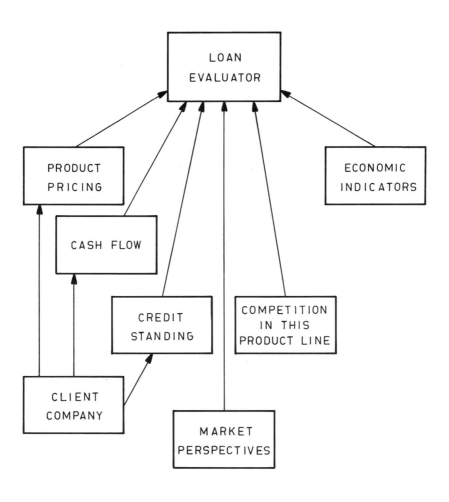

3.   The investor's attitude to risk must be balanced with the outlook on interest rates and the time horizon.

4.   The investor's outlook on the future course of interest rates will determine an appropriate investment mix.

In other words, a longer bond is more sensitive to interest rate changes than a short one; bond prices rise as interest rates fall, and vice versa. If the investor is averse to risk, then bonds should reach maturity at the end of the time horizon, thus allowing exact matching of assets and liabilities.

If the investor is not averse to risk and interest rates are likely to fall, then bonds with long maturities should be selected because the potential for capital gain is greater. The reverse also applies; if interest rates are likely to rise, the investor who is not averse to risk should invest in short gilts with a view to reinvesting later.

Hence, an expert system should seek out the investor's viewpoint on the future course of interest rates. This can be done by using a profile analyzer, a module which, through a question-and-answer session, maps the investor's goals and attitudes. The results are then stored in the investor's database.

A properly designed expert system will ensure that the essential principles of investment expertise are adequately reflected in the construct as well as in practice. The program should proceed as an expert would, sifting through the data for securities that approximate given criteria.

In this process, it may be possible to determine that a certain issue is without doubt unsuitable, but it is not usually possible to state that an issue is certainly suitable.

As in science, it is easier to reject a hypothesis than to accept one. This is because there is a solid basis for rejection, while acceptance is conditioned by the fact that no basis for rejection has been located. Hence, every acceptance is tentative most likely will be evaluated again.

5. Parallel Processing and Anomaly Switching

A knowledge-based system will generally be a significant improvement over manual investment practices. It will be even more efficient if it is designed for parallel processing and handled through supercomputers. There are a number of reasons for this statement, the factor of real-time trading being one of them.

There may be purely mathematical grounds for selling security x and buying security y, which may be identified merely by number-crunching extended over a day's period. However, this switch may not be possible for a particular investor, because by the end of the day, the market has changed. This is one of the risks of operating in a serial manner.

Trading decisions must be learned, and this means experimenting. It may be that switching x into y will provoke a heavy tax penalty under particular circumstances; or, because the investor's financial year-end is approaching, a switch, though justified in the long run, might cause the investment portfolio to do poorly in the short term.

It is therefore crucial from an investor's standpoint to meet market requirements instantly, to avoid being left out of the switch. Hence, the use of parallel computers has attracted considerable interest from securities companies, and super-computers are now an instrument of choice on Wall Street.

Parallelism permits taking an integrative approach to the algorithmic and heuristic modules of the complete model. There are three basic stages in this process:

    1.   Form a view of interest rates that indicates that a policy switch may be profitable.

Figure 6–2   Investment Advisor for High-Net-Worth Individuals

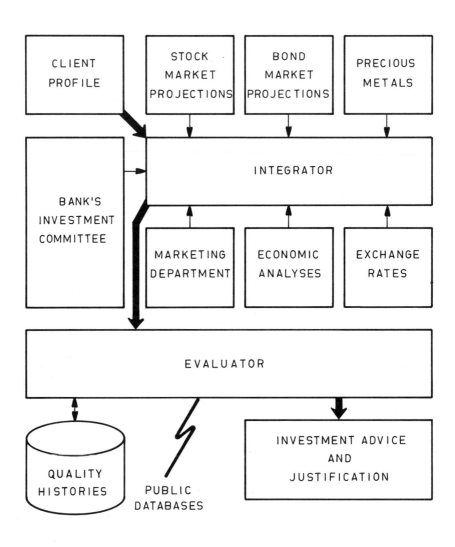

2. Make sure that timing is taken into account in regard to, for example, cash flow and tax position.

3. Select actual stocks and bonds to switch out of and into, and take into account taxes and other issues specific to the investor.

A number of rules may be developed at the level of individual issue selection. For example, an investor may wish to switch in order to slow down or speed up the flow of income.

Because of the polyvalence of requirements, portfolio design, portfolio maintenance and investment analysis require both simulators for forecasting and expert systems for optimizing along established criteria. When using simulation, settled industries such as mining and energy are amenable to handling through mathematical models. When dealing with technology start-ups, qualification rather than quantification is appropriate.

Profile analyzers, simulators, and optimizers all have a role to play. As a result, an investment-advisor system will be an aggregate of modules, each reflecting decision criteria defined by the investor and the bank's specialists. Figure 6–2 shows the modular construction of an expert system specifically designed to give investment advice to high-net-worth individuals. (See also Section 6, on the use of fuzzy engineering for buy/sell decisions.)

Both parallelism in the execution of modules that affect investment decisions and real-time response are crucial in operations such as securities switching (i.e., the practice of attempting to increase the return on a portfolio by simultaneously buying and selling stocks and bonds, without adding cash or taking it out. Policy switching and anomaly switching must also be considered, and their aftermaths experimented with.

Policy switching refers to the practice of moving between stocks and bonds that are different in term (and therefore have different sensitivities to changes in interest rates), with the aim of producing a portfolio that performs better if a predicted change in interest rates takes place.

Anomaly switching is the practice of moving between stocks and bonds that are similar in term (for instance bonds similar in coupon), with the aim of exploiting the small pricing anomalies that occur from time to time.

The fundamental rule of policy switching is that the switch be made as an expression of a viewpoint on interest rates. For this reason, an interest-rate simulator can make a valid contribution. The same is true of a portfolio simulator that will permit experimentation.

Regarding anomaly switching, some of the rules may be the same, but others change because the basic principles are different. The concern is no longer with forming an opinion about interest rates, but with analyzing the past performance of stocks and bonds and detecting ongoing anomalies.

Applying the principles brokers use in the evaluation of anomalies, we must look at all possible pairings of stocks x and y that are fairly similar. Then we must attempt to determine if either the ratio of their prices or the difference of their yields shows signs of oscillating between reasonably well-defined limits. A considerable amount of number-crunching will be required before beginning to make any rules.

Stock markets and bond markets are heavily analyzed; individual stocks do not deviate much from the resulting tight price structures. Therefore, most stocks produce very small unit level profits, perhaps 0.5 percent of the money invested. Only a fast evaluation capability can give a firm a competitive edge; thus, expert systems and supercomputers are important.

6. A Heuristics Implementation at Yamaichi Securities

A number of features of switching have implications in terms of decisions. In order to make decisions quickly and accurately, specialized expertise is needed within a reasonably agreed procedure that can be codified as rules. These rules can be quite mathematical; implementing them requires access to an extensive database as well as number-crunching power. Also, there are highly subjective areas in which rules become vague at best. Hence, heuristics is the instrument of choice.

In line with this thinking, Yamaichi Securities has developed the Integrative Expert System (IES) which provides users with advice on securities investments.[2] Its rules reflect not only information collected on corporations by analysts, but also securities investment know-how built up over years of experience. Its key components are an alarm system and a reasoning process.

The alarm system's function is to give buy or sell signals when signs of change are detected in the market. This module classifies all companies listed on the first section of the Tokyo Stock Exchange (approximately 1,100 issues) into sixty-five industry sectors and takes into account each industry's sensitivity to macroeconomic indicators.

One company and its stocks can belong to several industry sectors with weighting in each sector being determined by sales breakdown. The model works on-line and has access to databases listing the latest stock prices as well as financial and corporate statistics. The reasoning process applies fuzzy engineering rules, incorporated in the models, to the latest data available, including forecast figures. Figure 6–3 uses the example of a graded buy/sell signal to show the method of this fuzzy logic.

For simplification, let's assume that there are only two rules: One is to sell when the price-earning ratio of a given stock is high; the other is to sell when there is significant stock-price deviation from a given moving average.

Figure 6–3   A Fuzzy-Logic Reasoning Process for Buy/Sell in the Stock Market

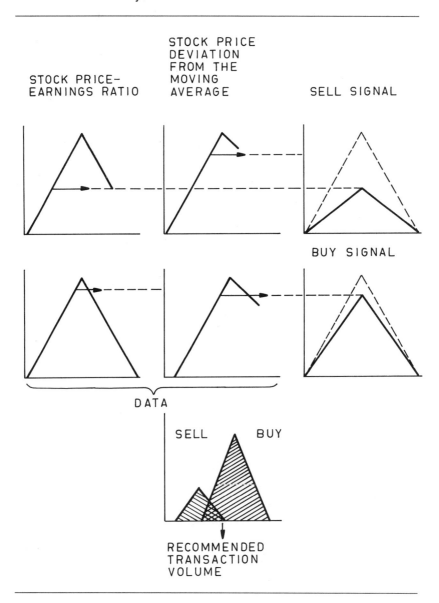

Each stock could have several graded buy/sell signals, depending on how many industry sectors it belongs to. In this model, the grades given to a stock are weighted averages determined according to sales breakdown by industry sector.

Transaction volume is established by the gravity method. First, the height of each membership function polygon is adjusted to the grade of the signal; next, the centers of gravity of these polygons are weighted by their area; the weighted center of gravity is used for the recommended transaction volume.

The result of the fuzzy logic process is presented in bar charts for each stock. Each chart reflects only those grade and volume figures above certain levels that will trigger an alarm. This chart is useful in determining which rule resulted in the grade given to a stock.

The "If...then" sections of the rules take into account the specific industry and specific stock. Rules incorporate standards by which buy/sell signals for each stock can be given as market conditions change. These rules have been determined by an intra-company rule-study group. Also, besides having basic arithmetic operations, Yamaichi's IES has been designed with its own data-processing functions, for example, lag, moving average, and volatility.

System rules operate on four levels in accordance with the structure of the model. Macrorules imply standards for overall market-related economic trends in choosing industries and stocks. They use variables such as commodity prices and interest rate trends.

Industry rules imply a reference for each industry-related economic indicator. They help determine, for example, if the housing construction materials industry should be selected for a given growth-rate of floor space of housing starts.

Microrules are instrumental in developing standards for selecting individual stocks without reference to industry data.

They can be described using variables such as, stock price deviation from moving averages and market volatility.

Individual rules map the preferences of individuals and reflect investment restrictions imposed by the investor or by regulatory authorities. These become exogenous factors.

Fuzzy reasoning is done independently for each level. Subsequently, a weighted average of the resulting buy/sell signals is used. The relative weights represent a particular view of the market. For instance, if the investor thinks it is an earnings-driven market, then more weight is put on microrules; if the investor believes it is a market driven by cash availability, then more weight is put on macrorules.

A rule-management subsystem is able to analyze rule structure and rule sensitivity, as well as having the capacity to register rules. Rule structure can be evaluated by determining the consistency of rules governing buy and sell signals. This is done through equilibration.

Rule sensitivity is studied by determining the effects of a rule change on a buy or sell signal. The goal is to make the expert system work more efficiently.

Once such a sophisticated construct has been built, it can serve not only to evaluate new investments, but also to periodically review existing portfolios, thus improving their return. Improvements in portfolio composition are carried out by switching investments, with the expert system making documented proposals.

Artificial intelligence constructs of this nature make it possible to look at portfolios globally by evaluating single stocks. Each portfolio component has a yield, duration, volatility, and pattern of cash flow. The expert system also helps to optimize the return on a portfolio, subject to certain constraints, by using relatively simple fuzzy engineering rules rather than heavy mathematics.

7. Contributions to Asset Management and Inventory Valuation

That financial analysis calls for algorithms, heuristics, and databases is evident; less evident is the fact that it requires clear management policies and tax expertise. The many facets of analysis—determining inventory values, computing depreciation expense, accounting for the difference between tax expense and taxes that are really paid, correctly discounting for past commitment and future projections relating them to the present—add up to a demanding task.

In Chapter 5, capital budgeting and depreciation were discussed, and it was noted that every company has its own policies for dealing with fixed assets. When we buy an asset we are spending cash today for a stream of income services over time. This asset has a useful life cycle, but we may wish to charge expenses against its purchase over a different timespan for tax- and book-reporting purposes.

To help administer its capital assets, IBM has written the Capital Asset Expert System (CASES); its goals are

1.   to simplify operating procedures in ordering, acquisition, transfer to/from, storage, utilization, and disposal;

2.   to give a comprehensive advice on asset management;

3.   to provide overall guidelines for interdepartmental procedural application;

4.   to eliminate unnecessary procedures and directives;

5.   to integrate signature authorizations for transaction validation;

6. to reduce time wasted and avoid unnecessary frustration.

CASES offers on-line consultation, provides users with information, and merges procedures and forms from many sources. Also, a factory knowledge bank has been created to store written operating procedures and directives. This system is available twenty-four hours a day, seven days a week.

Special tax treatments reward business for buying, selling, and depreciating assets. AI deals with these issues, as well as that of handling inventory, in an expert manner.

Each of the methods used in calculating depreciation expenses for accounting purposes can be expressed in algorithmic terms and enriched with knowledge engineering. Four examples of depreciation are straight line, flexible declining balance (to be set parametrically), double-declining balance, and time-and-a-half declining balance.

The computation algorithm typically reflects generally accepted accounting principles. Tax depreciation parameters can be set in an algorithmically described procedure such as the accelerated cost recovery system. The same is true of handling investment tax credits.

Another asset-management notion that can be expressed as an equation is pretax asset recovery. This refers to the economic value of an asset (i.e., its market value) which is not the same as its book value (i.e., original cost less the total of all book depreciation expenses taken to date) or tax value (i.e., the original tax status less the total of all depreciation expense deducted to date).

It is helpful to be able to see the pretax asset recovery value in each year for each fixed asset as well as for the total of capital investments. This value indicates what the worth of an asset would be at the end of any year in which selling it off is being considered.

In fact, in many leveraged buyouts, mergers, and acquisitions, as well as in securities evaluations, a given stock's worth in the market is sometimes listed as being below the book value per share. This is misleading because the book value itself may be too low or too high in relation to the asset's real worth; thus, pretax asset recovery is a useful accounting tool.

Many ledger valuations cannot be followed successfully in a manual or even in a classical data processing manner. Establishing an asset's real worth requires expertise that, while often impossible to express in a procedural, algorithmic sense, can be mapped into an expert system.

8. Learning How to Learn from Experience

As discussed in section 4, there are fundamental similarities between military and industrial logistics and finance. To learn by anology, consider the following case from a production environment and see how it applies in finance.

An AI construct used by a manufacturing firm is programmed so that if an asset is general-purpose it is projected with a declining economic value; however, company valuators can modify the curve for each individual asset as they see fit. Sometimes, they may lower it by the amount of unrecoverable costs associated with the installation. In contrast, specialized assets can be set to drop their salvage value immediately because they are presumed to have no resale value beyond the present one.

This and similar scenarios permit experimentation with the investment module (in manufacturing or in banking) by setting asset recovery parameters and subsequently showing asset recovery estimates for all assets. Also, through scenarios, the experimenter can estimate the liquidation value of working capital at the end of a chosen period, for instance, by taking accounts receivable at a chosen discount rate, accounts

payable at book value, or inventory at cost (excluding depreciation expense and taxing at the marginal rate for ordinary
income).

Inventory valuation should always be subject to experimentation. A simulator enriched by an expert system will
typically accept units sold, units produced, and on-hand units
as inputs. It will peg inventory as a percent of

1. revenue,

2. cost of goods sold,

3. the number of months of production in inven-
    tory,

4. inventory turnover in function of sales.

Any efficient system will provide several inventory valuation methods, such as, weighted average cost, last in-first out,
(LIFO), first in-first out (FIFO), to assign a value to the units
in stock. Both the parametric expression of alternative methods and the chosen approach itself can be expressed algorithmically. Experimentation done by an expert system will allow
operators to choose the best alternative.

This system contribution can be instrumental in tax calculations (an important factor in determining the bottom line).
Taxes are of an algorithmic computational nature; but, an
expert system can contribute a multicountry, multicurrency
perspective of before-and-after tax values, including what-if
experimentation. Such a system should calculate taxes both
for book purposes (tax expense) and to determine cash flow
(taxes paid).

These numbers may not be the same because the book and
tax-depreciation parameters can be set differently if, for instance, depreciable lives and salvage values are not the same
for book and tax purposes. Typically, book and tax deprecia-

tion methods are different; in other cases, investment tax credits change from time to time according to changes in legislation.

Investment tax credits are direct reductions of taxes that arise from the purchase of depreciable assets. The amount of credit depends on the asset's class and the expert's knowledge. The latter has three main components: facts, rules used in judgment, and procedural guidelines. Facts are reflected in the organization of collected experience; but, many of rules are typically in fuzzy logic and can only be represented through heuristics.

In other words, while algorithmic approaches can simulate tax procedures, there are issues that knowledge engineering is better equipped to handle. One of these is change in deferred taxes, that is, the difference each year between tax expense for books and taxes paid. This nets out to zero over the life of a project because differences are due to timing and are not permanent. However, the intricacies of the subject require expert knowledge, which will reside in the rules of the AI construct.

Algorithmic approaches enhance procedural knowledge, which is based on practice defined through government regulations. Heuristic logic, however, capitalizes on analogies and associations as well as hypotheses, reasoning, intelligent defaults, and everyday experience.

Though being used by an industry other than banking, the approaches discussed in this section can be universally applied. Three basic steps in problem solving are to

1. develop a comprehensive underlying framework,

2. link planning concepts and components, and

3. produce useful solutions that are action-oriented.

Quite often, AI applications are instrumental in recognizing that management strategy and technology planning must be linked, with the former driving the latter. The challenge is to align management strategies and infosystems plans, which has been one of the major weaknesses in classical data processing.

9. Knowledge-Based Approaches to Responsibility Accounting

Expert systems support has been instrumental in improving the quality of responsibility accounting reporting systems. Since their inception, these systems have been directed toward controlling costs, often at the divisions and branches of the bank. Modern management accounting includes

1. defining responsibilities and grouping them within the organizational structure,

2. determining and assigning income and expenses to appropriate organizational levels and activities,

3. emphasizing cost control and the importance of profit planning.

Such activities require skill and know how. Therefore they should incorporate knowledge engineering.

Emphasis should be placed on details (hence on the component parts of the system) regarding not only internal operations, but also product and customer profitability reporting. By exploiting standard costs and associating them with specific daily activities, expert systems can provide management with profitability information on each service. This allows a firm to plan and direct its activities and to qualify/quantify goals. Expert systems can also be adjusted to determine the profitability of clients over a given period of time.

A sensible approach to profitability analysis is inevitably based on skillful handling of client accounts. Because of deregulation and stiff competition, this approach needs to go beyond simply acquiring accounts and doing subsequent "handholding." Sound evaluation policies and rules, the latter handled through the development and use of expert systems, are now required.

For the last ten years, the banking industry has been experiencing rising levels of loan defaults as well as expenses associated with the management of client investment accounts. Bank capital and profits are not meeting general expectations; yet, at the same time, financial services are being expanded beyond electronic fund transfers to globalization and twenty-four-hour banking. As a result, banks now have a renewed interest in assessing the profitability of individual services and accounts.

Traditionally, banks have tended to cost and price only a small group of standard activity services. Most services have been offered free of charge. By setting prices on the costed services to cover expenses, banks have been able to obtain a rough indication of the costs of servicing individual customers.[3] However, this method of costing may not be sufficient.

It is necessary not only to set standard costs, but also to establish in detail the cost of specific banking services. These services should then be priced. Also, standard costs must be upgraded as the introduction of new technology changes the basis on which they have been set.

This work is demanding and need not be done manually. Expert systems are ideal for helping to upgrade a costing system because of their ability to focus on essential issues while measuring changes in standards and in work flow.

Expert systems can also isolate cases in which costs have been understated or overstated, for example, in regard to customers using mostly non-costed services.

Through the use of AI, numerous aspects of a customer relationship can be combined into a single analysis. This creates a detailed picture of customer profitability. Furthermore, because each stage of the analysis involves difficult choices, and because results must be viewed in light of various underlying assumptions, the implementation of knowledge-based systems is critical.

10. Using Industrial Engineering in Finance

To use customer profitability analysis intelligently, it is necessary to understand the methods by which costs and fund transfer prices are derived and to recognize the implications of alternative hypotheses. Properly used, information technology is the most reliable form of assistance for the professional and the manager who need to do their work efficiently.

Within the realm of responsibility accounting is a knowledge-based profit-planning system. This system formalizes, through rules or statements, the plans and goals of the bank, including not only medium- and long-range goals, but also specific short-range objectives.

Rules can be used to design and implement a reporting structure able to supply data to each level of management, with the data varying according to the degree and field of responsibility of the individual manager. One implementation along these lines is based on the following steps, some of which relate to industrial engineering (IE) and others, to artificial intelligence (AI).

1. Review and identify areas of responsibility for income and expenses at division and branch levels of the bank's activities (IE).

2. Determine the cost centers to be established and designate specific responsibilities (IE).

3. Finalize a coding system applicable to such cost centers to assure responsiveness to future organizational changes, permitting accumulation of data for reporting at several management levels for all the bank's planning and control purposes (IE).

4. Develop expert systems and interactive formats to supply detailed information to first levels of supervision, such as, small branches and banking platform teams in main branches (AI).

5. Develop expert systems able to evaluate details and proceed with graphics presentation of actual versus plan—that is, deviations from expectations—for top-level interactive reporting (AI).

6. Review and revise, where necessary, the chart of accounts, in order to assure its adequacy in exploding income and expense by cost centers/profit centers (IE).

7. Determine a basis for allocation of service-center costs to profit centers and identify unallocatable costs of service units that represent an unabsorbed overhead factor (IE and AI).

The success of this implementation depends, to a large degree, on the direct participation of, and support from, senior management. The best solutions will incorporate system expertise and the technical knowledge of bankers. They will also guarantee that the resulting system is fully understood by its users, who should participate to a significant extent in its design, implementation, and operation.

One vital contribution of computer-assisted solutions to administrative duties is the creation of interactive on-line queries. These may relate to clients, accounts, chapters in accounts, trade or settlement date basis, specified date ranges, and consolidation perspectives.

Queries concerning positions may focus on current and past holdings. They should be detailed by account, investment type, or other criteria. They may, for instance, reflect position of cash and focus on current cash in user-defined classes such as principal, income, forex transactions, accrued dividends, and bought/sold securities.

Queries may also concern transactions from the viewpoint of gain/loss, taxation, actual or projected income, broker commissions, actual versus planned performance, and so on. These analytical queries should be differentiated from the simple queries that characterize a current accounts environment.

Queries based on transaction processing are wide-ranging; they may relate to cash and holdings maintained on trade and settlement date bases, input from a trade support system, or observance of client restrictions, both generic and specific. Accounting queries will typically involve accrued interest, current yield, yield to maturity, yield to call and put, and credit/debit by currency. This last area is important because transactions may be booked in multiple currencies, with conversion rates provided for each transaction. The system should allow cash rebalancing across accounts with a given client.

These ideas are valid from both a national and an international market perspective. Not only do firms need to make a first-class product, but they must also be able to deliver it. The following financial domains are open to AI implementation:

1. foreign exchange

2. money markets

3. interest accruals

4. commercial lending

5. syndicated loans

6. arbitrage

7. mortgage-backed securities

8. different types of options

9. financial futures

10. dealer aids

11. securities trading

12. portfolio management

13. risk and exposure management

14. cost control

Each of these fields requires a considerable amount of industrial engineering and organizational groundwork, which is best handled by computer. Once this is done, artificial intelligence constructs can aid in efficient management.

While deep AI models have been successfully developed and extensively used in major financial institutions, expert systems have been used to support agile end-user interfaces, including transparent linkage to discrete modules. The example shown in Figure 6–4 is end-user oriented, but it also integrates old DP and AI modules, hence, a real-time operating hybrid system.

With the help of expert systems, real-time calculation of exposure is a realistic goal; the same is true of global-risk evaluation. Today, taking advantage of these opportunities will allow a firm to prosper; ignoring them will be courting financial disaster.

Figure 6–4   End-User Interface through Expert System

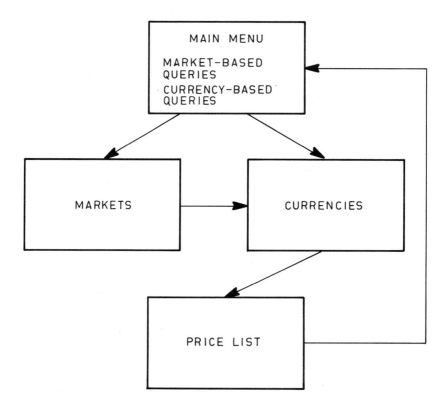

Endnotes

1. See also D.N. Chorafas and H. Steinmann, *Expert Systems in Banking* (London: Macmillan, 1990).

2. This information is based on a meeting with Yamaichi Securities in Tokyo; and on 1989 papers by Bunji Kaneko and Om Sarda of Yamaichi, and Prof. Michio Sugeno of the Tokyo Institute of Technology.

3. See also D.N. Chorafas, *Bank Profitability* (London: Butterworths, 1989).

Chapter 7

Simulation and Optimization in Securities Decisions

Chapter 7

Simulation and Optimization in Securities Decisions

1. Introduction

In his visit to ancient Egypt, the Greek Solon (640–560 B.C.) was received by an old priest, to whom he spoke with pride about his country of origin. The host interrupted him:

"You Greeks are like kids: There are no old people in Greece."

"What do you mean?" asked Solon.

"You are young in spirit," responded the Egyptian priest, "because you have no really old traditions, no concepts fine-grained by time."

The Egyptian priest was right. Even if we use Pericles (fifth century B.C.) as a reference point, there is as much chronological distance between his time and that of Egypt's Pharaoh Djeser and his pyramid of Saqqara, as between his time and ours. When Herodotus visited the Nile Valley around 450

B.C., he discovered that the pyramid of Cheops was already more than twenty centuries old—and that the passage of time had deepened the sophistication of Egypt's mathematicians, philosophers, and savants.

The relationship between early applied mathematics and current mathematical modeling is similar to that between the ancient societies of Egypt and Greece. The experimental models developed by mathematicians such as Rene Descartes (1596–1650) and Gottfried Wilhelm Leibniz (1646–1716) were first put into practice in the physical sciences three to four hundred years ago. Econometrics, on the other hand, is a form of math dating back only a few decades.

Hence, there is much to be gained by studying what the physical sciences have achieved through mathematics, and in particular through *simulation.* Currently, the major invest-ment banks and brokerage houses on Wall Street are investing heavily in this domain, employing rocket scientists and, more recently, supercomputers.[1]

The science of mathematics has no boundary as such. Its theories apply in many different domains, such as chemistry, physics, engineering, and now economics. Mathematics is a game of signs and rules: signs have a semantic meaning; rules describe behavior, and in particular, constraints.

The theories of mathematics aid in making discoveries. Hypotheses (tentative statements) are made and tested. The use of mathematics also improves cognitive ability, which aids in understanding complex financial problems.

2. The Concept of Optimization

Managing money is just as important as making it. A scientific approach to money management involves locating the best possible product mix, called an *optimum,* within an acceptable level of risk. To draw an analogy, in biology an optimum is the combination of light, heat, moisture, and food that best promotes growth and reproduction. In finance, choices are made in an attempt to balance risk and return. The main challenge in money management is to determine the best possible asset mix in regard to a given investment horizon, which may be short-, medium-, or long-term. This horizon will be based on quantifiable expectations of risk and return.

No one can work miracles in terms of controlling risk and improving upon return on investment. However, winners in the equity and debt markets are usually players who have superior models and timely information. The goal of optimization (and the use of mathematical models) is, therefore, to approximate the higher level of community intelligence. In other words, no one of us is as smart as all of us (i.e., as intelligent as the market).

Approximating this higher level of intelligence is the objective of mapping the market into the computer and then applying *simulation* (more fully explained in section 3 of this chapter). It should be noted, however, that building this mathematical model is one thing, using it is another.

Optimization models usually focus on historical returns. Although they direct themselves toward the future, they also assume that risk and return patterns will not change significantly. This is not always true.

◆ Past performance in equities, debt, and currency management does not necessarily imply future success.

◆ Past growth rates do not necessarily forecast future growth rates.

◆ Past market booms and depressions are not duplicated in future bulls and bears, though they can function as warning signals and indicators.

In the absence of a fundamental theoretical framework, that is, one able to pass the twin test of empirical verification and experimental evidence, attempts have been made to construct theories that at least reflect some basic factors. (See Chapter 9 for a discussion of Modern Portfolio Theory, Efficient Market Theory, Capital Asset Pricing Model, and other constructs.)

Models used for optimization purposes are important in securities trading and management (provided the theory on which they rest is solid); the major considerations, when evaluating an investment opportunity, are portfolio performance and investment risk. The development and use of appropriate models can make all the difference between *Active* and *Passive* portfolio management. A passive portfolio does not involve futures arbitrage or asset liquidation models, which require frequent contributions and changes—and therefore more powerful tools for their administration.

Yet, a passive portfolio, too, can profit from simulation as it involves *indexing*, that is, a composition with the explicit intent to match a particular index. Such equity indices are typically weighted for market capitalization. They are also broadly diversified; hence, they can benefit significantly from experimentation.

"A financial genius," a proverb says, "is a short memory in a rising market." No senior investment advisor can afford to follow this track. Experimentation based on mathematical models, and with it optimization, is a means for better documenting securities, as well as for unearthing investment opportunities.

Furthermore, sophisticated investors, who provide some of the most lucrative business of a securities house, often choose a combination of active and passive strategies for investing, called quantitative fund management. In this approach, traders and investment advisors use simulation studies and knowledge engineering to plot strategies (see Section 6).

3. The Meaning of Simulation

Simulation is essentially a working analogy. An analogy is the similarity of properties or relations: when analogous systems are constructed, measurements or other observations made of one of these systems may be used to predict the characteristics of the others. Simulation may be analog (e.g., scale models, differential analyzers) or digital. Only the latter will be discussed in this book.

Simulation involves analogical reasoning. The usual method of digital simulation is to construct a computer-based mathematical model with properties, or relationships, that are similar to those of the system under study. This system may be physical or logical; two examples of the latter are economic and financial systems.

By using analogical reasoning, it is possible to conceive or restructure a given system without having to work with a real-life construct, which may be awkwardly big and complex, or not yet built. Through experimentation, the optimization of a given system's characteristics can be predicted. This draws attention to the close links between simulation, experimentation, and optimization.

As society changes—some would say develops—human needs increase, bringing into perspective the need to obtain more products from limited natural resources. An enduring effort to improve upon the use of resources has gradually given rise to the notion of experimentation done for reasons of optimization. As resources are further depleted, this optimization process has to be accelerated, so that rapidly expanding demands can be accommodated with what is available.

In building up a mathematical model for simulation, the first step is to visualize the behavior of a familiar system, then exploit the resemblance between the two, thus extending beyond the familiar system to new domains.

If the model is the first done on this particular system, past behavior of the system is analyzed by considering historical data and reasoning by analogy. On the basis of this analysis, the researcher may build a tentative mathematical model, test it with actual data to verify the reliability of its output, and modify it accordingly for better fit with real-life situations.

In almost every case, the modified model needs to be tested, then remodified, and so on, until a simulation results that is reasonably close to reality. How close to reality a simulated model can be is subject to several constraints including time and cost, experience with the system under study, and simplicity of the model itself.

Simulation studies do not need to be complex. Even simple models provide a foundaton for research and experimentation on systems that cannot be constructed in complete physical form for laboratory purposes; or that we have not yet been constructed but whose behavior is a desirable subject for study; or that may be simply impossible to build because they are too vast and imprecise (such as the national economy or the stock market).

The purpose of computers and mathematics is to help us better understand complex situations. For this, a system methodology is needed, which typically involves two processes (see Figure 7–1):

1.   The first is a *deduction* in which basic rules are unearthed from a large volume of data.

2.   The second is *induction* in which basic rules are used to project data (as is done in forecasting).

"If you don't believe in induction, you don't believe in anything," said Bertrand Russell. Although he was referring to the physical sciences, his statement holds true for economics and finance (with the added virtue that rules in these areas are not crisp).

Figure 7–1   Induction and Deduction Are Two Pillars of System Methodology

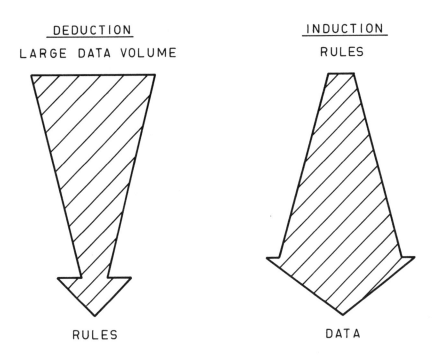

DEDUCTION

LARGE DATA VOLUME

RULES

INDUCTION

RULES

DATA

THE RULES MAY BE:

1. CRISP: DETERMINISTIC,
          PROBABILISTIC

2. NON-CRISP: POSSIBILISTIC, FUZZY

◆ *Crisp* rules typically are expressed through algorithms, whether deterministic or probabilistic.

◆ *Non-crisp* rules are appropriate for fuzzy engineering. They involve vagueness and uncertainty, and
   typically are possibilistic.[2]

Today, the business of building simulators of economic and
financial systems is at about the same stage as the automobile
business was eighty-seven years ago, when innovators such
as Henry Ford were experimenting with internal combustion
engines. However, the fact that economic modeling is in its
formative years is an opportunity rather than a constraint.
Financial institutions that are able to capitalize on modeling
can leave competitors miles behind.

Concerning a supercomputer with simulators and artificial
intelligence (AI) models recently installed at an investment
bank, senior officer remarked, "This gives us solutions fifty
times faster than what we were getting before with the mainframe." And, he added, "Even those competitors who know
how to work with models but operate them at lower speeds
are at a disadvantage," because "they can either react fifty
times slower to achieve the same calculations, or they can
react as fast but with much less information and poorer
understanding of the market."

Mathematical models are aids in the art of solving problems, and problem solving is at the heart of learning. Simulation, experimentation, optimization—and the supercomputers
needed to handle these models—are key steps toward greater
competitiveness because they are reducing cognitive complexity.

4. Cognitive Complexity and the Trader

Cognitive complexity can exist in all of the four quarter
spaces (see Figure 7–2) that describe the essence of human

Figure 7–2   The Four Quarter-Spaces of Human Ability

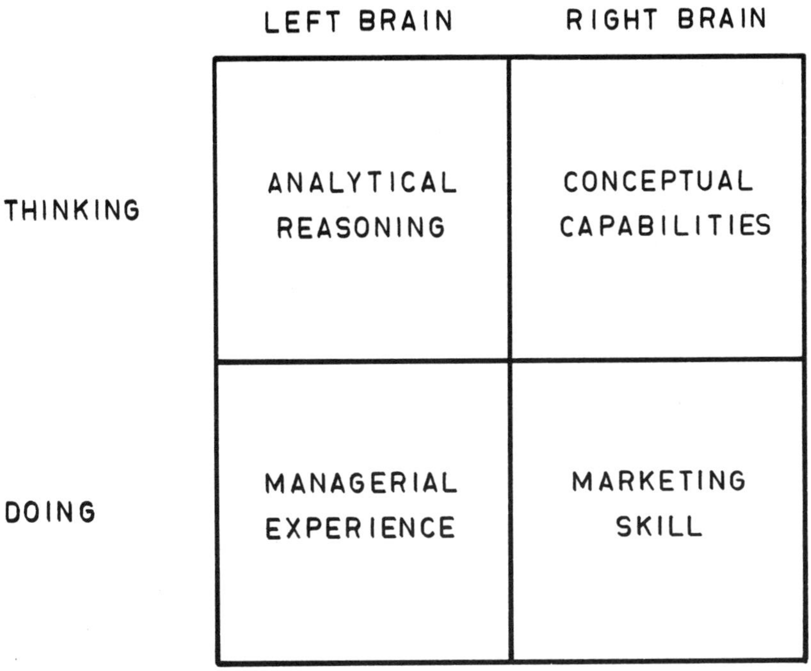

	LEFT BRAIN	RIGHT BRAIN
THINKING	ANALYTICAL REASONING	CONCEPTUAL CAPABILITIES
DOING	MANAGERIAL EXPERIENCE	MARKETING SKILL

ability. Some people tend to be analytical, others, conceptual; some lean toward management, others toward marketing. All, however, have the ability to extract imbedded information, derive insights from patterns, and reinforce a viewpoint based on prior knowledge or experience.

Perception and cognition are powers of the intellect, and cognitive complexity has conceptual and descriptive components. Both can be reduced through methodology and technology (see Section 4). This process of reduction is fundamental to the ability to comprehend market movements and to act accordingly.

The cognitive process assisted through methodology and technology in no way implies uniformity. Whichever basic style of reasoning they use, people differ in their approach to problem solving. However, the data on which reasoning is based must be shown to be correct and representative of the process we try to master. A person—using in this case the example of a securities trader—can do this through simulation and optimization.

As would a skilled financial analyst, a trader examines several types of market data (prices, ratios, etc.) and judges each of them individually or in relation to the others. Various types of data may appear too high, too low, or about right. Subsequently, these largely subjective judgments are used to draw qualitative conclusions about concepts at a higher level of abstraction, such as liquidity or profitability.

Typically a person will mentally sort through a collection of values, which are then constructed in the sense of building a fuzzy network whose nodes may connect values partially and/or temporarily or connect nothing at all.

This approach to qualitative reasoning cannot be sustained through data processing because DP is of the all-or-nothing type. But it can be supported through modeling, particularly by using fuzzy engineering. Furthermore, whether this fuzzy system runs on a computer or in the trader's own head, it must be executed in real time, and its performance must be evaluated by means of imprecise qualitative assessments in shades of grey rather than black or white.

Usually, clarifying a market trend requires a significant amount of number-crunching; hence, the inclusion of computational complexity.

◆ If more than one independent variable is involved, and if these variables can vary simultaneously, it is probable that partial differential equations will be involved.

◆ If the system is nonlinear, it may have to be transformed to a linear one by using logarithms.

◆ If statistical processes are involved, models incorporating probability, such as the Monte Carlo method or operating characteristics curves, must be used.

◆ If reasoning is at the core of the problem, it is best to apply semantic network-like representations, which are useful for describing the mental models of managers and professionals.

Both computational and knowledge-representation formalisms have a long history. The method of solution often depends on the type of problem involved. But, both methods and tools evolve.

One of the major objectives in using simulation is to develop new approaches to the never-ending need for research—specifically, research geared to finding a system that can be used in the process of determining the optimum allocation of finite resources among competing ends. This process consists of five parts:

1. dividing significant functions into key variables

2. constructing the model based on these variables

3. estimating the derivatives of the functions

4. assigning values (a process enhanced by data collection)

5. processing these values through a computer

Models need not be expressed only through equations. A networked semantic model, for example, will consist of nodes interconnected by various kinds of associative links. Links from one concept node to other concept nodes collectively form a definition of the original concept, in the sense of a semantic network.

Often, these concepts are formal objects that represent attributes and relationships of the domain being modeled. A concept is thought of as representing an intensional object, a callable entity that involves rules as well as data to be manipulated by these rules.

Today, object orientation is considered to be a trend in computer programming; but, the manipulation of rules and data in an object-oriented fashion is what has always been done in modeling. A semantic network is a model, its nodes being intensional, extensional, or both.

The general framework of an analogical reasoning methodology will capitalize on the use of intensional objects and proceed through a number of orderly steps:

1. Identify applicable analogies in tackling a given problem.

2. Retrieve examples similar to that problem (i.e., data from the database, and rules from the knowledge bank).

3. Elaborate on the retrieved examples in order to turn them into forms better suited for the present case.

4. Map parts of the current problem to parts of the retrieved examples present in the original statement (of a given problem).

5. Infer key features, even components of solutions that may not be present in the original statement.

6. Establish justification for the intensional approaches that have been chosen.

7. Learn from successful passes through the preceding steps and insert the learned lessons in memory.

The methodology that is used plays a major role in problem solution. Simulation should never be thought of as a monolithic approach consisting only of equations. As does analogical reasoning, analytical thinking requires flexibility and can be well served by inventiveness, provided a solid methodology is followed.

5. Interactive Computational Finance

Modern finance needs analytical studies. The investment advisor and the trader must be capable of designing and carrying out experiments involving alternative courses of action. They need to evaluate underlying market trends, stock and bond tendencies across currencies and country boundaries, market psychology, human reactions and interactions, political problems, and more.

On the basis of incoming data, financial analysts must draw conclusions and make inferences. The validity of these inferences depends on the proper manipulation of algorithmic and heuristic processes, whether done with computer assistance or manually.

The term Interactive Computational Finance refers to the real-time processing of heuristics and algorithms, which is necessary to handle analytical queries from traders, investment advisors, and researchers. Results should be made available, using visualization, at subsecond speed, and any variables relevant to the situation must be specified in advance. Also, experimental conditions must be spelled out, and those factors that cannot be immediately determined must be controlled, not forgotten.

Often variations of uncontrolled factors will affect the outcome of a projection or experiment. Experienced financial analysts know that properly prepared simulation studies are powerful tools for real-life experimentation.

Examples from everyday experience may lend themselves to mathematical modeling. Using simple terms, it is possible to express variables in the form of mathematical equations, then determine the outcome by identifying key variables, finding the weighting factors, and making a rough draft of the model.

This procedure usually involves five steps: (1) initialize, (2) analyze, (3) design and develop, (4) apply, and (5) sustain. Each step is then analyzed into finer elements. Table 7–1 shows in detail what the first two steps involve.

Completing the two steps shown in Table 7–1 leads to proper design. At this stage, the conceptual and computational complexities previously discussed are joined by a third factor to form a coordinate system (see Figure 7–3), whose axes of reference are conceptual, descriptive, and computational.

Table 7–1   Basic Steps in Developing Models for
                 Interactive Computational Finance

Initialize: 1. Define the problem.

                   2. Identify its scope.

                   3. Determine opportunities and constraints.

                   4. Undertake an initial study.

                   5. Establish the model's requirements.

                   6. Estimate time and costs.

Analyze: 1. Reflect on organization and structure.

                   2. Identify policies, procedures, roles, and re-
                      sponsibilities.

                   3. Define the proper equipment.

                   4. Establish the model's layout.

                   5. Describe the information flow.

                   6. Make a first draft of the rules.

                   7. Estimate strengths and weaknesses.

**Figure 7–3   Conceptual, Descriptive and
                  Computational Complexity Characterizes
                  Many Financial Products**

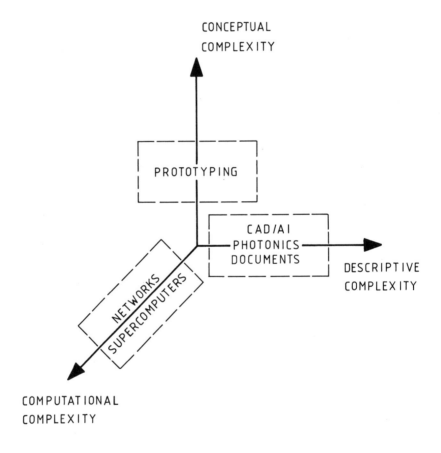

Prototyping may be used to reduce conceptual complexity. Prototyping makes it possible to adjust a basic pattern of reasoning to the cognitive complexity of the expert. According to Dr. Alan J. Rowe,[3] the individual's frame of reference is the basis by which the world is seen, and it differs with each expert.

The creative part of conceptual study is describing the problem and developing relevant alternatives. Problems are seldom, if ever, presented with relevant alternatives identified a priori and with the procedures listed. The analyst working on interactive computational finance must, therefore, be aware that conceptual studies are by necessity *pragmatic,* that is, the cost of inaction is weighed against the cost of being wrong.

Japanese financial institutions, for example Nikko Securities, employ computer-aided design (CAD) to reduce the descriptive complexity of financial systems that its specialists study. Originally designed for engineering studies, CAD can be used for tasks such as checklisting the features that go with different qualitative levels of reasoning.

To deal with model design problems, it is necessary to examine the reasoning patterns followed by financial experts and their descriptive perspective. Descriptive analysis goes beyond the conceptual issue of how experts reason and arrive at judgments and into paradigms able to explain what kind of reasoning can be expected, when (i.e., under which conditions), and how it can be formulated.

This knowledge is important when attempting to construct a set of rules. Reasoning must be examined from the viewpoint of analogies, data aggregation, pattern recognition, value judgment, and even fixation.

As its name implies, a descriptive complexity often involves a significant amount of documentation whose storage and retrieval should be on-line but cost-effective. Hence, the best technology to use is photonics (optical disks), which is an efficient means for handling compound electronic documents.

Descriptive requirements include the bill of materials and focus on the characteristics of all the component parts. The use of CAD is particularly helpful in this connection. It has good graphics capabilities, and there is good document-handling software and file-transmission standards such as the graphics kernel system by ANSI.[3]

The computational challenge has been approached in many ways. The problem of maxima and minima, for instance, has been widely treated in conventional differential calculus. Other approaches include linear programming. More recently, heuristic solutions have been followed, with the choice of the mathematical tool often depending on the skill and imagination of the rocket scientist.

Computational complexity can be affected by the method of calculation. Once a functional relationship is formulated between a decision variable and a stated variable (i.e., the objective function), it is possible to directly calculate the value of the stated variable for one decision variable. This is the direct method of calculation.

Whenever the value of the function is increased by using another value of the decision variable, the second value can be picked instead of the first. This process is typically repeated until no improvement can be made on the value of the objective function.

The direct method of calculation is applicable whenever there is a master decision variable or when there are few variables with limited choices. Whenever the domain of the decision variable(s) increases and/or there are many extremal values for the stated variable, the task of computation can become inhibitive if classical mainframes are used.

The best approach to solving the computational complexity is to use supercomputers. This is a subject that merits significant treatment; therefore, Chapter 11 of this book will be devoted to it.

6. The Concept of Prototyping

Prototypes may be built for a variety of purposes—emulating a given process or product, making scale models or digital simulators, or using the latter for identifying and clarifying requirements. Building working versions of parts or of the whole system is a good learning method; it is easier to focus on working versions than on paper documents. Combined with visualization, prototyping can be a powerful tool.

There are several models of prototypes. The most rudimentary is a throw-away demonstrator. A more complex model is built for identification, clarification, and mapping requirements.

Still more complex is the incremental prototype, which is built, evaluated, and modified according to user feedback. This can become a first version of a simulator, or any other solution in interactive computational finance, with the understanding that it will likely be refined (and possibly rewritten) as experience is gained.

The fourth model, an evolutionary prototype, evolves such that dynamic changes are incorporated without disruption, and there is no reason for rewriting (with the exception of optimizing its code, i.e., software, for reasons of response time).

Prototypes can be classified not only by model, but also by functionality, that is, the reasons for which they are built. These could include rapid prototyping, specifications analysis, and software experimentation.

Rapid prototypes are usually developed in response to situations in which it is not precisely known what to build nor how to build it. This is crucial when the identification of specifications as well as software requirements are processes subject to change. A rapid prototype supports the development of snapshots, which helps in finding subsequent solutions.

Specifications analyzers are useful because one of the important contributions of prototyping is that no system specification need exist a priori; it can be developed through prototype usage. The process produces the specification; it leads, interactively, to a functional description.

Prototypes are also used both for interface design and for determining software requirements. A software prototype, which is an approximation of the intended product, concentrates on modeling particular aspects of a system. This is usually the case with rapid prototyping.

While there is no standard approach to the development of functional financial simulators and optimizers through prototypes, there is general agreement that a prototyping approach is appropriate in most, if not all, cases. This arises from several characteristics of the use of mathematics in economics and finance:

◆ Some significant system requirements are unknown when development starts.

◆ A very effective way of eliciting knowledge is by showing experts the results of implementing their rules; this requires interactive prototyping.

◆ Representing and structuring knowledge accurately sometimes calls for experimentation through prototyping.

◆ It is often impossible to determine requirements for the user interface when development has just started; prototyping helps to structure the human window.

Figure 7–4   The Real World and the Role of Modeling

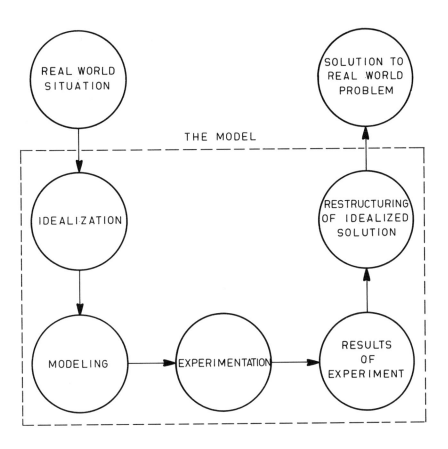

Because product planning in banks and securities houses is a complex affair, the user should determine how long the design continues and when a prototype successfully captures the critical aspects of the envisioned product. Interactivity is important because a number of iterations may be involved when developing new financial products. Figure 7–4 shows an example of model construction, the sequential steps which are involved in prototyping a real-world situation.

A successive approximation method needs a user to determine the initial approximation and, having seen how close that is in practice, to identify the next increment of change. Thus, prototyping needs inputs of requirements from the user and, at the same time, helps the user to refine and evolve those requirements.

The backbone of many new financial products is software development. This is true in R and D, financial product design, production proper, distribution functions, account management, and accounting.

Software is not developed in a vacuum but for specific reasons. One question should be asked in regard to any financial product: Can it be successfully sold on the market?

Prototyping makes it possible to "buy" knowledge and thus increase the likelihood of success of a financial product. The knowledge sought may relate to clarification of requirements, user acceptance, marketability, market behavior, or critical performance factors. Thus, prototyping is a means of reducing the risk that arises from incomplete knowledge of what is required or how to achieve it.

Through prototyping, customers can be encouraged to help design the products they want. This breaks down communications barriers between the bank and its customers and encourages innovation. For instance, a demonstration prototype may be used to show the potential value of a proposed financial product to prospective customers or sponsors. A research prototype may be concerned with feasibility and fundamental functionality in a particular problem domain. A field prototype may support other areas of concern to end users, such as effectiveness in actual operation.

Prototypes allow reviews to be conducted in an orderly way, focusing on one issue at a time or a combination of factors. To do effective prototyping, however, it is important to have the cooperation of people who will be using the resulting product or system.

7. Optimizing Results under Given Conditions

Optimization refers to obtaining the best results under given conditions. This process converts an experiment into a mathematical problem in which a certain function or variable is maximized or minimized, with some constraints imposed on it.

Optimization techniques typically focus on the search for the extremal value of a function. This function is usually a performance criterion of the system and is called the objective function. The maximization or minimization of this objective function should lead to a solution.

The optimizer has several variables, known as *decision* variables, under its control. The problem is to find the values of these variables within the allowed boundary that maximizes (or minimizes) the objective function.

As with more general experimental approaches previously discussed, an optimization procedure starts with a definition of objectives, system boundaries, endogenous variables, and exogenous parameters. Restrictions, boundary conditions, and external parameters should be clearly defined so that the solution for a system is consistent (see Figure 7–5).

Because real-life systems can be very complex, analysis often involves simplification, which may reduce the cost of modeling. Simplification, however, may also distort some of the variables. Thus, it is best to restrict simplification to the

Figure 7–5   An Optimizer Is a Special Type of Model

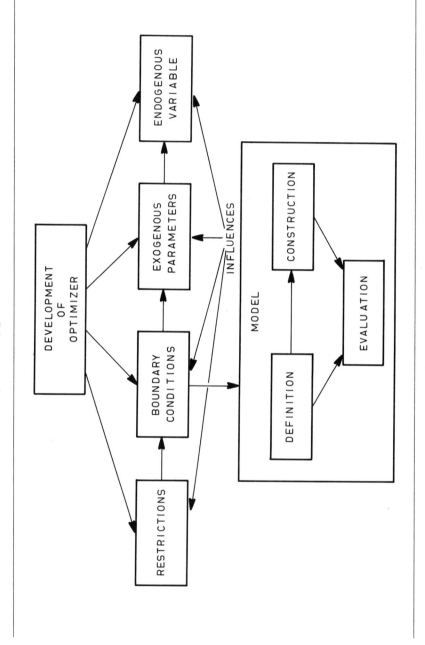

reduction of insignificant variables and of secondary processes. Also, a process of many variables can be restructured into another with several stages of few variables.

The process to be simulated, and subsequently optimized, can be deterministic, stochastic, or possibilistic. A path of the process may represent any real or abstract entity; it can be, for example, a space path, a time path, or a sequence of continuing economic activities. Variables that are transformed along each path are called *stated* variables; each variable's transformation along each path is completely described by a set of performance equations. The objective function can be described in terms of its stated variables.

Processes subject to optimization can have more than one initial or final value. The first step in optimizing a continuous, dynamic financial process is that of mapping it into the computer (hence simulation); the next step is experimentation, with the results of this experimentation analyzed. This could create a need to restructure the simulator in a pragmatic way—which would likely elicit a reasonable approximation to the real-life problem.

As shown in Figure 7–4, in order to study a real-world situation that may be too complex to experiment with, it is best to proceed with abstraction and idealization. Through algorithms and heuristics, this abstract prototype is subsequently concretized into a model. The fit of the model determines the possible success or failure of subsequent optimizations.

The algorithms and/or heuristics developed for emulation purposes, and the robustness of the software, play a key role in the success of optimization. Some developers establish a table of project features listed by stage of software dependability.

If failure means only that an early exploratory prototype must be repaired by its developers, software dependability is relatively high, and the effect of this failure is an easily recoverable loss. On the other hand, software dependability is relatively low if a defect results in moderate loss to users, and very low when the effect of a failure can be loss of most of the investment (caused, for example, by a faulty indicator of market patterns).

Thus, it is important to ensure that the whole cycle from analysis to design and programming is thoroughly understood and tested. It is also advisable to establish what characteristics the project needs to ensure software dependability.

8. The Modular Construction of a Program

In the financial industries, it is not uncommon to find a system that consists of several interconnected and often interacting logical and/or computational paths. Optimization in one of these systems is no longer a matter of determining the values of the decision variables in a single path of the system; values of the decision variables in all the interconnected paths must be simultaneously worked out.

Interdependence increases the complexity of the solution, but also presents opportunities. The best way to approach the problem is by using modularity, which makes it possible to follow self-standing yet interconnected paths. These paths are called modules.

Each module is a unit that should be designed, written, and reviewed independently of other modules—though with the final interaction in mind. Within each of these units is a collection of programs and what are often called access programs.

The designer of the interactive financial system must ensure that the structure allows independent development and change. All programs must be included once only, and interfaces to the modules must be precisely defined.

In true modularity, component parts will be compatible, and together they constitute a system that meets functional requirements. The correct procedure involves several steps:

1.   Perform a requirements specification.

There are risks with modularity. One of them is that a function, if not properly planned, will be duplicated in more than one component part, sometimes in an incompatible manner. This can be avoided through requirements specification in a systems sense, followed by the appropriate definition, not just description, of each module.

2.   Make a document describing the responsibilities of each module.

The purpose of this module guide is not only to make it easy to find all modules relevant to a particular aspect of system design, but also to review specific subjects in functionality, identifying compatibilities and incompatibilities.

3.   Perform a precise interface specification.

This typically provides a complete description of the module interfaces. There should be one specification for each component part mentioned in the module guide as well as a system-wide definition of interfaces. (The quality controllers of these documents must be experienced software engineers with knowledge of similar systems, able to note omissions in the module structure and in the interfaces.)

4.   Describe the data structures that will be used, as well as each module's effect on the data.

This information must be defined in a way that is independent of the programming language being used—without ever forgetting the role of prototyping.

    5.   Perform algorithmic and heuristic documentation.

This is written in connection to programming and abstraction functions. Each module has one programming function, which gives the mapping from the state before the module is executed to the state after it terminates. The abstraction functions are used to define the meaning of the data structure, mapping between the data states, and conceptual values visible to the user(s) of the module.

Whether algorithmic or heuristic approaches are applied, there must be no ambiguity about the responsibilities of each module. The specifications must be consistent with the module guide and its requirements. Each module design document should include evidence that the internal design satisfies the module specification; if the module specification is mathematical, mathematical verification of the design correctness is also necessary.

Furthermore, the module design document that describes the heuristics and algorithms must be clearly mapped onto the code. The processing components must be described in an abstract notation or via structured diagrams, and the test plan must show how the tests are derived and how they cover the requirements.

There is a significant amount of detail that must be taken into consideration in the software of any worthwhile model. Hence, each module should be designed through prototyping, preferably using an expert systems shell, and all documentation should be done and updated (maintained) on-line. (Some major software errors occur when documentation is allowed to get out of date while software engineers make notes with pencils on their own copies.)

Testing of both the modules and the system must be thorough. Also, configuration management will be needed to assure that every designer and reviewer has the latest version of the documents and is informed of any change in a module that might affect the review.

Endnotes

1. See also D.N. Chorafas and H. Steinmann, *Supercomputers* (New York: McGraw-Hill, 1990).

2. See also D.N. Chorafas, *Knowledge Engineering* (New York: Van Nostrand Reinhold, 1991).

3. Professor of Management, University of Southern California.

4. American National Standards Institute. See D.N. Chorafas and S. Legg, *The Engineering Database* (London: Butterworths, 1988).

Chapter 8

Expert Systems in Trust Management

Chapter 8

Expert Systems in Trust Management

1. Introduction

Throughout the First World, money managers are attempting to improve investment performance with the help of new theories and technology. Managers are also aware of the benefits, both for their own companies and for clients, in implementing advanced methods based on artificial intelligence.

In Japan, despite the fact that brokerage firms are currently locked out of the pension market (only large trust banks and life insurance companies can manage pension assets), the most advanced Japanese securities houses are way ahead of their European counterparts and slightly ahead of the Americans in implementing computers, communications, and AI. As a result, these firms are selling software for securities trading, investment advising, and equity risk modeling to institutional investors and money managers, both in Japan and in other markets.

Nikko, for example, started marketing computer-based services to U.S. pension funds in 1988. That same year, General Telephone and Electronics gave Nikko $100 million to manage an active Japanese equity portfolio, using the Niba system, in its $10 billion pension fund.

GTE is noted for applying quantitative strategies to its corporate pension plans and for hiring international managers to focus on different markets and currencies. This approach provides for better hedging and greater profits; hence, other pension funds will likely take similar approaches.

A recent initiative by GTE is to pay Nikko on an incentive basis. Instead of paying a percentage on assets under management, GTE pays Nikko a fee that varies with how well the broker performs in relation to Topix, the index of eleven hundred stocks listed in the Tokyo Stock Exchange.

Deals such as this will multiply in the 1990s, providing a stimulus for financial institutions to implement high technology in order to keep their present clients and acquire others. Expert systems will play an increasing role in this process, from providing simple customer profile analyzers to devising complex investment management constructs.

The time is right for investment banks and securities houses to do a thorough appraisal of technology policy (most likely by the mid-nineties). Today's data-processing approaches will disappear; there will be radical changes in the work of the programmer/analyst and the packaging of technology in order to meet competitive business needs.

Investment banking is making a transition from a time in which technology consisted of data-processing chores to one in which technology will be a competitive weapon. The emphasis will be on how technology can help the bottom line, that is, how it can best serve the end user.

2. The Various Aspects of Managing Trust Accounts

A trust account is created through an agreement between a client and a bank as *trustee*. The trustee manages a trust property (i.e., it invests, reinvests, administers, collects, and disburses income) in accordance with the terms of agreement. Such trusts may be revocable or irrevocable; the agreement may provide for one or more co-trustees or advisors (who are generally private individuals) to be consulted on administrative matters, investments, or both (see Figure 8–1).

With the exception of the U.S. (because of the Glass-Steagall Act) and Japan (because of Article 65), the custodian and brokerage firm may be two divisions of the same financial institution. When this is the case, it is to the advantage of both client and bank to create a computer-integrated investment management system with similarities to computer integrated manufacturing (CIM).

If clients wish to benefit from investment portfolio management expertise and its associated technology, they are usually required to sign a discretionary investment management agreement giving full powers to the financial organization. The trustee should use a client profile analyzer to obtain exact information on the client's investment desires (see Section 3).

There are a number of types of trust accounts, each with their own specialties and procedures. *Personal active trusts*, for example, deal with stocks and bonds (though occasionally real estate may comprise a portion of the property held). *Personal inactive trusts*, on the other hand, involve life insurance, savings accounts, long-term bonds, and other static investments. The client retains all rights under the policies, and the trustee has no duties except to hold the policies until the client gives written orders specifying otherwise, or until the client's will is executed posthumously. When this occurs,

Figure 8–1   Procedures Supported by a Model for Investment Management

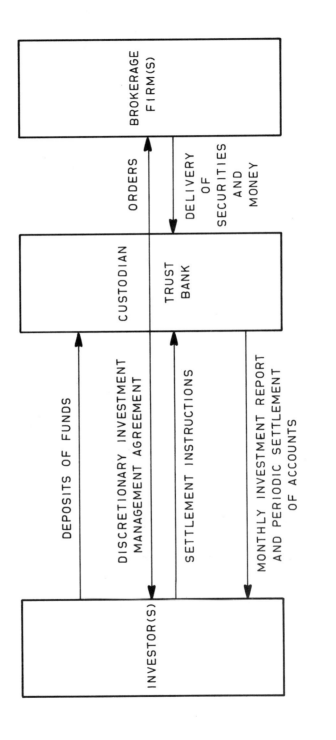

the trustee collects the proceeds, invests the money, and administers the trust in accordance with the terms of agreement. The bank may also have one or more co-trustees or advisors to assist in the administration of the trust and offer consultation on investments.

An important class of trusts is pension and profit-sharing, or living-trusts. Such trusts are held by banks for corporations. The trustee usually receives administrative directives from the client's committee which, in most cases, consists of officers or employees of the trustor company appointed under the terms of the agreement.

Sometimes, however, the trustee may have sole investment responsibility, or may offer suggestions for the approval of the committee. The bank may even have a co-trustee. In profit-sharing trusts, the bank may maintain detailed records of participants' interests. (These are generally in stocks and bonds, although occasionally life-insurance policies, annuities, or more aggressive investments are used.) Distributions to participants are generally made under the direction of a committee whose bylaws are provided for by the plan.

In a pension plan, the bank may issue checks on a monthly or other regular basis. In some instances, a lump sum is paid to the client's administrative committee, which in turn issues checks to pensioners.

Agency accounts are established for the management of property under an agreement between the principal and the bank, as agent. Where stocks and bonds or other securities are involved, the bank may offer investment advice and may make changes in the portfolio with the approval of the principal.

Under some arrangements, the bank neither offers investment advice nor makes actual purchases, but only receives and delivers securities as the principal directs. Usually, the bank collects income generated by the property it holds and disburses it as per the agreement. (In a few cases, the bank might not hold actual securities; it receives income from them and disburses it.)

Securities are usually held in the name of the principal (although, the bank's nominee is sometimes used for registration). And, while the property held under the majority of agency agreements consists of securities, the bank also acts as managing agent for real estate.

Agency accounts may be established for individuals, trustees (including pension and profit-sharing trusts), executors, guardians, institutions, or investment funds. Some agency accounts represent escrow arrangements, under which property is held for a limited time, subject to distribution in accordance with the agreement.

Testamentary accounts consist of administratorships, executorships, testamentary trusts, and guardianships. In the U.S. when a deceased person has no will, administrators are appointed by the probate court. The administrator gathers the property, pays the taxes, expenses, and administrative costs of the deceased, and distributes the property as provided by law.

Property held by the administrator may be cash, bonds, stocks, bank and building association accounts, jewelry, automobiles, or furniture. Approval for sales or distribution of the property must be obtained from the court.

A testamentary account is generally on the books for a period of a little more than a year. An inventory of the property of the deceased, as well as an account of subsequent receipts, disbursements, and distribution, is filed with the court.

Under *executorships,* the bank carries out the same duties that it would under a testamentary account, but in accordance with the terms of the will of the deceased.

Testamentary trusts are designed usually to provide for a deceased person's spouse, children, or other relatives; or, they may be established to benefit an institution. Some testamentary trusts, in the manner of living trusts, are perpetual in nature, particularly when a charitable institution is the beneficiary.

Under a testamentary trust, the trustee may have one or more co-trustees, or advisers, who must be considered when carrying out investment and other administrative duties. Property held by a testamentary trustee is usually in the form of stocks and bonds; although, real estate is also held. Under U.S. law, it is necessary to file a report biannually in probate court showing receipts, disbursements, and other distributions. The trustee may also provide the beneficiary with more frequent statements of account.

Trust accounts may also be set up as guardianships. The bank, by appointment from the probate court, serves as guardian to the estate of a minor or incompetent. As with administratorships and executorships, an original inventory is established on the date of appointment. Biannual accounts, showing receipts and disbursements, are filed with the court.

The guardian has statutory investment powers but all investment changes and disbursements must be made under court order. Property held by the guardian may be cash, bonds, stocks, real estate, bank, and building association accounts; or, it may be contributions from the state, such as pension payments.

All trust accounts have processing requirements. The areas classically handled by computer are audit of disbursements and income distribution, security review, maintenance of security master file or issue record, and computation of profit-sharing trusts. Nevertheless, portfolio management and investment decisions add domains that require considerable know-how; hence, the use of expert systems is advisable.

3. A Client-Profile Analyzer

Socrates once said that the first thing a person should do is to know himself. In an investment context, it might be said that the first thing a trust bank should do is to know its clients.

Each client has a profile, which can be mapped into an investment template that reflects customer wishes, drives, and criteria. This profile analyzer can be used to select securities as well as to manage a portfolio. As Figure 8–2 shows, a profile analyzer can become the cornerstone of a knowledge-based approach to account management.

Some may argue that an investment advisor does not really need an expert system if he or she is experienced in doing customer-profile analysis. In fact, while every investment manager asks clients questions about their preferences, no two managers ask the same questions.

Also, these questions are usually unstructured, and the answers to them are rarely stored in the bank's database.

Thus, an expert system can be useful; it helps an investment advisor to establish a client's views on portfolio selection and management through a well-established constraint set. This program is structured; hence, it can be easily handled by computer. It is invaluable in subsequently establishing a recommended investment list.

A profile analyzer is based on the premise that to manage a client portfolio efficiently, a financial institution—not just its investment advisor—needs to know the client profile in detail. With the use of computers, an interactive dialogue can take place between the account manager and the client, resulting in the rules (to be stored in the database) that constitute the decision-style template.

For this interactive questionnaire, a number of queries are written to cross-validate answers for consistency. This feature allows the investment advisor to systematically monitor cli-

**Figure 8–2   Component Modules of a Portfolio
                  Management System**

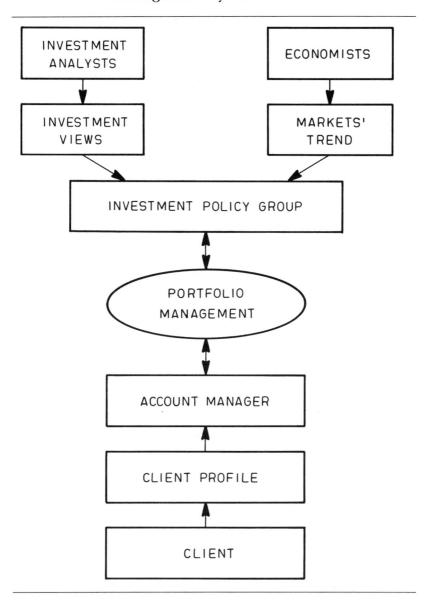

ent responses to queries regarding, for example, investor age, investment outlook (optimistic, neutral, pessimistic), earnings level, family and other financial obligations, pensions plans, liquidity requirements, and percent of net worth to be invested.

From these responses, a client template can be constructed. This profile analyzer will have an investor code that indicates the quality and dependability of the client. It will also focus on the client's sophistication and investment preferences (in terms of relative percentages, i.e., what percent bonds, what percent stocks, cash, precious metals, and so on).

The profile analyzer may, by default, accept the recommendations of the executive committee of the trustee bank, particularly if the customer has decided that such recommendations are a better alternative. Nevertheless, this client choice will be written in the corporate memory facility supported by the expert system.[1]

Other queries posed by the expert system concern the client's income versus capital-gain choices (high, medium, low risk); the type and time profile of this and other investments; and the reference currency chosen by the investor (an alternate currency or currencies can be selected if the client so desires). Profile analyzers can also be written for corporate clients and institutional investors.

Based on this input, expressed in expert systems rules, the computer can filter the list of investments and help structure the portfolio. This particular reference can be instrumental in investment reviews.

The computer does not need to generate mandatory sell recommendations if the portfolio has holdings in stocks that violate the profile filters; other modules will address themselves to advisable transactions and act as on-line assistants to the portfolio manager. The goal of the profile analyzer module is to accurately reflect the rules that define the client's investment policy.

One such rule regards preferred currency, which must be explicitly stated to measure profits and losses from a multinational, multicurrency investment. The profile expert-system module does not contain domain knowledge on shares, bonds, prices, or foreign currency markets. (These will be input by the bank's specialists in the securities and Forex domains.) It does, however, contain a clear statement of customer preferences—typically done in an interactive manner, with the expert system asking the questions on all relevant rules and facts.

Returning to Figure 8-2, we see that in a complete investment management system more modules are necessary to reflect market trends, select, and optimize. Input, for instance, comes from the bank's research department, economists, securities analysts, and other sources. But deciding what investments to recommend is determined by, for example, whether the client is income-oriented and would rather take less risk, or is capital-gains oriented, that is, driving for more growth but also taking more risk.

Though high, medium, and low graduations in risk taking provide a guideline, given the complexities of the securities market, this guideline may be too fuzzy for the trust manager.

To structure new investment portfolios, or revise existing ones, greater detail is necessary, and this is what the client profile analyzer can give. For each stock or bond, as well as futures or options position, it can help the investment advisor make a client-oriented rating and determine whether or not existing entries are dynamic (i.e., on the recommended investment list).

Based on client wishes and recommendations, as well as market inputs, an expert system can generate or evaluate a target portfolio for each client. After comparing the current portfolio composition with the target portfolio, the system makes recommendations and provides the infrastructure necessary for experimentation and for optimization.

Furthermore, this process can be completed with the client present. Visualization makes it easy for him or her to accept or reject the expert system's recommendations.

Alternatively, through computer-to-computer communication, there may be downloaded to the client's database a report detailing the initial state of the portfolio, the selected transactions, and the target state. This allows the investment advisor, the client, or both to make choices regarding investments.

Because of the amount of input that they receive from the client template, from research results, and from financial market prices, investment management expert systems can handle complex portfolios. Working backwards, they prune different types of investments in a documented manner. Smaller systems can be used as telebanking product for important clients (as Sanyo Securities is doing with a smaller version of SIRNIS, called Passport).

Aggregates of expert system modules integrate different services, giving the account manager and the client company a unified frame of reference. They can analyze corporate statements to help a bank determine whether or not to invest in or make loans to a given firm. They try to answer questions such as, Are revenues steady and rising? Does the company's cash flow enable it to pay the interest and repay the principal? Is the company's balance sheet in order? Is the price/earnings ratio reasonable?

As would an expert investor, AI constructs look at the numbers, then at intangibles. An expert system can also provide predictive comparisons between current and previous financial status. An accompanying radar chart provides visualization, showing the differences or similarities between consecutive graphs or these graphs and a standard reference.

4. An Investment Advisory System by Nomura Securities

Nomura Securities was founded in 1925. Less than a year later, its research division started publishing the financial report Zaikai Kenkyu, as an investment advisory service. In 1927 Nomura established a New York branch and began publishing a weekly report, still in print, called Nomura Weekly.

In 1952 Nomura opened the Tokyo-Nagoya-Osaka teletype line and in 1955 held its first stock symposium. Also in 1955, a Univac 120, said to be the first commercial computer in Japan, was installed. Ten years later the Nomura Research Institute was established, and in 1966 the Nomura Electric Computing Center was inaugurated as a service-bureau operation.

An on-line system began operations in 1970; by 1979, a second-generation on-line system (CUSTOM) had evolved. In 1980 and 1982, an overseas on-line system and a securities information on-line system (CAPITAL) were added on.

The domestic integrated information system named COS-MOS began operations in 1983. A year later the Securities ANSER system was phased in; with it, Nomura started home banking operations in Japan. In 1987 it began using the Famicom home-trading data system with monitors and in 1988, Famicom's home-banking trading services.

Some of the expert systems designed and implemented by Nomura Securities for investment advice to clients relate to this network. One of them is designed to run on Nintendo game computers, because these are widely distributed among Japanese families, can easily link on the telephone network and, although inexpensive, can support quality graphics.

"We must take account of changes in customer needs and customer technology, adapting to them," says one Nomura executive. The goal of Nomura, now the largest securities house in the world, is that of popularizing investment procedures through widely spread economic and financial information. The algorithm of this strategy is as follows:

Information communications media development bring consumer interest and attention to economic/financial information.

Nomura's management recognizes that newspapers, TV, satellites, broadcasting, and money magazines are efficient vehicles for dissemination of information; transactional capabilities and home-based investment management can now reach the consumers at home, thus providing an effective, low-cost but wide-spread investment vehicle. Thus, Nomura's approach is focused on individual investors and is a legal way of bypassing Article 65, since its mass marketing perspective is instrumental in siphoning money out of savings accounts and into securities.[2]

Using a home computer, a consumer can work with Nomura's investment expert system on-line, interactively. The first module is a profile analyzer which asks questions concerning, for example, the consumer's reasons (such as purchasing a home or car, marriage, children's education) for wanting a savings-type investment account. Appropriate questions are also directed to consumers interested in retirement plans, annuities, and pension plans. Queries are posed interactively through a short, simple questionnaire, or a more complete one with explanations that, if necessary, can be faxed to the client.

The online system gives a visual presentation of all products offered by Nomura. One of the expert system modules, the best portfolio integrator, then gives investment advice based on the sum the consumer plans to invest.

A savings profile is established through queries such as, How much are your living expenses? How much do you earn per month? How old are you? Do you have any financial obligations? The client's answers trigger the interactive systems to move to the next list, which contains queries such as, Do you have savings accounts? Money market accounts? What is the return? The maturity? Do you have stocks? Do you have bonds? Are they government bonds? Short or medium term?

In a manner similar to that of the client profile analyzer, the Nomura expert system poses the type of queries to an investor that an experienced investment advisor would, How should your fund grow? Slowly but steadily? More aggressively? Very aggressively? What is the return you look for?

Depending on the client's responses, the interactive system will orient itself toward stocks and convertible bonds (aggressive portfolio) or toward more conservative Nomura products, such as government bonds. The investor is offered product mixes and options from which to choose. Based on choices that have been made, the consumer receives on-line proposals for investment and may act upon them. (A more sophisticated structure, which runs on networked PC, is available for institutional investors.)

Some other Japanese investment houses, Nikko Securities for example, have programs similar to Nomura's. Nevertheless, every investment bank and securities house, whether in America or Japan, has a somewhat different approach. Two examples, which both contrast and complete one another, are shown in figures 8–3 and 8–4.

The first approach shown in Figure 8–3, is made for private investors, particularly lower- to medium-net-worth individuals. It runs on personal computers and works on-line, thus capitalized, from the central resources of the securities house. This solution is satisfactory but could still be enriched with

**Figure 8–3   An Investment Model Assisted by a
                 Profile Analyzer**

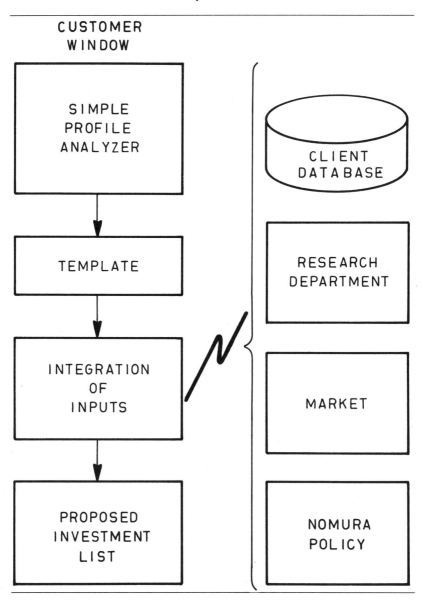

Figure 8–4   Modular Investment Advisor for Wealthy Clients and Institutional Investors

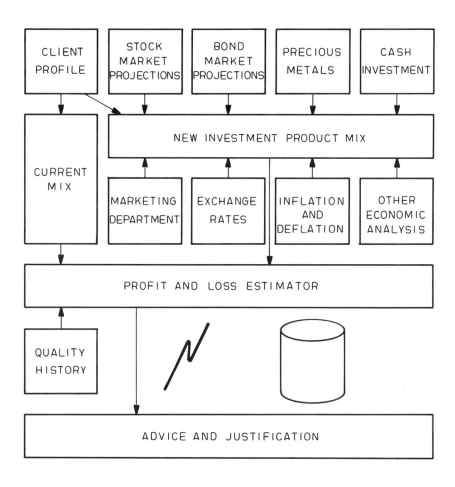

more modules; one, a life plan which will include several more functions, is in development in other departments of the securities house that advanced this approach.

Included in the life plan are a taxation expert system and a real estate knowledge construct that is smart on tax breaks. The tax module advises the client on which course to take as a function of income and obligations. Figure 8–4 shows a complex AI structure for institutional investors and high-net-worth clients. This structure is actually a synthesis of the modular AI structures used by two different securities houses. This system features a variety of specialized input modules, which address equities and debt as well as cash and precious metals to produce a new investment product mix.

This synthesized structure takes into account both current and new investments, and it utilizes modules that can project exchange rates, analyze inflation and deflation, and more. Quality histories and profit-and-loss estimation are also part of the aggregate.

When writing expert systems addressed to sophisticated investors, investment banks try to ensure that these systems are supported by rich databases. One solution has basic information on the characteristics of about twelve thousand different stocks and bonds and on the behavior of several hundred portfolios of stocks, bonds, and bond investment trusts. This system also incorporates a time series of daily quotes for about four thousand equities and debt instruments, totaling some 2.3 million points, and features a data filter that edits the input flowing from information providers.

The intelligent software that the securities house has developed analyzes patterns, reflects on entity-relationships and adheres to ad hoc data representation requirements.

This whole system handles in real time a dynamically varying and potentially large number of information elements. For elements such as attributes of stocks, bonds, and whole portfolios, the system can focus on time intervals and prices, including both bid and ask in the bond domain. (In an ad hoc query, the user might want to know the monetary value of the calls made by the issuers of a given bond—which is a function of the bond's current price, price volatility, time to maturity, and remaining call schedule.)

Another implementation for sophisticated investors is a currency-investment/portfolio-management program, a new type of investment vehicle that uses currency forward contracts and interbank currency options in a portfolio of long and short cross-currency positions determined by optimization. This system simultaneously computes price trends, interest-rate differentials, cross-correlations, and volatility; also, it recommends a combination of positions to yield a good return-to-risk ratio. It has a global view and uses short as well as long positions. Diversification of investments is a sound method of reducing portfolio volatility. An expert system has been written handling several asset classes with the goal of offering investors and investment managers the potential for improving portfolio performance and controlling diversification. These will become the standard goals of the 1990s.

5. Improving the Sophistication of Investment Management Procedures

As we have discussed, expert systems can help investors, traders, and portfolio managers to assess current positions, evaluate financial products, determine the extent to which the financial products they use are keeping pace with market growth rates, and identify repositioning strategies. Simulators and AI constructs can also be used to forecast future evolution in a range of financial products. They provide investment alternatives, as well as help in evaluating the impact of different investment allocation strategies. They do so not only through algorithmic and heuristic models but also by means of a well-structured conceptual framework.

Yamaichi Securities' Integrative Expert System (IES) is intended to provide users with up-to-date information on securities investments. The system's knowledge bank consists of securities investment know-how garnered from the brokerage house's years of experience and from corporate information collected and processed by the securities analysts.

One of the basic modules of IES is its alarm system, the function of which is to give Buy/Sell alarm signals when a change in the market is detected. The core model is Japanese spot stock Transaction One (TSE 1st section), which classifies approximately eleven hundred issues into sixty-five industry sectors, taking into account each industry's sensitivity to various macroeconomic indicators.

The stock of one company can belong to several industry sectors, with its weighting in each sector determined by a sales breakdown. (See Chapter 9 for a discussion of the trading theory behind the Integrative Stock System.) The information incorporated into the model is the latest taken from the stock price database and other databases, such as financial statistics and corporate finance.

The rules of another key module reflect the broker's reasoning process. This expert system's reasoning rules rest on fuzzy logic using graded buy and sell signals. Each stock could have several graded buy/sell signals, depending on how many industry sectors it belongs to. The grades given to a stock are weighted averages from determining sales by industry sector.

Transaction volume is established by the gravity method. The results of the fuzzy logic process are indicated in the form of bar charts for each stock. Only grade and volume figures above certain levels, reflected in the chart, trigger an action alarm.

The expert system's rules incorporate standards by which buy/sell signals for each stock can be given as market conditions change. These rules are based on how investments are managed by securities experts. In the case of IES, such rules are determined by an intracompany committee established by the management of Yamaichi Securities.

IES includes information-processing functions, such as lag algorithm, moving average, and volatility factor. Many variables are qualitatively expressed and therefore complement the quantitative arithmetic operations.

The reference rules are a vital part of the knowledge bank. This expert system uses a large number of rules to produce a small number of answers. This approach is designed to reflect the way a human would behave. "For a small number of rules, we do not need computer assistance," says one Yamaichi executive.

The IES rules operate on four levels, in accordance with the structure of the specific module to which they belong:

1. *Macro rules* are market-related and reflect economic trends. They are useful for choosing industries and stocks and can be described by using variables such as, commodity prices and interest rate trends.

2. *Industry rules* imply a standard for each industry-related economic indicator. They help the operator to compare different industrial sectors.

3. *Micro rules* focus on the selection of individual stocks without reference to industry data. They include factors such as, stock-price deviation from moving averages and volatility.

4. *Investor rules* qualify the preferences of investors but also reflect a number of investment restrictions.

As we have discussed, fuzzy reasoning is done through weighted averages that work independently for each level. These weights represent the investor's view of the market in the sense that certain levels are weighted more than others, according to the client's profile template. Particular attention has been paid to rule sensitivity to such choices.

The IES rules system is designed, as are similar AI constructs, to provide agile, user-friendly, and forgiving human-machine interfaces. The idea is to offer computer-based solutions while giving the end user a sense of dealing with a person behind the machine.

This policy of basing designs not on the limitations of silicon, but on the limits of human imagination, is a bold approach. Ingenious human-window solutions can be implemented by keeping in mind that expert systems, through the use of non-procedural methodology, reflect human knowledge in handling fairly complex situations. Also, their inference mechanism is able to provide justification, and some knowledge-based constructs exhibit a learning capability.

The first step is know-how-through-show-how. The end goal is to refine knowledge through an integrated process of deriving, measuring, testing, and even transforming embodiments of useful investment management knowledge.

An expert system investment advisor should run on the executive's networked personal computer; though, an AI construct for traders may also require a supercomputer to do number-crunching. This advisor should have, in addition to its specialized capabilities, wide range of conventional applications, featuring extended usefulness of the personal workstation, and low-cost delivery.

A typical application is as an aid to making investment decisions and financial analyses regarding equities and bonds, capital financing projects, and the tax consequences of all these. These are the ideal knowledge domains.

One of the foremost banks in Japan built an expert system that works on-line and advises its clients in response to queries regarding the best financial investment available for assets. (This system also includes a module that addresses itself to tax law.)

This knowledge-based construct asks why the user is posing a query; it records the user's answers (or no answer) to the system queries; and it accesses distributed databases in order to acquire enough information to form an opinion. The system is designed to help users get to know the markets (including interest and taxation), analyze different types of investments, learn how to develop alternative investment plans, and evaluate the return on an investment for each alternative. The system also gives an opinion on a contemplated investment solution and justifies this opinion.

As it has grown more sophisticated, this AI construct has been enriched with risk-management tools. Presently, it is able to generate market models and does far more than collect and maintain securities and price information.

For example, it has the ability to calculate the susceptibility of a financial product to adverse market conditions and to elaborate an analogical base to produce knowledge relevant to the current situation. Furthermore, the construct has the ability to learn from this analogy. New analogies are added to the memory, which is restructured to account for newly recognized financial products' similarities.

6. Using AI in the Payments System

Trading generates considerable follow-up paperwork, which uses up time and costs money. This process can be fully automated with the help of expert systems. Specifically, expert systems can be used to handle payments traffic at three levels, those of exceptional (large), spontaneous, and regular payments.

At CHIPS, *exceptional* payments average 750,000 per day, each $3.2 to $3.5 million in mean value. *Spontaneous* payments include all one-time personal payments made, for example, those to retailers.

Regular payments are those made on a steady basis to meet a range of commitments (e.g., mortgage repayments and utilities payments). It is projected that in the early 1990s, in Britain, there will be between 1.6 and 1.8 billion non-cash payments in this category, approximately 60 percent of which will be made electronically. Per capita, American statistics are similar.

The on-line electronic execution of payment transactions presents business advantages ranging from improved competitive position to cost control; nevertheless, electronic payments also pose challenges. The least of these is renting telephone lines and buying computers (though, with the current incompatible telco standards, for a multinational bank, the experience of international dealing can be frustrating). Among the challenges is software to handle payments, developing imaginative applications, and selling them to user organizations in an on-line, networked manner. Figure 8–5 shows a layered approach to the efficient use of AI constructs in a telecommunications network.

At the lowest layer is the physical plant (leasing lines and buying computers). The expert systems that can assist at the physical plant level typically focus on fault diagnostics, reliability/availability calculations, and quality histories.[3]

The next layer up deals with software support for the network. Useful expert systems will look after error control, ensure fast delivery of messages and files through rerouting, and optimize the use of resources (for instance, by selecting among alternative tariffs) in order to help provide low-cost operations.

The top level in network sophistication is applications-oriented. Fundamental to the automation of payment handling is the use of imaging. Expert systems automatically exploit the imaging database, face-lift documents and signatures, and select and transmit information elements to the client.

Figure 8–5   Expert Systems Support to the Different Layers of a Communications System

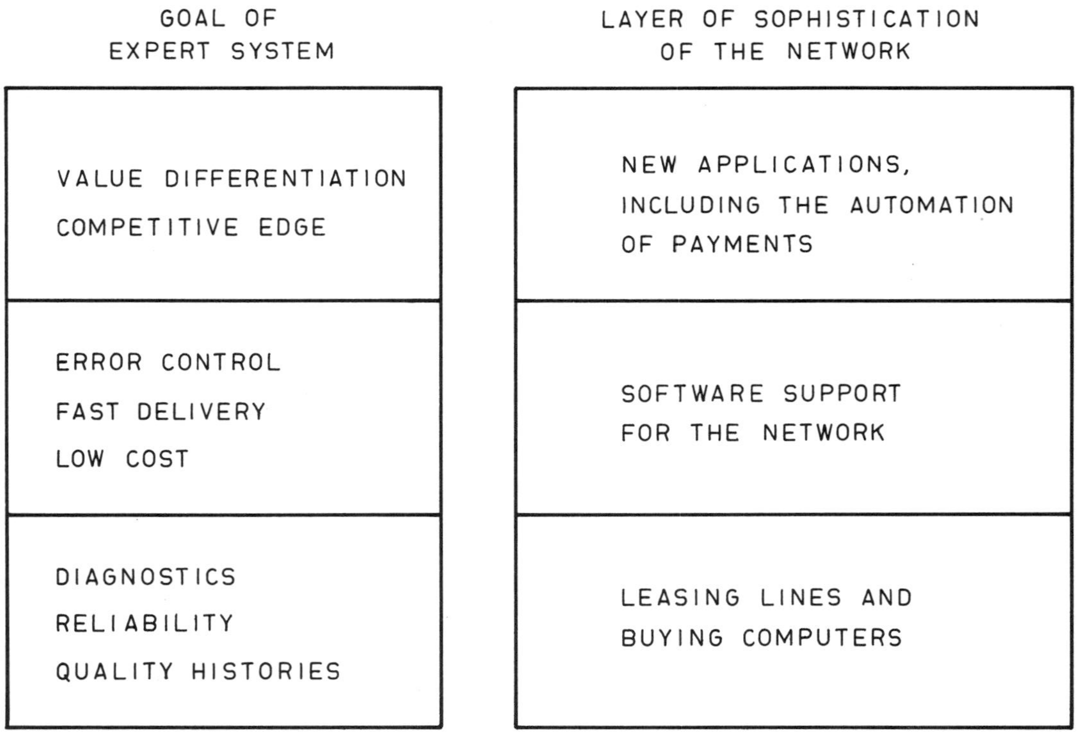

GOAL OF EXPERT SYSTEM	LAYER OF SOPHISTICATION OF THE NETWORK
VALUE DIFFERENTIATION COMPETITIVE EDGE	NEW APPLICATIONS, INCLUDING THE AUTOMATION OF PAYMENTS
ERROR CONTROL FAST DELIVERY LOW COST	SOFTWARE SUPPORT FOR THE NETWORK
DIAGNOSTICS RELIABILITY QUALITY HISTORIES	LEASING LINES AND BUYING COMPUTERS

Leading banks and securities houses understand that since deregulation, a financial company can successfully compete only if it

1. is a key node in the global electronic trading network;

2. makes it easy and cost-effective for multinational clients to do business;

3. provides a means for clients to link with their international communications networks;

4. spreads fixed costs over a large range of activities worldwide;

5. adapts its policies and its technology to changing conditions.

Since the emergence of twenty-four-hour trading and associated settlements procedures, financial institutions have little choice but to adopt these five procedures. Sophisticated customers want to trade any currency or security on any exchange, any place in the world, at any time of the day. Thus, an investment banker must access and analyze activities through an on-line workstation, be able to reach all major money markets immediately, execute buy/sell orders, and move funds from market to market and currency to currency, and evaluate client portfolios and optimize them.

Financial institutions are not the only ones to move in this direction. Information providers have also developed into network operators, sometimes going into competition with the exchanges. According to an article in the *London Economist*,[4] "Reuters is also pinning its hopes on automated trading ... Foreign exchange, commodities, futures, and shares will be able to be traded anonymously simply by posting bid and offer prices which are then matched automatically."

7. Computers and Communications in Securities Trading

Using computers and communications in securities trading enables a bank to stay competitive. Efficient trading tools, if properly designed, also help to control risk. Management-oriented programs should aim to provide quick and comprehensive information for traders, investment advisors, and customers, and to rationalize administrative work, thus reducing clerical costs.

Computers and communications can enhance the technical base for the global custody function. They expedite dealing with and monitoring securities, by linking on-line to relevant clearing institutions and depositories, and provide efficient base-portfolio management, including consolidated asset valuation.

Effective solutions do not address items individually; they focus on a systems approach and take a global view. Shares, options, bonds, participation certificates, bank-issued medium-term loans, money market papers, certificates of deposit, mortgage notes, bills of exchange, borrowers notes, and precious metals and coins are all items covered in the securities trade.

While a securities house front desk must execute deals efficiently, its back office must provide interactive reports for processing and control purposes. Bookkeeping operations need to be done automatically, and the reporting structure should provide up-to-date, comprehensive information. A fully automated back office can handle securities transactions such as, receiving and delivering for custody accounts, transfering custody accounts and/or security numbers, transfering depositories, matching open deliveries, and making or canceling security administration entries.

Custody account bookkeeping typically holds all positions for customers. The inventories must be correct. Market information, leading values, management and custody fees, and taxes must be automatically calculated and available interactively on request.

Depositories bookkeeping can be fully computerized, with detailed mapping of all positions conserved at each depository. Transactions not yet confirmed should be indicated as open deliveries to permit their control. Repayments, dividends, and interest must be credited for custody accounts, with the respective advices forwarded to customers, preferably on-line. For repayment, securities must also be booked out of the custody account.

Collection and redemption of bonds coupons can also be automated. Answers to queries concerning securities administration, including custody account analysis, income projection and performance statements for investment counseling and portfolio management, need to be given on-line. (Expert systems can capture the know-how of people who once performed these tasks manually.

Managing profit margins is critical to the survival and success of any financial institution. By controlling product and service costs with the use of AI, management can achieve the profit margins required to be competitive and profitable in the securities business.

Computer-based models can also be used for pricing. Aggressive pricing in investment advising and administration aims to maximize margins while recognizing the need to serve different customers and market segments. Pricing options should include the possibility of fine-tuning market strategies. Some of the options are customer-specific pricing, quantity breaks, and product-class pricing.

A financial institution gains a competitive edge by providing more complete information for clients than other firms do. Thus, a bank's information system must be on-line for faster response and better customer service. As well as information, computers should provide experimentation tools;

A financial institution gains a competitive edge by providing more complete information for clients than other firms do. Thus, a bank's information system must be on-line for faster response and better customer service. As well as information, computers should provide experimentation tools; that is, flexible solutions with the ability to make evaluations and give advice.

Offering value-added-services is necessary to stay competitive. Generally, banks charge service fees for expertise and for client hand-holding. As more of these functions are performed by computers, added values will make the difference. Value differentiation is designed by expert bankers and implemented through communications and computers.

Endnotes

1. See also D.N. Chorafas, *Risk Management in Financial Institutions* (London: Butterworths, 1990).

2. For low-net-worth individuals these are mostly guaranteed government bonds.

3. See also D.N. Chorafas and H. Steinmann, *Intelligent Networks* (Los Angeles: CRC/Times Mirror, 1990).

4. *London Economist,* 23 July 1988.

Chapter 9

Theories That May Help in Trading

Chapter **9**

Theories That May Help in Trading

1. Introduction

In contrast to deposit and loan bankers, traders are in the moving business. They cannot operate without creating and holding positions and evaluating the different components of risk and opportunity in order to make reasonable deals as well as hedges when necessary.

Prior to managing a fund, traders must create it. This requires asset-allocation procedures that are responsive to market trends. Computers are more necessary than ever as firms continue to offer a growing range of financial instruments around the globe. Thus, there is a need for trading theories capable of assisting in asset allocation, in one or more stock exchanges and in different currencies, both in capital markets and in money markets.

Also, the knowledge of the most experienced people in an organization should be made available to all traders. This can be done with the help of expert systems. Both trading proper and alarm algorithms (as well as heuristics) must be easy for traders to understand and follow. A moving target can be identified by overlaying two or three images with market values taken less than a second apart, as on a radar chart; subsequently, its relative positions can be compared, keeping in mind that the scene, as it evolves, will make a comprehensive pattern.

If the trading theory is worthwhile, then microcomparisons will suggest either that there is a trend or that there is no movement worth noticing.

This presents, in a nutshell, the solution we seek. It is helpful to remember that while a number of technology-enriched solutions with marketing flavor must be addressed to clients, efficient and personalized support systems are also necessary to help traders do a better job.

2. Fundamental Analysis and Technical Analysis

Commodity traders basically rely on either technical or fundamental analysis (and sometimes a combination of both) in order to make trading decisions. Technical trading strategies are designed to identify and follow existing and incipient trends in the market. Fundamental trading strategies are designed to forecast possible future developments on the basis of relative strengths and weaknesses in the markets.

Technical trading uses data on price, volume, and the number of outstanding contracts to identify profit opportunities. Price levels represent the general assessments of fundamental traders; price trends occur as new and changing information is considered by fundamentalists. Technical traders usually employ carefully researched indicators to identify trends early and to exploit them.

The basic idea behind technical theories is that, at any given point in time, market prices will reflect all known factors affecting supply and demand for a particular commodity.

This is not necessarily true in every case; therefore, technical analysis has its critics.

As used in futures trading, the term technical refers to the recording (usually in chart form) of opening, high, low, and closing prices, as well as volume of trading. From these factors, a technical analysis attempts to project the future price trend, show a possible price objective of the move, and indicate when this objective might be met.

Critics notwithstanding, the technical approach is now probably used more than any other type of analysis, particularly in futures markets. This is partly because of the ready availability of the few factors required for such analysis.

Technical analysis, however, is based not on the anticipated supply and demand of a particular cash (actual) commodity, but on the theory that the study of commodities markets themselves can provide a means of anticipating the external factors that affect the supply and demand of a particular asset, thus, making it possible to predict future prices.

The fundamental approach is based on the study of factors external to the trading market that affect the supply and demand of a particular commodity. The user of this approach aims to predict future prices by considering issues such as the economy, government policies, domestic and foreign political and economic events, changing trade prospects, and the weather.

By monitoring supply-and-demand information relevant to a particular commodity, fundamental securities analysts try to identify a current or potential disequilibrium of conditions that has not yet been reflected in the price level of that commodity. An important assumption behind fundamental analysis is that markets are imperfect.

The fundamental approach is the traditional method, that is, attempting to project prices by analyzing what data affect the supply and demand of a commodity. The assumption is that the price of any commodity will ultimately be determined by the interaction of the fundamentals affecting that commodity. Careful analysis and weighing of relevant factors is the basis of the fundamental trading approach.

One of the problems in analysis today is that fundamental and technical trading is still one-market oriented. Neither approach has yet been revised to incorporate the concept of a country and its exchange(s), currency, credit rating, resources, political stability, and state of economic development (see Figure 9–1).

Despite different approaches to the problem of predicting and explaining the market, both fundamental and technical analysis focus on market perception, the concept of movements, risk evaluation and pattern recognition. Both also attempt, more or less, to test market inefficiency (in prices) against the hypothesis that markets are efficient.

For example, one question might be, Should IBM shares be at $100 because the market says so at closing? At this point, traders and securities companies develop different theories to test the distribution of prices and determine possible trends.

One of these theories suggests that the correct price is not the closing price but the one on which volume trades. That is, the closing price is a basis of performance evaluation; and the price on which volume trades (weighted average) plus trend and psychological factors is the decision basis.

These assumptions dictate the wisdom of assessing patterns in prices and markets looking for a real-time and real-space response on how to improve trading efficiency in an imperfect market. This assessment requires a valid methodology able to go beyond current macroeconomic models. Some brokers focus their efforts (in line with the New Wave Economics of Dr. Edward Yardeni et al.) on manageable microeconomic models of market valuation.

One challenge is to identify anomalies and to establish a dynamic methodology able to follow market movements and

Figure 9–1   A Multimarket Model for Country- and Industry-Oriented Studies

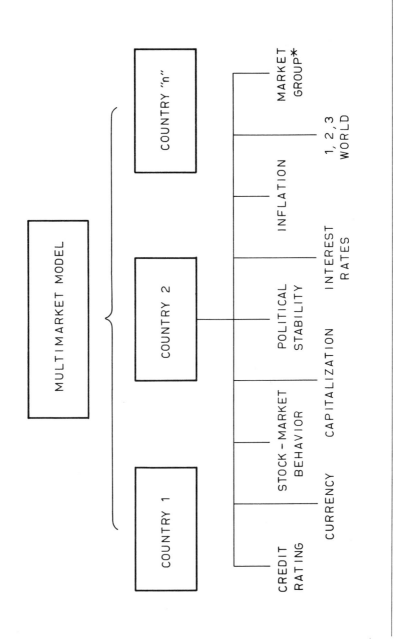

explain at least some of them. Will the market gravitate around an expected value? What is the risk in downside? This reference is just as valid when dealing with money as when dealing with securities. Both are, after all, traded by the same market participants.

An expert system should help traders and fund managers to select a portfolio consistent with a client's investment objectives and to maintain or adjust that portfolio in response to changing circumstances and investment views. The system should also provide facilities for compliance as well as for monitoring performance and other variables. It must be able to link to a variety of databases holding client and securities information and to support a user-friendly interface to make it easy to access.

Future developments will most likely be integrative. Instead of making a fundamental or technical analysis per se, a securities expert will call the appropriate modules into a process of reviewing a portfolio. Then he will define an investment scenario by specifying the client fund in question, the securities to be added to or deleted from the portfolio, and further investment objectives or constraints that are consistent with the aims of the fund.

The optimization of a portfolio is a two-stage process of asset allocation and stock or bond selection. Options should be available for both standard quantitative techniques and a user-defined style of optimization, subjecting the portfolio under examination to a variety of analytical procedures before commitment to actual purchases or sales is made.

During the 1980s, investors discovered the benefits of asset allocation and began switching between stocks, bonds, and cash, as well as investing in various markets and currencies. The strategy was to take advantage of market inefficiencies but also to hedge—with the overriding goal being that of obtaining higher returns, at least on a projected basis. This led to novel portfolio management approaches: indexing was one of the innovations (see Chapter 10, Section 4), and currency hedging was another.

Asset allocation, also known as Tactical Asset Allocation (TAA), is a popular form of investing. It is similar to what used to be called market timing (see Chap. 10, Section 5). One difference, however, is the use of computers and analytical models to predict returns.

Many analysts consider asset allocation to be a major success story in the structured investment management business. This is because of TAA's ability to establish optimal exposure to asset classes and to follow guidelines defined by an investment manager.

Stocks, bonds, and Treasury bills are selected as asset classes, and an asset-allocation model is used to determine the best possible portfolio allocations. More complex asset allocation approaches can be taken for international equity markets.

While it is fairly common for an investment manager to determine an appropriate mix of stocks, bonds, and cash in a portfolio, such work becomes cumbersome as the investment choices increase. It is no longer enough for investment managers to adjust asset mixes based on their feel for the market. Quite often these adjustments are based on recent market activity, rather than on a long-term perspective; hence, the need for experimentation.

Such experimentation typically includes a comparison of projected risk and return (investment objectives), as well as exposure to factors the user considers to be of investment significance. To increase accountability, actual performance is tracked against technical and fundamental analysis, and use is made of specified benchmarks, such as indices or model portfolios.

Also important is the incorporation of an automatic compliance mechanism; it monitors how well the deals made and overall portfolio composition conform to rules set out by the client, senior management, or governmental constraints.

This facility should be used with any intended portfolio change; it must include monitoring of drift against objectives, bringing such cases immediately to the investor's attention.

3. Market Volatility

As discussed in a previous chapter, volatility is the quality of being volatile, that is, evaporating rapidly, changeable, or transient. Most of these terms can be applied to the market behavior of stocks, whose value can change sharply and suddenly at any given time.

Volatility greatly affects the banking industry; banks are vulnerable to changes in interest rates. Credit volatility adds to their desire to get into the business of underwriting the growing securitized credit market. It yields a steady source of income. But, credit markets are also subject to volatility though of a different kind.

Evaluating market volatility requires perspective on the financial markets of the First World, the principal market in which we invest, the currency in which investments will be made, industry risk within the principal market, the specific stock or bond in which an investment will be made, the expected dividends (or interest rate), and carry. Precisely because of volatility, successful hedging requires a global market viewpoint as well as the consideration of trends in currencies and in industry sectors.

Because volatility affects market behavior and the values traded in the market, it should be measured as much as possible. For many professional traders, portfolio managers, and investors, a key factor in successful securities handling is an understanding of the volatility metric beta, which they consider a risk-management tool.

Beta is a measure of a stock's volatility relative to the broad market. Beta figures, which are published by large brokerage houses and by analysts such as Standard & Poor's, show aggressive or defensive strength in the market.

Mathematically, the volatility factor is calculated as standard deviation in stocks price movements, as if these were forming a normal distribution. These can be minute movements; although, volatility was formerly measured by using annual statistics. Volatility is an indicator of price differential.

The first step in calculating volatility is to examine how closely the distribution of all available data approximates a bell curve. The next is to use powerful mathematical models and supercomputers to experiment on implied volatility at the same speed that stock and commodity prices change in the exchange.

Supplied with a steady stream of real-space data, supercomputers make it possible to instantaneously calculate the standard deviation of the distribution of total return (i.e., the yield plus capital change). This provides a measure of an asset's volatility.

For a given expected value of return, investors generally prefer securities with the Lowest volatility and Predictability of return. However, this does not necessarily correspond to the intuitive concept of many investment decisions, since the chance of underperforming some benchmark depends on both the relation between the expected return and the benchmark and the dispersion of return about its expected value.

High beta stocks are bought in the hope that they will outdistance the general market (assuming that there is a bull market and the investor's timing is right). But, volatility is also a source of worry and of potential risk. (Based on daily reports after October 1987, the Dow Jones average began fluctuating by roughly 3.5 percent. This degree of volatility had not been seen since 1929, and up to a point it eroded investor confidence—most exchanges took a couple of years to return to pre-October 1987 levels.)

If a stock has a beta of 1.2, then theoretically it moves faster by 20 percent in either direction. A beta of 1.6 means that the stock moves 60 percent faster than the market. Such volatility promises good capital gains on the upside, but is risky on the downside. The risk is even greater when capital markets work in sympathy with each other.

One explanation for the variety of declines in different markets is that an underlying worldwide variable causes upswings and crashes. One related theory is that the movement of each market is based on the relationship between that particular market and this underlying variable. Accordingly, data is used to construct a world-market index weighted across countries using local currency-denominated returns; then, a market model is fit to the time series of monthly returns for each country.

Indices can be constructed on both a common-currency and a local-currency basis and treated in either equal-weighted or value-weighted manner by the dollar value of total country capitalization. Time-series regression between individual country returns and the various indexes sometimes yields surprisingly similar betas (slope coefficients), even if exchange rate adjustments add a noisy random variable to the local currency return.

In this multinational, multimarket model, beta measures the relative magnitude of response of a given country to changes in the world-market index. One goal of the model is to determine whether or not this country has a statistically significant relationship to the index.

Some economists, by examining the magnitude of a country's response to a world market movement, attempt to determine whether this response is itself a function of the institutional arrangements in that country's stock market. Margin requirements and limits on price movements can reduce the beta in the market model from the level it would otherwise achieve. Such analyses are important given the global marketplace of the First World and the financial instruments which are being handled.

Certain financial institutions, while they use beta, also establish their own metrics. For instance, Yamaichi Securities has instituted alpha as an indicator of how much investors try to beat the market index. In that sense, each volatility metric is focused on a target; alpha helps to measure company-specific risk, and beta reflects the amount of market risk.

This alpha factor has proved to be of value to Yamaichi traders; thus, when this securities house sells stock trading and bond trading computer-assisted solutions to competitors, it releases the beta, but not the alpha. (These Yamaichi solutions extensively use Modern Portfolio Theory, to be discussed in the next section.)

Whichever metrics are applied as a guide to trading, the fact remains that the opportunity for profits and the risk of loss increase as volatility in the markets grows. By using metrics and an associated methodology to measure volatility, traders merely exercise some control over this risk factor.

By identifying risk and measuring it, it becomes possible to balance it across different investments, accordingly adjusting the level of trading when markets become volatile. Combined with adequate capitalization and diversification, a balanced risk operates to preserve equity.

4. Modern Portfolio Theory

Fundamental to a structured portfolio management approach is a theory of portfolio risk and return as well as elements of a general equilibrium theory describing the pricing of risky assets. Both require computationally demanding testing of investment alternatives, the subject of which will be discussed in a later chapter.

This chapter will examine the basic components involved in structuring a portfolio theme with reference to the seminal work in the field of investment risk management done by Dr. Harry Markowitz (then a scholar at UCLA) in 1952.

Portfolio managers have long known that risk can be reduced by increasing the number of investment instruments in a portfolio and spreading them across different sources; prior to 1952, however, this task had not been mathematically defined. Markowitz presented a mathematical approach for determining the portfolio that offers the highest expected return for the risk taken.

According to Modern Portfolio Theory (MPT), the steps necessary to quantify risk and return are to calculate the mean and standard deviation of expected returns for each investment being considered and to correlate returns for each pair of investments. Within this setting, the class of portfolios offering the highest return for a given level of risk is said to be on the efficient frontier.

Investors should choose a portfolio that suits their risk preference, since to do otherwise is to accept lower return for the risk taken. (The notion that investors should diversify their portfolios seems self-evident now. But at the time that Dr. Markowitz first proposed his systematic method, even the renowned economist Dr. Milton Friedman said to him, "Harry, what is this? It is not mathematics; it is not economics; it is not finance."[1])

In essence, MPT is simple: it focuses on portfolio diversification on a statistically precise basis. This thorough mathematical evaluation can be financially rewarding because shares are inherently risky (since they were first exchanged in Amsterdam in the seventeenth century, they having risen and fallen in cycles).

Dr. William Sharpe has built upon the Markowitz statistics-in-investments concept by demonstrating that the risks and rewards of holding an asset are linked to its volatility in relation to the rest of the market. The concept, that highly volatile stocks are the biggest winners in bull markets, but suffer the heaviest losses in downturns, is simple and may even sound self-evident; the challenge is to quantify it. Dr. Sharpe's approach extends the idea of portfolio diversification by introducing the beta coefficient of volatility as a precise indicator of the relative risk of a particular asset.

If one knows the degree of a stock's volatility in relationship to that of the market, it is possible to manipulate investments. For example, one monitoring of a basic game with stocks consists of zig-zagging a share upwards in a way that attracts maximum attention and, therefore, public following. This permits operators to exit with big profits before the share collapses.

Recent market panics, such as the October 1987 Black Monday meltdown, have led to a renewed emphasis on diversification, as well as increasing acceptance of the Markowitz principle that investors need diversify their portfolios only slightly to significantly reduce risk, provided the separate holdings do not move in tandem. Markowitz says, "It is enough to have a portfolio of twenty stocks, provided they have different characteristics. Adding another one hundred or one thousand stocks will not reduce your risk much more." The caveat is that those twenty stocks should represent a variety of industries (hence, multidimensional analysis, which will be examined later in this chapter).

Thus, investment should not be only in, for example, technology companies that move in lock-step. Nevertheless, investing in only growth-stock funds is unwise, since they tend to reinforce or to weaken each other. A mixed portfolio of stocks, bonds, cash, and real estate helps reduce risk substantially. On this principle rests the concept of hedging.

Still, more complex moves are necessary in order to meet market challenges today. In the original version of MPT, exchange-rate risks were not diversifiable. By contrast, today, this function is not only possible, but is also, to a considerable extent, mandatory.

In risk/return terms, a portfolio that holds hard currencies is perceived to have relatively high volatility which may add incremental value regardless of the degree of market efficiency:

♦ Short-term currency deposits in a portfolio will give the investor a pure currency scenario, which can be balanced in terms of risk.

♦ A hybrid approach will involve not only a global approach to portfolio composition but also debt, equity, and foreign currencies.

The effectiveness of equity portfolio management has sparked interest in a parallel approach to bonds. A rapidly developing subset of the government and corporate sectors is the market for cross-border bonds. These are bonds issued by a country, or one of its corporations, in the currency of another country. They may also be held primarily by residents of another country.

Cross-border bonds include traditional foreign bonds and various categories of Eurobonds. Today the cross-border bond market has reached nearly $1 trillion, having grown at an 18-percent annual rate since it began in the mid-sixties.

5. Portfolio Diversification on a Statistically Valid Basis

All investors are really portfolio managers; although, they may not be skilled, particularly if their investments are overly concentrated. Far too many do not consider their overall holdings when they invest, but instead evaluate each investment on its own merits. Unfortunately, even if each one of its individual components is sound, an investor's portfolio may make no sense from the standpoint of risk and return. (This is true even for banks and institutional investors.)

Modern Portfolio Theory (MPT) can help investors to systematically construct and modify their portfolios to increase performance and control risk. MPT uses two methods of stock market analysis and valuation. One is based on the microeconomic-oriented stock price index; the other is based on macroeconomic indicators as interest rates and inflation. Modern Portfolio Theory addresses the valuation of individual securities and the construction of portfolios, demonstrating that portfolio selection can be divided into three distinctive areas:

1. asset allocation,

2. investment analysis, and

3. selection proper.

The first two of these are judgmental processes to which artificial intelligence and heuristics tools are applicable. The third is an algorithmic process that uses estimates of risk and return generated by investment analysis, as well as compositional constraints produced by asset allocation.

According to MPT, the utility of a given portfolio to its owner should be a maximum, with the exact nature of the utility function varying from one individual to another. A number of variables may characterize the individual investor—the amount of money he or she has available to invest (which is part of his or her broader resources), investment preferences, obligations, and requirements, and a certain degree of risk aversion (see Figure 9–2).

In the case of equities, an investor may be concerned with a given industry sector; in the case of debt (bonds), he is concerned with sourcing, maturity, yield, currency, denomination, or guarantees. Pricing preferences may be expressed by an investor (or advanced by a portfolio advisor) in absolute terms or in terms relative to alternatives (see Figure 9–3).

These are all issues that an investment theory must address if it is to be a vehicle for sound choices.

An important premise of MPT is that any asset held has varying risk implications, depending on whether it is self-standing or part of a larger portfolio.

Expanding on this premise, MPT emphasizes that a significant factor in reducing portfolio risk is correlation, which reveals the way the securities, loans, and trades in the portfolio move in relation to each other.

MPT utilizes risk and expected return as parameters in asset selection. From this standpoint, some combinations of securities are preferable to others because they promise a greater return for a given level of risk or a lower risk for a given level of return. Much of MPT, therefore, concentrates on the analysis of expectation and variance for portfolio returns. (The quantification methods MPT provides are inadequate for the analysis of loans.)

The variance of return (standard deviation of return, hence related to beta) can also be interpreted as a measure of investment risk; but, as discussed in Section 3, this is more a measure of the volatility (i.e., unpredictability) of return. The implication is that optimal portfolios can only be identified by effectively testing every possible combination of securities weightings to establish which is the best under given investment risk perspectives.

Market changes make it necessary to rebalance portfolios with short-, medium-, or long-term planning horizons. Using short-term ones leads to tactical asset allocation, in which positions are turned over within a day. In principle, by following the beta factor (see Section 3), the risk of a security (defined as its standard deviation of return) can be estimated from its historical price behavior, and these historical estimates form the basis for future risk values. Alternatively, a mathematical model of security returns can be constructed using the statistical techniques of factor analysis and princi-

Figure 9–2   An Integrative Approach to Account Management

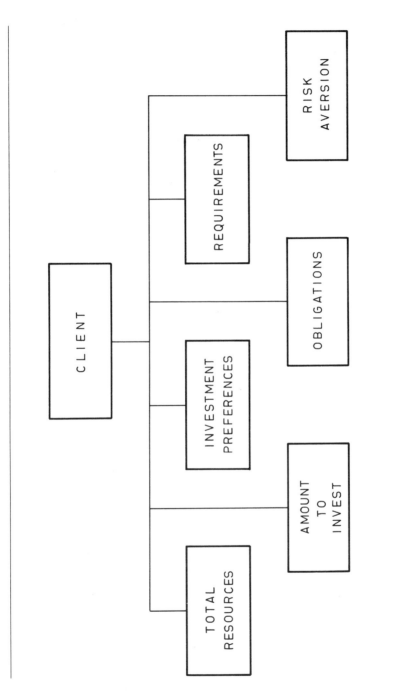

Figure 9–3   Critical Factors Characterizing Bond Investments

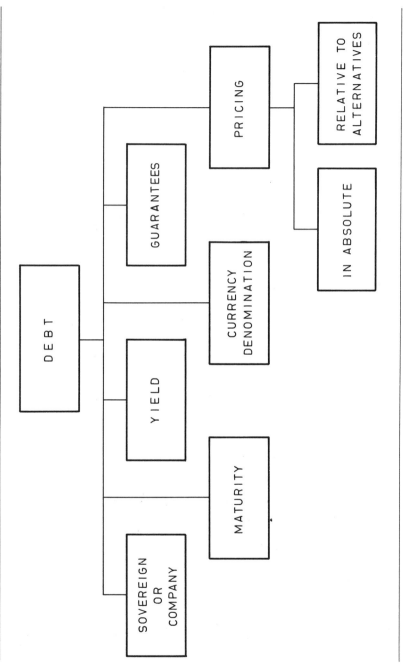

pal components analysis. To do this requires an intimate knowledge of how and to what extent markets are driven by objective forces.

These are the basics of Modern Portfolio Theory. In the next section we will discuss how this theory can be implemented by investment bankers who wish to define investment styles that will be subject to analysis and control within the context of a complex and dynamic market environment.

6. The Capital Asset Pricing Model

Traders and investment managers who can demonstrate to investors that they have well-defined and controllable investment processes will enjoy an advantage over those who cannot. Merely understanding Modern Portfolio Theory is not enough—it must be put into action.

One practical application of MPT is the Capital Asset Pricing Model (CAPM). It analyzes the return of a specific stock and compares it with the return of the market index.

In the early 1960s, a Ph.D. candidate named William Sharpe developed, with the help of Dr. Harry Markowitz, a general-equilibrium model for the pricing of risky assets. Sharpe's idea, which was based on Markowitz's theory of portfolio selection (see Section 4), became known as the Capital Asset Pricing Model. By quantifying individual factors, Sharpe demonstrated that the ideal market portfolio is one that provides the highest return per unit of risk. The premise of CAPM is that investors should value stocks in such a way that their expected return falls on a security market line. How investors can formulate these return expectations is not explained by CAPM.

In 1971, Wells Fargo's Security Analysis Group produced estimates of expected return by employing a version of the Dividend Discount Model (DDM), which was first suggested by J.B. Williams in 1934. Taking twenty-five years of earnings statistics and dividend forecasts, the group calculated both the internal rate of return for each stock (discounting the forecasted stream of dividends) and a common terminal dividend growth rate for each stock, all the way back to current price.

The internal rate of return calculated from this process was annualized and labeled the expected return. Its determinant is the implicit expectation of return on equity capital. According to the group, dividend policy should be governed by how relatively successful the company is likely to be in investing retained earnings. Also, if the projection of future dividends is accurate, the actual rate of return to be earned in the long run by investing in this stock will equal the expected return.

Other researchers have offered models consistent with CAPM. Academics Myron Scholes and Fischer Black helped to formulate a leveraged low-beta mutual fund, called the Stagecoach Fund, by using Modern Portfolio Theory in conjunction with empirical data supplied by the Center for Research in Security Prices (CRISP).

The idea of this model was to get pension fund sponsors to invest in a collective approach that would borrow short and invest in a portfolio tracking the performance of low-beta stocks. The work by Scholes and Black revealed that high-beta stocks had not produced investment returns commensurate with their systematic risk. This stock-market pricing inefficiency was called the alpha effect.

Leveraging is another concept with a theoretical approach to managing portfolio risk. Professor James Tobin, winner of a Nobel prize in economics, demonstrated that the choice of stocks held in a portfolio is separate from the decision of how much risk to take. According to this concept, an investor always owns some combination of the stock portfolio offering the highest return per unit of risk and lends or borrows a riskless asset. This investment approach is known as the Separation Theorem.

Different versions of CAPM use some or all of the foregoing notions. For purposes of portfolio management, CAPM's concept is that all factors affecting stockmarket volatility are reflected in the market-price index. Therefore, CAPM calculates risks (beta) and associated returns by performing a simple time-series analysis. This computation often adds fundamental data related to the company concerned. An example of factors coming into play in this equation is shown in Figure 9–4.

Not every economist agrees with this approach, nor is there a unique way for building the necessary mathematical model. Multiple regression analysis, binomial lattices, Monte Carlo simulation, and the use of possiblity theory (fuzzy sets) can all be helpful.

Another relatively new, application of risk-and-return analysis, known as Arbitrage Pricing Theory, takes into account macroeconomic factors such as inflation and interest rates. The assumption is that a corporation's fundamentals can be measured by their sensitivity to these variables. (This issue will be treated more fully in Section 7, with the presentation of ISS by Yamaichi Securities.)

As discussed in Section 3, investor choices may be directed toward the lowest volatility and, therefore, lowest unpredictability of return; nevertheless, a conservative strategy may not be acceptable to investors (from individuals to mutual funds, institutions, and securities houses) who set benchmarks and prefer to use intuitive approaches.

Closer approximations to the intuitive concept are provided by so-called safety-first risk criteria, which emphasize limiting the risk of adverse outcomes.

◆ The Roy criterion is that the portfolio should have the lowest probability of producing a return below some specified level.

Figure 9–4   Component Parts of a Multidimentional Analysis

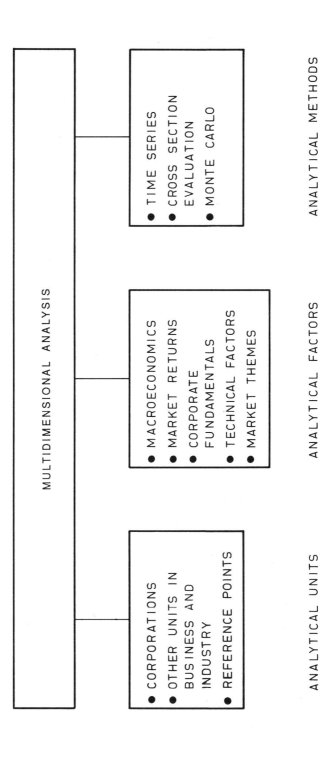

MULTIDIMENSIONAL ANALYSIS

ANALYTICAL UNITS

- CORPORATIONS
- OTHER UNITS IN BUSINESS AND INDUSTRY
- REFERENCE POINTS

ANALYTICAL FACTORS

- MACROECONOMICS
- MARKET RETURNS
- CORPORATE FUNDAMENTALS
- TECHNICAL FACTORS
- MARKET THEMES

ANALYTICAL METHODS

- TIME SERIES
- CROSS SECTION EVALUATION
- MONTE CARLO

- ◆ The Kataoka criterion is that the portfolio should have the highest value for the level which has a 5 percent chance of being underperformed.

- ◆ The Telser criterion is that the portfolio should have maximum expected return subject to the probability of a return less than or equal to some predetermined limit being not greater than some specified value.

Other criteria of portfolio optimization have also been suggested. One of these, the expected geometric mean return, tends to produce diversified portfolios, since it penalizes high volatility. Among others, stochastic criteria, such as the mean-variance portfolio, are usually based on broad characterizations of investor preferences. Using mean-variance portfolio theory, it could be shown that optimization is a quadratic programming problem involving the covariance structure of security returns.

In terms of mathematical models of financial problems, there is no reason to use quadratic programming if heuristics and simpler models can render better service. With a single-index model, for instance, an explicit simpler solution to the quadratic programming problem can be found. Modified Modern Portfolio Theory, as applied by Yamaichi Securities, is another possible alternative.

Significant improvements can also be made by using chartist solutions with an emphasis on pattern recognition. A radar chart uses the large storage capacity of a computer to identify market movements in the field of view and uses the processing power of a supercomputer to calculate a multivariable change in subseconds. Visualization is employed to convert complex value tables into images.

Pattern parameters can be developed through careful research to include virtually everything "normal." If a pattern does not correlate in real time with the financial database, it will be flagged and the alarm will sound—thus making it unnecessary to sit patiently in front of the screen and study thousands of frames of data as they develop. Computers and intelligent networks will do this job in real space, provided that there is a valid trading theory.

7. The Integrative Stock System (ISS) by Yamaichi Securities

The Integrative Stock System (ISS) is a practical application of the Capital Asset Pricing, Multiple-Dimensioned (CAPMD) theory, which was jointly developed by the Global Advanced Technology Corporation (GAT)[2] and Yamaichi Securities, in conjunction with other researchers.[3] CAPMD is an integrated version of the CAP and APT models of Modern Portfolio Theory. Its developers felt that while these two models were both constructed on sophisticated and well-established theories, CAP did not seem capable of measuring macroeconomic influence, nor did APT accurately reflect ever-changing corporate business performance.

CAPMD combines the features of CAP and APT, while remedying some of their deficiencies; it also incorporates new analytical methods. ISS, a computer-based system that uses CAPMD, integrates previous models. It features a stock investment management system capable of performing multidimensional market analysis. This type of analysis enables ISS to manage various risks and maximize investment returns. Analytical units, market factors, and evaluation methods are introduced; thus, risks and returns can be measured with a certain precision.

Whether this method or a similar one is used, the emphasis should be on what factors influence market movements. Since stock valuation models extend to the strengths and weaknesses of individual companies, the key factors entering the equation must be reflected in the model (see Figure 9–5).

Since no two financial simulators are the same, no two models behave in precisely the same manner. In the case of CAPMD/ISS, the component parts that were selected reflect four basic design choices:

1. risk/return evaluation based on the multidimensional analysis of macroeconomic, microeconomic, and theme factors[4]

2. projected degrees and trends of various factors in the market

3. simultaneous calculation of risk and return

4. construction of a portfolio to suit users' needs

Of the various types of portfolios made available by ISS, the Index + alpha portfolio is fundamental. It can

1. mirror a profitable performance by the stock market;

2. provide an edge when the stockmarket resembles an efficient market;

3. make it possible to use index futures effectively for hedging and other purposes;

4. employ the concept of excess return potential of Multiple Dimension/alpha (MDa), which allows construction of a value-added, index-linked portfolio.

Using the concept of multiple dimension, ISS utilizes three parameters based on alpha (as defined), beta (volatility), and gamma. The latter handles the six most important factors affecting the Tokyo stock market (as chosen by Yamaichi

Figure 9–5   Critical Factors Helping to Define a Company's Health

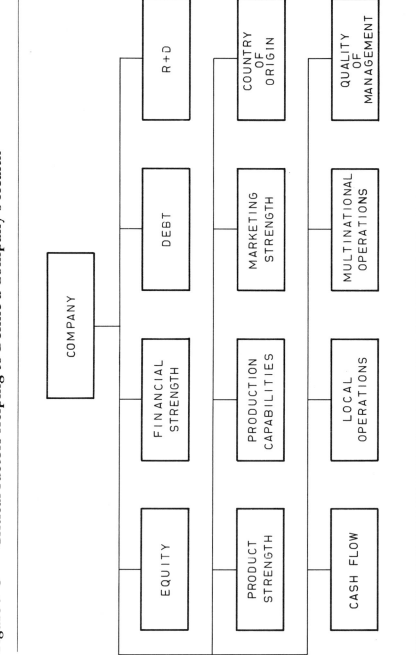

research economists and investment experts) and focuses on the possible variation on each one of them (see Figure 9–6).

Figure 9–6 is a radar chart known in Yamaichi jargon as MDgamma. Its parameters are handled as follows:

- When MDbeta fluctuates between 0.95 and 1.05, the portfolio has a price movement similar to that of the stock market.

- With MDalpha at maximum, it offers maximum excess return potential.

- With MDgamma at zero, the portfolio has the same sensitivity to macroeconomic factors (such as interest rates and the national economy) as the Tokyo Stock Exchange (TSE) index.

The developers have seen to it that industry diversification is implemented during portfolio construction in accordance with CAPMD industry classifications. The Capital Asset Pricing, Multiple-Dimensioned theory provides the theoretical background for ISS.

As discussed, a theme is a Japanese government directive specifying the parameters of individual industries. The observance of themes therefore requires a detailed classification of industries. Because ISS is geared to this system, its "as is" portability to other stock exchanges is restricted (though an adaptation to NYSE has been done). In the context of the Japanese financial environment, however, the investment advisors at Yamaichi International Capital Management have a market edge.

An ISS portfolio is constructed by taking the following steps:

1.   Create a master list.

Figure 9–6   Radar Chart for MDgamma

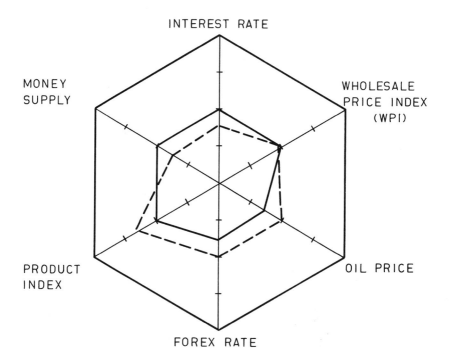

ISS automatically selects issues from each industry that is represented on the first section of the Tokyo Stock Exchange and includes them on a master list. Those issues are chosen that have better-than-average financial ratios, liquidity, and so on.

2.   Construct a portfolio.

Key parameters such as risk level and extent of diversification are decided upon in accordance with the need of the portfolio to be managed. Contingent on the amount of risk and the rate of return that clients are prepared to accept, the Asset Allocation System (AAS) calculates the percentage of stock value to be incorporated in the portfolio.

An optimum structure for a given portfolio is worked out by determining the issues and volume of stocks to be purchased. The system further specifies the transactions necessary to construct the portfolio.

3.   Review the portfolio.

Once constructed, the portfolio is regularly reviewed by the system and, if necessary, reorganized to best suit changing market conditions. Such reviews are performed automatically, bringing to the investment advisor's attention the possible need for changes.

Yamaichi makes decisions and executes transactions on behalf of investors based on the results of these analyses. The computer includes workstations networked through a local area network, for which a supercomputer serves as number-cruncher and calculates parameters, including MDalpha, MD-beta, and MDgamma. Then, industry classification is determined by CAPMD. The asset performance appraisal leads to construction review (and the revision of an optimum portfolio) as well as the calculation of risk accompanying the portfolio. The system regularly monitors asset management performance.

An associated portfolio manager support system automatically executes analyses of portfolio composition and the market. Another analyzes stock futures by determining optimum hedging positions and portfolio insurance. Simulation is carried out to assess the performance of a previously constructed optimum portfolio.

Two markets are covered by these multidimensional analyses—Japanese markets, especially the first and second sections of the Tokyo Stock Exchange and American markets, including S&P 500 and three thousand issues in the U.S. and Canada. (European markets will be analyzed in the future.)

With the supported environments, all data and materials related to portfolio analysis are available interactively. Also available are regular and by-exception (ad hoc) statements, such as return on investment, appraised securities value, and dividends received.

Statistics derived from calculating the MDalpha parameter are presented in tabular form by code and by the names of the companies included in an optimal portfolio suggestion. Each company is identified by weight, capital, traded volume, equity ratio, and more. An MDbeta synopsis is offered in both graph form (plotted as "1.00, 0.00.,...1,000 vs. time") and tabulation (particularly in terms of weights and residual risk). The MDgamma synopsis has been offered through the radar chart in Figure 9–6.

8. Alpha, Beta, Gamma, Delta, Theta, and Tau Functions

As discussed, CAPMD does advanced stock valuation in three dimensions—units (e.g., corporations), elements (economic factors), and method (e.g., time series). Also each company analyzed is defined as a combination of several industries: the traditional method of classifying a company in one industry (e.g., motors, chemicals, electronics, or finance) is not sufficient to reflect the diversity of modern companies. Nor does this method allow for extensive coverage of the variables affecting a corporation and its market value; though, these can be numerous.

The matrix in Table 9–1 shows company K, for example, to have an involvement of 40 percent in industry I, 20 percent in II, 30 percent in III, and 10 percent in IV. Using ISS to do a detailed search of financial data, an operator can place a company's business in any of 101 industrial categories. The analytical factors that enter the model focus on macroeconomics such as inflation, rates of interest, employment, foreign exchange, and microeconomics, including market return resulting from overall market movement as well as corporate fundamentals and technical indices.

The inclusion of this range of factors in the analysis results in a more thorough assessment of stock than is possible by using simpler stock models. Table 9–2 demonstrates this by comparing CAPMD with APT and CAP that uses historical data with CAP that uses fundamental alpha/beta.

With the tools of time-series and cross-sectional analysis, CAPMD attempts to provide an ongoing interactive picture of changing events in the marketplace. This falls somewhat short of the consistent pattern-recognition process that is needed in a highly competitive environment; nevertheless, it still allows for the analysis of events at any given time and gives an overview of trends from past to present. Changes within a single corporation and changes in its relationship to other corporations can be grasped at the same time. This integrative feature is one of the model's most important assets.

While there are a number of different key factors—alpha, beta, gamma, delta, theta and tau—embedded in this market model, some securities analysts do not like to work with so many that focus on establishing a relationship between assets

Table 9–1   Multiple Classification of Industrial
                   Companies by CAPMD

	Industries					
Company	I	II	III	IV	V	VI
K	40%	20%	30%	10%		
L	30%		30%		40%	
M		70%		10%		20%
N		25%	25%		20%	30%
P			35%	15%	50%	
Q	10%	10%		50%	10%	20%

Table 9–2

	CAPMD	APT	CAP Historical Beta	CAP Fundamental alpha/beta
Macroeconomic factors	X	X		
Market return	X		X	X
Corporate fundamentals	X			X
Technical indices	X			X
Investment themes	X			

and liabilities (though each from a different angle). These analysts believe that beta is enough to assist in assessing market volatility and associated risk.

For financial analysts who subscribe to this approach, beta indicates the level of the premium to apply, as if buying market insurance to cover the associated risk.

Yamaichi Securities, nevertheless, has chosen the following factors for its market models:

Multidimensional alpha (MDalpha) indicates, by using the Capital Asset Pricing, Multiple Dimensioned theory, whether a portfolio (or single stock) is priced at an appropriate level upon analysis of risks, fundamentals, and other information. When MDalpha is positive the stock or the portfolio is undervalued, and the analyst can expect a future return that exceeds the return commensurate with risk by the value of MDalpha. By contrast, when MDalpha is negative a return that is lower than the return commensurate with risk by the value of MDalpha is forecast.

Through the use of MDalpha, ISS makes it possible to manage a portfolio so that its yield is higher than that which corresponds to the associated risk. If the MDalpha of an existing portfolio is positive, the portfolio price is judged to be relatively low. By contrast, a negative MDalpha indicates that a stock's (or the portfolio's) price is considered to be relatively high, and a careful review of the portfolio's contents is desirable.

When a portfolio is modified or a new portfolio is prepared (excluding an index-type portfolio), the standing instructions are to sell issues for which MDalpha is negative and buy issues for which MDalpha is positive. On this basis, an efficient selection of issues can be made.

Due to MDalpha relationships, Japanese investment managers now endorse plus-alpha (enhanced index) funds. This is part of a policy of trying to out-perform broad market averages by tilting holdings to specific fundamentals, industry sectors, or themes.

Multidimensional beta (MDbeta) is an application of the beta factor. MDbeta measures the sensitivity of a stock or portfolio to movements in the market index. Although it is of the same nature as the conventional beta value, MDbeta is calculated on the fact that CAPMD theory tends to respond to changes in the company's fundamentals and the market environment.

MDbeta is a short-term parameter, and its developers advise that it can be used to hedge a portfolio. One of its applications is in connection to the TOPIX futures, which started trading in June 1988.

Multidimensional gamma (MDgamma) indicates the degree of response of a portfolio to macroeconomic changes, with the reaction of the market as a whole shown as a standard value of zero. When MDgamma is positive, the portfolio shows a movement more advantageous than the average market movement in response to an upward change of macroeconomic factors. MDgamma features a more adverse movement than the market as a whole when macrofactors turn downward.

As discussed in Section 7, ISS utilizes MDgamma to measure response to changes in six macroeconomic factors—interest rates, general price level, crude oil price, exchange rate, economic activity, and money supply. Table 9–3 shows a method of interpreting MDgamma in case interest rates vary; Table 9–4 shows the method to use in case exchange rates vary. These tables reflect relative values and can therefore be used in conjunction with possibility theory.

Delta factor and the degree of industry diversification. The value of the delta factor indicates the degree of diversification by industry. Based on the CAPMD classification by industry, it shows the gap between the industry composition of the

Table 9–3   Interpreting MDgamma Factors in
                   Risk and Decline of Interest Rates

MDgamma	Under Conditions of	
	Rise in Interest Rates	Decline in Interest Rates
+1.2	A more advantageous movement than if MDgamma = 0.5	A more adverse movement than if MDgamma = 0.5
–0.5	A more advantageous movement than the index	A more adverse movement than the index
0.0	The same degree of movement as the index	
–0.5	A more adverse movement than the index	A more advantageous movement than the index
–1.2	A more adverse movement than if MDgamma = –0.5	A more advantageous movement than if MDgamma = –0.5

Table 9–4   Interpreting MDgamma Factors in the
                 Case of Exchange Rate Variations

	Under Conditions of	
	Yen Depreciation	**Yen Appreciation**
MDgamma		
+1.2	A more advantageous movement than if MDgamma = +0.5	A more adverse movement than if MDgamma = +0.5
+0.5	A more advantageous movement than the index	A more adverse movement than the index
0.0	The same degree of movement as the index	
–0.5	A more adverse movement than the index	A more advantageous movement than the index
–1.2	A more adverse movement than if MDgamma = –0.5	A more advantageous movement than if MDgamma = –0.5

market as a whole and the industry composition of a portfolio.

A value of delta zero (the standard value) indicates that the industry composition of a portfolio is exactly the same as that of the whole market. The larger the value of delta, the further the composition of the portfolio is from the composition of the market as a whole.

Some securities analysts employ the theta function; although, this is not being used by Yamaichi, it is included in this text for reasons of completeness. Theta reflects a theoretical change in a given option's price, holding futures price, implied volatility, or interest rates constant. This theoretical change is calculated over a possible small change in the time remaining until the option's expiration.

Theta is expressed in terms of a defined, discrete time interval such as one day or one week. In other words, it reflects the rate of option price decay with the passage of time.

As an outgrowth of option-pricing models, theta is computed as the first derivative of option price with respect to time until expiration. As theta is an incremental measure, it would be more accurate to state that, for instance over one day, the options will decline in value by, for example, 0.01, from 0.43 to 0.42.

Tau indicates the degree of inclination toward market themes by calculating the ratio of the number of issues falling under a particular theme to the number of all issues (with a standard value of zero). When tau for a portfolio is positive, the inclination toward the theme is larger than that for the market as a whole. When tau is negative, the inclination is smaller.

ISS offers tau analysis with regard to six themes—large-capital stocks, domestic demand-related issues, export-oriented, consumption-related, cyclical stocks (commodity market-related), and information/communication related issues.

By using ISS and the factors so far discussed, it is possible to prepare, diagnose, and adjust portfolios. Seven different parameters—investment account, upper limit to investment in a single issue, number of issues in portfolio, minimum daily trading volume required (liquidity requirement), minimum capital required, restrictions on the stockholder's equity ratio, and type of portfolio design the investment advisor desires—must be determined for portfolio structuring.

In portfolio diagnosis, various parameters are used to conduct analysis as well as to determine the extent of diversification. Data from the analysis of a portfolio is effectively used for portfolio adjustment, which must be done periodically in order to maintain optimal performance.

Endnotes

1. Markowitz and his theory were recognized by the market a quarter century later. Nevertheless, nearly forty years passed before, in 1990, the Swedish Academy awarded him the Nobel Prize for Economics.

2. A New York-based company run by Dr. Thomas Ho.

3. Two of these researchers are Stephen J. Brown of New York University and Toshiyuki Otsuki of the International University of Japan. Both men are experts in portfolio management and statistics.

4. Theme factors were discussed in Chapter 3. The microeconomics focus on corporate business fundamentals.

Chapter 10

Computer-Based Trading

Chapter 10

Computer-Based Trading

1. Introduction

For more than three decades computers have been used by the securities industry to process post-mortem transaction data, but not until the 1980s were computers employed as decision support tools in securities transactions. In the early eighties, financial analysts used Apple computers with the Visicalc spreadsheet for the analysis of balance sheets and other financial statements. As experience accumulated, by the mid-eighties, major securities houses were using computer-based, AI-enriched constructs as trading assistants.

Japan's Sanyo Securities was (in 1986) the first broker on record to develop sophisticated and highly integrated expert system to be an assistant to traders. The Sanyo Investment Research New Information System (SIRNIS) was at its time the most complex expert systems aggregate in the financial world. It included a stock diffusion index, inference modules for investment analysis, financial forecasting models, and a radar chart.

The radar chart reflected company performance by focusing on six key variables: profits, efficiency, productivity, growth, stability, and overall performance. Dedicated modules analyzed financial statements, and the research department of Sanyo Securities contributed another input. All this converged into the radar chart, which gave advice for investment purposes.

Still a prime example of automated trading, SIRNIS now operates around the clock in the new Sanyo headquarters at the Tokyo waterfront. Its output is available, in wall-to-wall and WS presentation, to 250 traders, and it highlights trading in Sanyo's new, unified dealing room, which is in a building bigger than the Tokyo Stock Exchange.

Passport, a subset of SIRNIS, is available to clients on-line and produces fees that equal the business contracted by a medium-size branch office of this brokerage house. New modules are added all the time; they now include futures for bonds and stocks, hedging and arbitrage, marketing and sales assistance, product-market evaluation, and before and after targeting.

Also under development are an intelligent network, expert systems for diagnostics and maintenance of SIRNIS asset-allocation modules and, most importantly, the use of imaging and AI in back-office operations. From trading to paperwork simplification, artificial intelligence is put to work for profits and survival in an increasingly competitive market.

2. Developing Intelligent Trading Assistants

Maurice Allais, the 1988 Nobel prize winner in economics, proved mathematically that, in an abstract model of a market in which goods are traded between households and firms, equilibrium prices are efficient. In other words, nobody can become better off without making somebody else worse off.

The essence of trading is, therefore, capitalizing on other traders' mistakes.

Performing better than the market average is also the aim of an intelligent trading assistant. These assistants should contain market experience and dealing expertise that has been built into expert rules or, even better, expressed in heuristics. A program should also use in-the-market experience to teach itself ways to improve upon its trading advice.

As discussed earlier in this book, it is unwise to buy expert systems. Unlike classical data processing routines, which should be bought as packages, AI constructs must be developed in-house in order to

1. reflect the securities firm's own culture and trading theories;

2. provide for close coordination between front desk and back office;

3. permit AI skills to grow internally;

4. fit the organizational perspectives of the financial institution.

No two banks or securities houses have the same structure, but they do organize their trading operations in reference to this structure; hence, the need to personalize expert systems solutions. Figure 10–1 shows two different organizational approaches, particularly with reference to placement R and D and marketing.

In the first organization, R and D marketing are done through a central department; in the second, each major operating division (securities, Forex, lending) has its own R and D and marketing operations.

Though both organizations focus on trading, the first is more integrative than the second, and its expert systems

Figure 10–1   Alternative Organization Charts of Financial Institutions

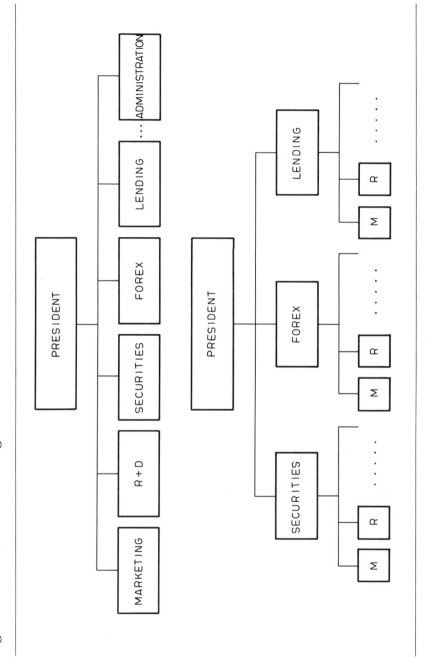

should be made to work accordingly. This does not mean that an integrative view is not necessary for the second organization, but the precise solution to be followed will most likely be different.

If an expert system is designed, for example, for the futures and options environment, it will scan all of the commodity and financial futures contracts the user asks it to track. It will then select potentially profitable markets and associated contracts.

Operating on-line, preferably in real space, an intelligent trade system should be able to prompt the trader immediately by

1. advising on the type and number of contracts that should be bought and sold, and at what price;

2. suggesting where stops should be placed;

3. identifying limits below which the deal should not be done;

4. handling all money and maintaining an accounting record of trading and open positions.

Through multiple windows, the intelligent trading assistant should offer traders and portfolio managers views of multiple aspects of the market, as shown in Figure 10–2. This should be done in an ad hoc manner, at the user's discretion.

A number of the expert system's modules should monitor the price and volume movement of any equities, bonds, precious metals, or other commodities that users want to track. Other modules will determine the expert rating for each result obtained in the preceding step.

For either organizational alternative discussed, the integrative approach should focus on five areas:

**Figure 10–2   Versions of the Same Basic Information for Different
Securities Professionals**

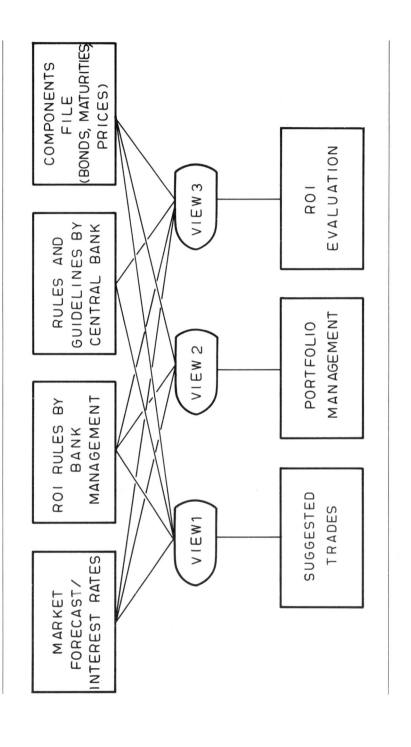

1. risk management

2. cash flow

3. P and L evaluation

4. general accounting

5. front-desk/back-office operations

The role of the front-desk system is to give market makers an edge on competition—identifying the deals' best bid and offer, comparing *this* market with the *other* market, and using color, graphics and position on screen so that the dealer does not need to read statistics to see that he must act.

Interactively on screen and on a real-time basis, the intelligent trading assistant should allow users to experiment with their hunches, doing tests with real-life data available through information providers. In terms of global markets, doing this experimentation will require not only AI software but also any-to-any networks and supercomputers for number-crunching.

Simple, yet comprehensive and documented, interactive reports should give traders advice on what to buy and sell, as opposed to only indicating which equities are going up or down. Also, the trading system should have access to an AI module that will act as a profit manager. This module is designed to protect investments, evaluate risk propensity, elaborate on profit objectives the user wishes to follow, and advise on buy, sell, and hold decisions.

Such intelligent trading support becomes important in direct proportion to the fact that the need to continue doing business in a turbulent financial environment stimulates a number of changes to current positions.

The back-office system should be integrated with the front desk in order to fully automate all the work being done in trading. Features of this system should include the use of imaging, in order to eliminate the paperwork associated with payments documents, and the use of neural networks to facilitate signature recognition.

Figure 10–3 shows an architectural approach adopted by one leading investment bank. Its front desk and back office share an integrated computers and communications (C+C) system; all its paper and microform records have been converted into optical disks.

Further, an intelligent network (long haul, local area and in-house) interconnects all workstations with mini- and maxicomputers, mainframes, supercomputers, imaging, and other databases. This new systems architecture goes way beyond what classical DP organizations can offer. The in-house network links together stand-alone applications, building bridges between formerly distinct islands of technology implementation.

Management, however, knows that before long, a new structure will be necessary, as the force-fitting of this growing number of information linkages is not made for the trading environment of the 1990s. "Only imaginative new departures can offer the required support," said an investment bank's chief executive officer.

3. Designing and Building a Trading System

The various data-processing-based management models formulated during the 1970s and early 1980s are fast becoming obsolescent. The new architectural approach focuses on the end user and emphasizes not only information, but also knowledge. Today, much of a securities house's business is in offering a full range of corporate advisory services. In addition to investment perspectives, these must cover capital raising, restructuring, mergers and acquisitions, disposals, and bid defences.

Figure 10–3   Main Component Parts of a Document Handling System

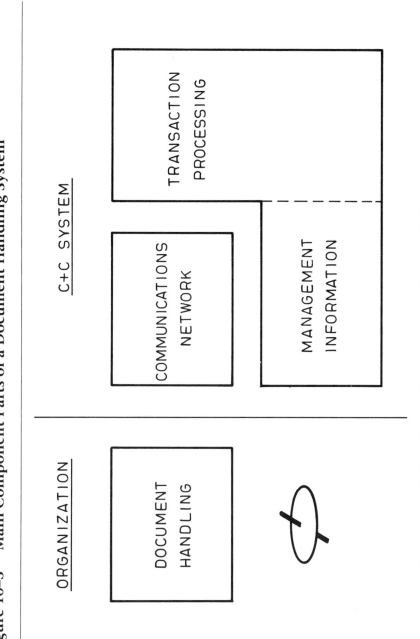

The specialist units of an investment bank focus on specific industries, and each can benefit from the use of AI constructs designed to satisfy the particular needs of client businesses. Expert systems can be built for industrial financing, property financing, international projects, asset finance and leasing, credit protection, and more. The aim of an investment house should be to equip each of its branches with top-level expertise in a full range of merchant banking services. This requires having an in-house professionals with background experience in investment, banking, accountancy, and knowledge engineering.

AI constructs can also help the investment bank to deal with risk capital, debt packaging and associated projects, as well as daily trading operations.

Trading assistants, implemented through expert systems, are the culmination of this process.

For example, ZETA, a real-time securities trading assistant, applies a set of knowledge-based rules to a real-time stream of market data (including stock prices, volumes, and market indicators) provided by Dow Jones Industrials and the S&P 500 Index. The rules in the ZETA expert system map a strategy that locates stocks that are moving in a direction opposite to the general movement of their industry group. According to the system's rules, the stock's motion must be on high volume to be considered significant.

The system monitors price changes both in the immediate past (two minutes in this case) and from the opening of the trading day. When the volume of trading in a stock is higher than average, the immediate price changes are examined. If these indicate long (buy) or short (sell), the change from the opening is examined to determine the strength of the recommendation (strong, average, weak).

Evaluation is done by an AI module, which bases its advice to the trader on the number of points on which rests a projection. When there is unusual motion in the volume of trading in a given stock, ZETA examines its price change over the several preceding minutes. If the price has been rising, the expert system proposes holding a long position and places a message to this effect in the advisory window; for falling prices, holding a short position is recommended.

When the AI construct evaluates a long or short position, it first examines the recent price movement of the stock relative to its sector. If these are in opposite directions, it suggests taking the position after examining the price motion from the start of trading. If the price changes of the stock and the sector are still in opposite directions, then the system advises that the position that was previously suggested should be based only on short-term price changes. The system also monitors price movements to detect any reversals and to retract advice that is no longer supported.

The example of ZETA shows that AI constructs can handle a layered set of trading rules that scan incoming market feeds for relevant trigger events. They can also do in-depth analysis in order to form conclusions, determine confidence in those conclusions, and justify the advice that they give.

Using AI in dealing equities is a major step forward from classical on-line transaction processing. The embedded expertise of AI allows traders to monitor current stock positions, to evaluate alternatives by taking a global view using in-depth analyses, and to issue buy-sell transactions relative to markets that are in constant flux.

As a result of increasingly sophisticated computer usage and the on-line handling through networks, average turnaround time of a transaction—from initiation (when new market data arrives) through decision (when a trader's buy or sell order is placed) to execution and completion (when confirmations are received that the order has been filled)—is now measured in seconds.

Buy and sell orders to the exchanges are increasingly placed over automated links, and information about these transactions is available moments after they occur. One such system, which automatically matches buyers and sellers, has been introduced by the Toronto Stock Exchange. Another (which connects on-line to the Tokyo Stock Exchange) is the Mitsubishi Research Institute (MIRI) trading expert system. According to its engineers, this expert system projects the next day's trends, which provides traders with more sophisticated solutions than a time-series approach can offer. Instead of this whole pattern approach (designed to offset stockmarket crashes or booms) allows dealers to identify and follow daily activity patterns, then examine individual stocks in order to determine their responses within that pattern.

The MIRI researchers have emphasized a pattern basis over a rule-based mapping of dealing knowledge; because of the variety of opinions among different securities specialists, individual traders' know-how was not found to be best suited for projecting stock movements. The expert system is, however, designed to be used by trading experts through fully interactive operation.

Figure 10–4 shows a radar chart projected by a European securities house. This chart gives traders a bird's eye view of financial market developments and is a good example of an interactive solution enriched with visualization. Solutions such as this are increasingly necessary to support the growing sophistication of trading strategies. Analytics for traders must be performed in real time, filtering large volumes of data to identify the crucial conditions that will trigger transactions.

Another trading expert system, by the Mitsubishi Group, classifies bonds as domestic or foreign and as straight, convertible, or bonds with warrants. This AI construct examines the special characteristics of every bond issue, evaluating its strengths and weaknesses. As major companies sometimes have some twenty different bonds each on the market, the system also compares one bond with another.

Figure 10–4   Radar Chart by a Leading Securities House

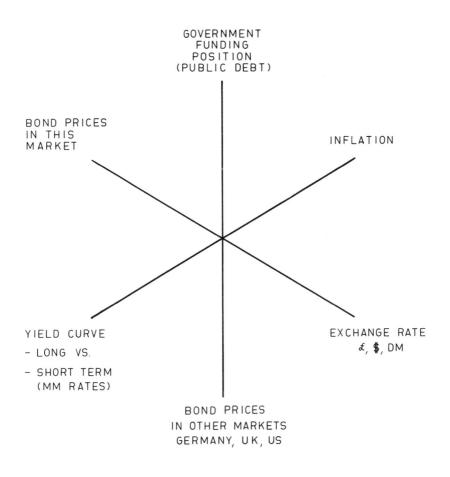

After making its analyses, this expert system produces a radar chart with documented evaluation of performance. Particular attention is paid to cost control, as shown in Figure 10–5. (By comparing this radar chart to the one in Figure 10–4, one can appreciate that there is no unique way of visualizing trading operations).

This bond selection expert system has been developed for underwriting. Its first version supports Yen-denominated bonds; a second version has been enriched with Eurodollars and Swiss Francs. Both the domestic (Japanese) and the international markets are being supported.

In a departure from other expert systems projects, the developers of this system did not restrict themselves to tapping the know-how of the bank's own traders. A questionnaire was given to the bank's client and the client's responses were included in the rule-base. How well the client's fund was managed last time he invested with Mitsubishi Bank—and what kind of improvements could be made—were among the relevant questions.

Mitsubishi's target population is corporate (not retail) clients, and its knowledge bank includes selection criteria for client accounts regarding the underwriting of bonds. Though Japan's Article 65 does not permit underwriting by city banks, Mitsubishi has subsidiaries that can legally use this model (e.g., Mitsubishi International Finance in Zurich and certain securities houses).

Also, detailed financial analysis of debt is of great importance to any bank. This particular application includes many criteria that center on financial standards and allow for evaluations based on performance results, all of which makes it possible to define the rate to attach to a given bond. The radar chart is also used to evaluate historical precedence, that is, respond to queries regarding what bonds have already been issued and what rate applies, and how successful these bonds have been on the market.

**Figure 10-5   Radar Chart for Bond Evaluation
by the Mitsubishi Bank**

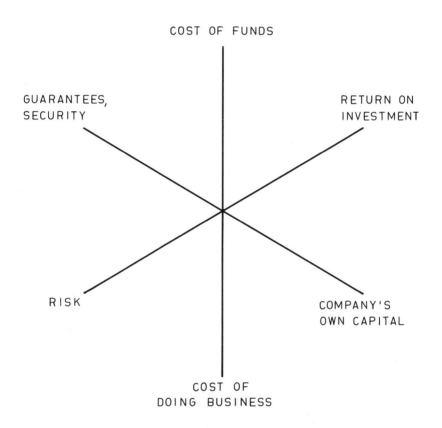

To do this the expert system uses six to seven rules divided into five main modules with ample database support, including

1. a P+L database of listed companies and an associated analyzer;

2. precedents of issued bonds and main underwriters during the last fifteen years (with all parties involved in an issue included);

3. the rules of underwriting and bond selection (based on questionnaires to underwriters and their responses);

4. proposal evaluation and development of an underwriting offer, including market conditions and scheduling;

5. feedback with links to No. 1 and No. 2, to provide a historical database and follow-up on underwriting cases and to make charts.

Significant parts of this AI construct are based on pattern recognition. Some modules provide the possibility for the specialist to add or delete selected clauses.

Completing this particular application, required thirty man-months of effort spread over twelve calendar months, compared with the time spent on classical data-processing projects in financial institutions around the globe, which may take thirty-six calendar months to complete and by then are often obsolete or give questionable results, twelve months is a minor investment of time for a successful project.

The bond selection expert system is based on another Mitsubishi expert system, in operation in the dealing room at the Mitsubishi Bank since late 1987. This system forecasts the prices and yields of Japanese Government bonds, implemented buy/sell orders, and makes recommendations in real time.

4. Systematic Risk, Specific Risk, and the Notion of Indexing

As discussed, a trading system must be built on a sound theory; it must also reflect risk and reward. Dr. William Sharpe originally suggested that the uncertainty of returns for a stock can be broken down into two elements: one can be diversified away, and the other cannot.

Sharpe said that investors should not expect to be compensated for taking on risk that can be diversified by merely combining stocks in a portfolio. The expected return for a stock should fall somewhere between expected return and nondiversifiable risk. A stock's nondiversifiable, or systematic, risk is determined by how its value is affected by system-wide events, such as real GNP growth, inflation, real interest rates, and foreign exchange rates. Systematic risks cannot be eliminated by reshuffling assets among portfolios; the only way to handle them is to reassign them. Based on the Sharpe hypothesis, we should expect to earn a lower return only if we reduce the systematic risk of our portfolio.

A stock's diversifiable or specific risk is determined by uncertainties specific to a firm (alpha factor) such as management quality, product innovation, product mix, market response, and capital structure. This deviation in performance, also called tracking error, indicates the difference in return between a portfolio and, for example, a target index. The terminology may be somewhat confusing. Technically, specific risk and tracking error are the same when the portfolio beta is equal to 1.0. Tracking error is usually reported as the standard deviation of returns.

Systematic and specific risk are becoming more significant as they filter into program trading, or portfolio trading (a successor to indexing; see Section 5). This is a mechanism that includes different investment strategies:

1. Index funds take advantage of market discrepancies.

2. Stock-index arbitrage generates returns above the level available on, for example, Treasury bills.

3. Index-fund arbitrage was developed when futures were created in 1982.

4. Index fund management is designed for large portfolios.

5. Index-arbitrage is designed for managed transitions.

6. Quantitative rebalancing can be done with a basket of stocks.

7. Portfolio insurance is designed for dynamic asset allocation.

8. Tactical asset allocation consists of shifting between equities, bonds, and cash.

The key word common to most of the items in this listing is index. A basic strategy with index funds is to create a portfolio able to track the performance of an equal-dollar-weighted New York Stock Exchange Index. The choice of NYSE is based mainly on the fact that it is a broad-based index; hence, by equally weighting it, investors bet on better returns due to its relatively high level of systematic risk.

To some extent, it was the disappointing performance of certain investments that led to index funds and other quantitative investment techniques. But also, the large amount of assets being managed in many funds has turned computer-driven approaches into effective strategies in investment.

These new solutions have been attractive to investors; index funds have grown from only $6 million in 1971 to $10 billion by 1980 and $250 billion in 1990. They currently represent 30 percent of institutional equity assets and may soon reach close to 50 percent.[1]

Stock-index arbitrage is a trading strategy designed to profit on gaps in prices between stock-index futures and the stocks that make up the indexes.

In a typical play, a trader buys a basket of stocks when they are trading at cheaper prices than their corresponding index futures contract. The trader then sells the overpriced future to lock in the resulting price spread.

Since the purpose of stock-index arbitrage is to generate returns above the level available on U.S. Treasury bills, it is often called interest-rate operation. If futures sell above their fair value, the investor who owns a cash position buys the stocks in the index and sells futures.

The index is adjusted for dividends and the interest rate to obtain the fair value of futures; thus, assuming a known dividend, it is possible to translate a futures contract with a price above its fair value into a better return. Theoretically, the investor is hedged because both operations will be of equal value upon expiration. In real life, however, the results may be more complex. If liquidity diminishes, there may not be enough futures-contract buyers to sustain the prices quoted on traders' screens.

Also, the aggressive implementation of index arbitrage and the buying and selling of packages of stocks may bring many variations, some of them difficult or impossible to foresee with present tools. One of these is that stock-index transactions are producing instability in the stock market.

Because these trades boost volatility, critics of index arbitrage argue that it is creating resentment among small investors. This argument ignores the fact that there are hundreds of reasons why small investors leave the market.

Although there is nothing illegal or unethical about the practice of stock-index arbitrage, another contrarian argument suggests that there may be potential conflicts of interest. The Brady commission, for instance, noted that a firm could use its prior knowledge of a client's index-arbitrage strategy to execute its own trades first, thus taking a profit for itself at the client's expense.

This argument seems weak, because institutional investors, whose trades weight heavily on the market, have the necessary know-how to do stock-index arbitrage on their own. And furthermore, no brokerage house controls enough of a market share to tip the balances even if it knew the index arbitrage strategies of some of its clients.

What is true is that stock-index arbitrage allows traders to profit from the price differences between stock index futures contracts and stock prices reflected in an index such as the Standard & Poor's 500 or the Dow Jones. A stock index futures contract is a promise to buy or sell a specific basket of stocks—at a future date but at a set price. This is where the opportunity to make a profit arises.

Stock-index futures have become an important medium for the portfolio manager since their introduction in 1982. They are present in portfolio hedging and are useful in program trading techniques; they can be employed as a tool in portfolio insurance, and they are helpful in achieving indexation.

The existence of an index-futures contract is not a prerequisite to conducting index arbitrage. If foreign options exist on the index, synthetic future contracts can be created through a combination of puts and calls. The latter, however, are not as flexible as normal futures because option exercise prices do not provide as comprehensive a price coverage as futures contracts.

Currency hedging may introduce more complexity. If an American investor is holding German securities, that investor bears exchange-rate risk. A German investor holding U.S. securities also bears exchange-rate risk. But, if they forward contract with each other, with the American investor agreeing to sell Deutsche marks and buy dollars and the German investor agreeing to do the opposite, then they can eliminate this mutual risk. Hence, exchange-rate risk is not systematic, but it is present.

Index-fund arbitrage by exploiting discrepancies between futures and their underlying stocks, boosts the returns of investors that own index funds. If the price of the future drops below the value of the underlying stocks determining the fair-value price of the futures contract, the index fund will sell part or all its shares and replace them with futures, while retaining the same equity exposure.

The investor thus replaces a physical portfolio with an identical virtual (synthetic) portfolio at a lower cost. When the futures come back in line, this scenario is reversed by selling futures and buying the equity.

One alternative to investing in an index is to purchase a basket of stocks that replicate the index. This core indexing can be significantly assisted by mathematical models—which is true of nearly every aspect of program trading.

Efforts have been made to bring indexing into the bond market. The practice has not found favor with investment managers, however, for two reasons. First, most bond investors have a more or less fixed planning horizon, which means that they have a specific preference for one type of bond, whether long-intermediate-, or short-term.[2] Second, a portfolio that is diversified across maturities, in proportion to the market capitalization of these maturities, is likely to be sub-optimal for many investors.

This sub-optimization occurs with global as well as domestic bond portfolios. Market capitalization weights may also mislead the investment manager who is seeking to diversify a bond portfolio across countries or currencies; the capitalization of a country's bond market may largely be an artifact of the country's financial and institutional pecularities.

Debt has become a more universally traded (and appreciated) commodity than equities. Nevertheless, both conceptual and real diversity exist for certain bond instruments that are unknown to many investment managers, which makes it difficult to handle them efficiently.

A good example of this is mezzanine financing in Ireland—a fairly mature instrument, but one not available in other countries. This financing is usually in the form of a loan holding a junior security position. This loan, in addition to its normal interest rate, carries a right to participate in profits. Profit participation is fixed by a formula, however, and usually only occurs when a certain threshold of profitability has been reached.

In theory, the profit participation compensates for a higher risk on the loan. Some mezzanine products have rights that can be converted into shares.

As with equity offerings, debt has to be analyzed for strengths and weaknesses before commitments are made. Both instruments involve risks, returns, and options available. Two bond portfolio risks—credit and interest-rate risk—have traditionally been measured when dealing with multinational bond portfolios; however, country and currency risk also come into play.

These factors have become more important as worldwide growth in corporate, government, and cross-border bonds has significantly expanded the opportunities available to fixed-income managers in any First World country. Also, need has been created for an international perspective.

Public databases could act as information providers to sophisticated bond investors with an international viewpoint; but, these databases are not yet available. Regardless of this limitation, passive bond management must be more than indexing. Country weights have to be set according to criteria other than market capitalization:

◆ Gross domestic product (GDP) weights capture the importance of a country's whole economy.

◆ Stockmarket capitalization weights make an indicative contribution as market capitalization correlates highly with trade volume.

◆ A passive country-weighting system is based on liquidity; this approach is used in the J.P. Morgan Global Government Bond Indices.

Morgan's benchmark portfolio reflects very few extremely liquid (on-the-run) bonds. Its active contents consist of the benchmark bonds plus other heavily traded bonds. A comprehensive portfolio is structured on these premises, and many portfolios include less liquid bonds.

While such approaches to debt and equity are sound, they do not account for fraud and crashes, which sometimes have the highest authorities' official blessing. A famous example of this is the formation in the eighteenth-century of the South Sea Company.

Basically a scheme to raise money to finance England's sprawling debts, the South Sea Company was at its time considered to be a brilliant solution. In 1711, the company received a royal warrant; King George I became its governor. From these auspicious beginnings, the company charted a course that some years later ended in disaster. It has since gone down in financial history as the South Sea Bubble.[3]

5. Program Trading

In the 1930s, medical experts theorized that travelling faster than the speed of sound would result in the disintegration of the traveller. Today were it not for a Mach meter, the twenti-eth Century Concorde's passengers would not be aware that they had exceeded the sound barrier.

A comparison may be drawn between the experts of the thirties and modern-day "experts" who maintain that com-puter-based trading started the selling spree of October 19, 1987. According to these critics, the fast pace and unpredict-able interplay of two different computer-trading strategies caused the stock market in New York and the futures market in Chicago to fall widely out of line with each other. A closer look at the evidence suggests that this crash was not the result of new technology, but of traders' inexperience in using it, combined with erratic investor behavior (see Section 6).

Far from being a concept alien to the exchanges, program trading responds to a changing financial environment as well as the advent of a global market. It is also capable of meeting the needs of investors who demand diversification in securi-ties as well as risk protection.

Program trading originally referred to the list of hundreds of indexes that institutional investors wanted to buy or sell in a day. Originally, it consisted of only those computer printouts with more than fifteen positions. This arbitrary dividing line originated with the New York Stock Exchange's identifying a program trade as any simultaneous transaction involving more than fifteen stocks. Index arbitrage fits that definition.

A key difference between Portfolio trading and Stock trad-ing is that decisions governing portfolio trading are generally based on macroeconomic factors and not the performance of individual stocks. Systematic risk rather than specific risk is in the background.

Another characteristic of portfolio trading is that available futures and options lead to the narrowing of spreads as well as the reduction of transaction costs. Stock-index arbitrage assures that futures remain in line with underlying stocks; even if investors perceive the current environment as more volatile, on average, the price level can be the same.

By being the mechanism through which different investment strategies or scenarios, such as index funds, arbitrage, asset allocation, and portfolio insurance, are executed, program trading responds to the changing needs of investors, whether they are individuals trading small amounts of stock or institutional investors doing block trading. (With the help of computers in planning and execution, block trading has grown from 3 percent of the market in 1965 to 50 percent in 1986).

A distinction can be made between the in-house trading assistants that have so far been discussed and program trading by drawing a parallel with telecommunications.

Individual expert systems for traders are similar to a private branch exchange. Trading programs can be compared with the telephone company's Centrex service, which downloads calls to a central network.

Program trading is associated with automated computer-driven techniques that eliminate manual intervention. This is true, but it does not necessarily mean that the computer makes all the decisions. Software is merely used to simplify the mechanics of the process: computers digest large amounts of data and produce real-time response.

There has been rapid acceptance of automated systems that forward and execute trade instructions, to the extent that nearly 15 percent of program trades by NYSE member firms are now done on London's International Stock Exchange

(ISE), where many big investors go to avoid stricter U.S. disclosure requirements. NYSE is losing revenue because of this trading migration (involving up to six million shares daily).

Hence, NYSE is seeking to bend some disclosure requirements and slash its fees to get big investors and their brokers to bring this program trading back to New York. Table 10–1 shows statistics on the execution of portfolio trading.

Computer-assisted program trading currently accounts for about 10 percent of average daily volume on the Big Board. To acquire more, NYSE plan launched two after-hours crossing sessions geared to further enhance program trading for big institutional investors.

Program traders participating in a crossing session are allowed to electronically trade exchange-listed stocks in Standard & Poor's 500 stock index. In a departure from the conventions of trading during normal NYSE hours, neither

Table 10–1   Statistics on the Execution of Program Trading by NYSE Member Firms*

On the NYSE	81.9%
In Foreign Markets**	14.8%
On the American Stock Exchange, over-the-counter and regional markets	3.3%
	100%

*   As of late 1990
**   Does not include trading by foreign units of NYSE members.

the names of the brokerage firms nor the size of the trades will be disclosed.

6. Portfolio Insurance

Portfolio insurance is provided through a computer-generated preset limit to buying and selling.

A program developed by University of California professors Mark Rubinstein and Hayne Leland enables investors to protect themselves against large portfolio losses by selling stocks or the index futures when markets decline. The amount of selling is determined through algorithms and heuristics; and as a market declines, the portfolio insurer continues to sell stocks until the mathematical program stops selling.

This technique, often called dynamic asset allocation, is based on theoretical trading options. Variations on the technique include replicating the structure of a put option, switching funds gradually into equity as the market rises and into cash when the market declines, and replacing the sale of stocks with the purchase or sale of futures contracts. The exercise of portfolio insurance requires selling into weakness and buying into strengths, which then amplifies the movement and volatility of the markets.

There is a risk inherent in portfolio insurance. Most traders and investors tend to cluster their limits in a narrow range; therefore, if some of these limits are broken by the computer, the plethora of available software might have a "snowball" effect. The avalanche that follows—as in the October 1987 crash—has been referred to as a "technical factor."

Limits have always existed in stock trading, but their paper-based manipulation involved errors and delays that attenuated the reaction. With current computer efficiency, there is a snowball effect which can only be avoided if individual securities houses and the Stock Exchanges of the First World act in unison, to prevent it.

Some analysts suggest that portfolio insurance is in fact a misnomer, and that this technique is actually a hedging strategy on the part of investors. When stock-index futures are sold in a falling market, losses in the stocks themselves are offset, at least in part, by gains in the sale of the futures.

If the market continues to fall, an investor can buy back the futures and close out in a profitable position.

Nevertheless, selling futures pushes down their price. A wave of selling can enlarge the disparity between the price of a futures item and the prices of the individual stocks that in the aggregate make up a certain basket.

Some traders think that computer-based observance of sell limits may have begun the 1987 wave of selling (as well as minor shocks in 1989) and that portfolio insurance programs helped create much of the turmoil that ultimately defeated them.

Proponents of portfolio insurance, on the other hand, argue that if the technique did not fare well in the October 1987 crash, it is because the model was not yet polished; confusion was created by a lack of timely information, which led to the withdrawal of index arbitrageurs. This withdrawal, they say, created large discrepancies between the futures and the underlying index.

Whatever the rationale for the performance of portfolio insurance on Black Monday in 1987, some market experts believe that computer-assisted techniques that were invented to reduce risk actually created more through simultaneous and coordinated trading in two distinct but related markets—the traditional stockmarket in New York and the relatively new financial futures market in Chicago.

The irony is that unlike earlier financial disasters, this one quite likely emerged not because of too much speculation but because of too much hedging. Another problem was a lack of matching capabilities, tied to the misconception that whenever the computer commanded buy or sell, there would be buyers and sellers. (Fully automatic matching capabilities should be fundamental to a global computer-based trading system, whether in the area of securities or that of Forex.)

Program-trading algorithms monitor minute changes in the two markets, in search of price differentials (spreads) between the two. These systems then execute a large series of trades, often involving millions of shares, at speeds nearly impossible to duplicate by hand or by telephoning the floor of the exchange.

This interlinking, and the global trading possibilities that it presents, is a totally new experience. With this available potential, it is important to remember that different markets buy and sell the same equities, debt, and commodities in different forms. To make matters more complex, the futures markets trade what amounts to baskets of stocks. One popular contract, for instance, is tied to Standard & Poor's 500 stock index. Theoretically, the price of these baskets will closely track the aggregate price of all stocks that make up the basket.

In practice, however, the price of the baskets reflects the stock market's overall prospects, while individual stocks may rise and fall in relation to news about different companies.

These price differentials provide an opportunity for arbitrage in the classic sense. Traders will buy whichever version is less expensive and simultaneously sell whichever is more expensive, executing in the process a matching basket of futures. This technique is not a new one, but with the use of computers, brokerage houses have turned it into a big moneymaker. (By October 1987, between $70 billion and $90 billion was estimated to have been invested in funds using some form of portfolio insurance.)

If we are to master the increasingly complex landscape of global networked exchanges, certain issues will need to be confronted in years to come. First, a fully automatic global trading network works well up to a point, but since experience with such large-scale systems is nonexistent, a lot of precautions must be taken, among them ensuring security and protection of privacy, using circuit breakers, and redefining the scope of regulatory authority (which may include an interventionist role).

Second, given that all trading transactions classifically end in considerable paperwork, an expert system must be developed to deal with this function (as discussed in previous chapters). It is pointless to use expert systems as trading assistants, or even fully automated traders, if the back office is a bottleneck in the circuit.

Trading solutions should focus on algorithms or heuristics; they should also be integrative. Attention should be paid to the aggregate front desk/back office within the 24-hour trading networks that link into one system the main exchanges around the globe.

7. Efficient Market Theory and the Crash of 1987

The October 19, 1987 stock-market collapse erased more than $500 billion in investor wealth in the U.S. alone (double that amount worldwide). It also struck a blow against one of the major theoretical ideas in finance—the efficient market theory (EMT).

EMT rejected the popular view that the value of stocks changes with buying trends or in reaction to speculative fever. According to this theory, investors act rationally and stock prices reflect whatever information people have about the fundamentals, such as present and future earnings. And because, as Dr. Maurice Allais demonstrated statistically, what one player gains, the other loses, stock prices change only with fresh financial news, and price movements do not necessarily reflect crowd psychology.

While not unknown in years past, the efficient market theory launched a market revolution in the 1980s. Finance professors as well as mathematicians and physicists built careers on Wall Street by exploiting EMT's real or hypothetical insights.

EMT says that one cannot consistently outperform market averages, since only unexpected news moves prices. But its theorems and postulates are useless in explaining Bloody Monday. What new information jarred investors into slashing their estimate of the value of corporate assets by some 23 percent in the six-and-a-half hours that the New York Stock Exchange was open?

None, apparently. Many people believed the price drops themselves signalled a crash, and many investors tried to cash in their assets.

The events that took place in the biggest New York stock-market calamity in fifty-eight years seem to have had several causes, among them shortcomings in trading practices. One significant problem was the inability of dealers to answer phone calls. This was simply a case of having too many phone lines for all of them to be answered manually.

Another problem was dealers' inability to process the flood of orders resulting from the crash. Normally, an offer-and-demand cycle corrects itself because there are a number of buyers and sellers in the market. In a market landscape dominated by institutional investors, however, big players move as one in the same direction. When there are too many sellers, there are almost no buyers, and disparities between offer and demand become very large. The result is that the old market mechanisms, which are based on the assumption that some buyers will be available, fail.

A computerized trading system could avert these problems by making it possible for a dealer to design a client's trade on a computer and execute it by phone or by hand on the floor of the exchange. This terminal-based trading will eventually predominate on the New York Stock Exchange (as it already does on the London and Toronto exchanges). At the same time, in order that traders may avoid other, unforeseen problems, program trading will require a set of regulations stating what can and cannot be done with technology. SEC experts, the Federal Reserve, and legislators must apply themselves to the long-neglected task of creating a modern, comprehensive system for regulating markets, one that takes into account computers and communications.

For example, breaker circuits may monitor programmed trades, the timing of which is a major factor in touching off a cascade of sales. Because each computer is programmed with a threshold set of prices, which kicks the program trade into action, it is important to know how portfolio insurance (intended to help limit an investor's risk) interacts with the arbitrage programs.

As well as putting circuit breakers in place, the computation of global risk[4] should produce a redefinition of financial responsibility and a new concept of market liquidity. (Liquidity has become problematic because computers and communications have tightened the links between markets, assuring that when one moves the other moves with it. As a result, many brokers will execute transactions for clients only if the other party to the trade has already been lined up.)

Some market professionals suggest that program trading can be successfully regulated under the current rules of the New York Stock Exchange.

These prohibit both computer-generated trades from being automatically dumped into the exchange's own computers and brokerages from program trading for their own accounts.

The practice of arbitraging dates to the beginning of civilization. What is new is an increased power to plan deals—that is, execute deals which makes it possible to buy and sell quickly in a number of markets simultaneously in order to take advantage of differences in prices. Thanks to computer technology, big investors can play one market against another and can rapidly move huge amounts of funds.

In fact, some recent large market swings can be traced to large investors' playing futures markets against what the assets were actually selling for. Today, when stocks, bonds, and other instruments are bought or sold for delivery at some specified future date, the calculations—which involve many currencies and products, and are extremely complex—can be made in a fraction of a second by supercomputers.

8. Stock Markets: Efficient or Inefficient?

Efficient market theory is based on the premise that all outstanding information about companies is built into their share prices. By extension, this means that such shares are always fairly valued. This is not true.

One implication of efficient market theory is that there is no sure way of making gains in the stockmarket unless one is trading on inside information. This is also not true, because even if a market is quick to digest earnings data, it can be grossly inefficient in valuing everything else.

In the long run, a variety of factors affect a company's performance. These may include the products in its laboratories, internal cost controls, the quality of its production facilities, inventory surpluses and shortages, the land on which the company is built, the loans outstanding, and the quality of company management.

Not only are financial markets a more or less inefficient operation, but they could not be otherwise; at least four different levels of inefficiency are built into the system:

1. Companies, whose equity and debt is traded in the market(s), are inefficient for the reasons discussed above.

2. Market(s), in which companies are quoted, are inefficient because pockets of corporate weaknesses are not easy to uncover.

3. The sprawling market-to-market transaction process, which overwhelms practically all securities houses, is inefficient.

4. Increased market complexity, introduced by global twenty-four-hour trading as well as currency risk and country risk, is inefficient because there are few theories on how it should be handled.

Taking currency risk as an example, if the market(s) perceived every currency as equally risky, implied volatilities would be similar. They are not, which is why it is difficult to evaluate and compare the implied volatilities embedded in currency option prices.

Option prices are generally used because they convey better information about risk and return than does the cash market. But, this approach only goes so far, and there are three other layers of inefficiency affecting the price of stocks.

Aside from the psychology of the markets, there are other reasons that all stocks cannot be fairly priced. If they were, investment managers would not be necessary; trading stocks would not improve investment performance; and brokers would earn large commissions for providing an unnecessary service.

In the 1950s, investors did not generally think about mathematical models when they set prices and built portfolios.

Most thought about earnings growth prospects when they assessed price-to-earnings ratios. They considered single stocks rather than portfolio aggregates when selecting investment strategies.

The fact that EMT is a dubious proposition does not hinder securities experts from taking a methodical approach to the market. Because they perceive market inefficiency, leading securities houses focus on locating pockets of overpriced and underpriced stocks. While some brokers believe that these can be identified by common factors such as price/earnings ratios yield, and market capitalization, the more scientific-minded investment analysts investigate also factors such as

1. a company's strengths and weaknesses,

2. forecasted growth rate in earnings and product leadership,

3. turnaround potential in P/E (documented by steps taken by management),

4. past surprises in company performance,

5. management quality (which must be evaluated on a steady basis).

On a national stock exchange (one on which country and currency risk are not factors), forward-thinking investment bankers and traders start from the premise that a market system is inherently inefficient because they know that this inefficiency can be exploited to their advantage.

The best way to capitalize on market inefficiency is by doing analytical studies through access to databases and by experimenting with simulators, knowledge engineering constructs, and supercomputers.

In the presence of market inefficiency, investors can expect to prosper only by possessing either better information than other investors or by having superior know-how that is supported through models. (If they hold a multinational portfolio, they should also have modules of the foreign exchange market.)

Opinions differ as to how this subject should be approached. Many market efficiency tests have used the forward rate to determine future spot. Recent studies, however, cast doubt on whether observed forward rates reflect the market's expectation of future spot. These studies suggest the existence of risk premia imbedded in forward rates.

Thus, when using statistical evidence alone to make judgments about market efficiency, it is best to proceed cautiously. More rigorous models are preferable, and these should have the ability to reflect risk despite the current polyvalence in investment perspectives and the large size of the foreign exchange market.

There is general concensus for this point of view, as shown by the fact that a growing number of highly trained professionals are constantly testing the currency markets for investment opportunities. This also means, however, that any perceived Forex inefficiency will be arbitraged almost immediately.

While speed is essential, decisions must be thoroughly documented. When large numbers of people are after the same commodity, whether it be a job, a stock, a bond, or a foreign currency, that commodity quickly becomes overvalued. Opportunity lies in the fact that some items become more overvalued than others. Operators will benefit from this trading environment if they know how to value different commodities, trade them at the right time, and capitalize on their purchase or sale.

Knowing the markets means knowing other people's strengths and weaknesses. This entails watching the important financial markets including New York, London, Zurich, and Tokyo as well as Frankfurt, Paris, Milan, Hong Kong, and Singapore twenty-four hours a day. It also means concentrating not only on stocks and bonds, but on currencies and commodities such as oil, natural gas, precious metals, and foodstuffs (i.e., anything that might in some way influence the market as a whole) as well.

Endnotes

1. Chapter 12 by William W. Jahnke in Brian R. Bruce ed., *Quantitative International Investing* (Chicago, IL: Probus Publishing, 1990).

2. Long-term bonds generally have ten years or more to maturity; short-term bonds two to three years. If its horizon is less than one year, the bond belongs in the money market rather than the capital market.

3. This company entered into legend after its predecessor scandal, that of the Great Tulip Bubble (late sixteenth century) but at about the same time as the Mississippi Bubble, and ahead of many real estate crashes, the Great Wall Street crash, and the more recent Silver Bubble. See also Robert Beckman, *Crashes* (London: Grafton Books/Collins Publishing, 1988).

4. See also D.N. Chorafas, *Risk Management in Financial Institutions* (London: Butterworths, 1990).

Chapter **11**

Networks

Chapter 11

Networks

1. Introduction

The great science of antiquity was philosophy. Rhetoric and literature came next, followed by history. In contrast, few people, with the exception of those devoted to geometry and astronomy, had engineering skills. The two most well-known engineers of ancient times were Archimedes of Syracruse and Hero of Alexandria.

The 20th Century, on the other hand, has been shaped by great team projects in engineering, from large dams and skyscrapers to energy production and telecommunications. The modern network is the infrastructure of a financial institution. (Its role was examined in Chapter 1 with a discussion of Project 2000.)

The communications revolution of the 1990s will make large-scale integration (VLSI) developments look like a child's play. Improvements in telecommunications and computer technology will permit many service firms to globalize their operations, much as industrial businesses have been doing for years by

1. accessing workers in low-wage countries where labor is plentiful;

2. improving the efficiency and productivity of their personnel worldwide;

3. delivering financial products on-line to their clients;

4. building layers of value differentiation on the existing sophistication and competitiveness of financial products.

The growth of the global office whose chores can be executed on-line, real time—and, therefore, can be largely automated—promises to change the way the financial industry operates. At the same time, operating networked workstations will raise issues of data security and integrity; it will also require an ongoing process of learning.

Peer-to-peer networks dismantle monolithic centralized organizations and diffuse points of control over computing. Intelligent networks, distributed databases, and powerful workstations lessen the demand for host systems, which are the domain of the data processing manager.

To survive, DP managers must become communications specialists who can operate comfortably in a culture of polyvalent products, one that focuses on end user support in the form of appealing, low-cost financial services.

2. Real Space: A New Communications Culture

In the knowledge-based society of the 1990s and beyond, all-digital communications services will help to produce efficient processes, distill information, save energy, and improving the performance of financial products. Real time and real space have already been defined in Chapter 1, page 17. However, as a refresher, let's recall that since the 1960s *real time* made possible speedy handling of local market and customer requirements. But as the latter grew in sophistication—and 24-hour banking came under perspective—though necessary, real time was no more enough.

A leading financial institution has to operate at any time, in any market, on behalf of any major customer. It has to trade in all key financial centers of the First World and, therefore, be able to see market patterns in *real space,* mapping in real time but in one geographic location[1] the behavior of financial markets in the four corners of the world.

The existence of real space facilities leads to value differentiation in financial services, and value differentiation is an important element in developing a new customer-oriented product. For example, capturing sales information at source means better and more immediate information for other departments.

♦ In financial product-design departments, a computer network links members of a design team, each work with screen-based workstations; the network allows them to share not only the computer's resources, but also work and know-how.

♦ Once a product design has been completed and is captured in the database it can be accessed by other departments, anywhere in the world.

♦ Consolidated reports on the sales of various financial services, as well as potential prospects, can be used by management to plan an overall strategy.

♦ A breakdown of sales figures by profitability (as opposed to standard activity reports) will provide the raw data that marketing needs for its strategic evaluations.

◆ The computer network must be used to link suc-
ceeding stages in the design, production, and
distribution of financial products.

Any computer network can be fine-tuned for maximum
speed, responsiveness, and accuracy. At the next stage, a
bank's technology officers must assist in enhancing the performance of financial products. They and their employees
should be aware of and exploit the potential communications
advances, in local, metropolitan, and wide-area networks.[2]
Bankers need to understand the competitive advantages
inherent in working on-line with the markets, a skill pos-
sessed by the new breed of Wall Street professionals called
rocket scientists (see Chapter 1). This group of technology
specialists and bankers focuses on new financial products and
employs supercomputers, artificial intelligence, and new
methods of risk control to support real-space systems—which
combine real-time operations with twenty-four hour banking—anywhere in the world. These real-space solutions,
which integrate multimedia databases, computational-in-
tense activities, and electronic messaging services, are a great
improvement over traditional real-time applications. Implementing them, however, requires a global approach, valid
interconnection methods, instantaneous response mechanisms, and the capability for consolidating the bank's capil-
lary structure.
    Now that the banking industry is moving toward relation-
ship banking, which emphasizes quality of service, customer
security, client consulting, and individual, personalized products, a bank's network is becoming its medium of financial
intermediation.
    In this new telecommunications perspective, information
technologists have a role to play that goes beyond projecting,
implementing, and maintaining the network. They must also
make the system and its elements understandable. They must

keep languages between processes consistent and must adapt requests posed on the network to the specific machinery existing in a given location, while making the non-homogeneity of software and computers transparent to the end user.

System professionals should also provide support for application and system activities beyond the fundamentals (i.e., the exchange of information between processes). Solutions must systematically integrate the individual capabilities of the user with those of various types of software and equipment and, at the same time, preserve the versatility necessary to create a system of more advanced intelligence.

This focus on advanced applications of the telecommunications system is applicable not only to investment banks and brokers, but also to the telephone companies themselves. General Telephone and Electronics (GTE), for example, is now going beyond offering basic telephone services to emphasize value differentiation. As Figure 11–1 indicates, GTE identifies basic services (assisted through AI) as consisting of network design, implementation, administration, and maintenance as well as high reliability, broadband channels, and efficient protocols. Value-added services are those that are user oriented, such as health management, electronic publishing, and frequent flyer, but also include intelligent databases and support for expert systems sold to the clients of value-added telecommunications products.

The general management of GTE is not the only management to believe in the need to invest heavily in knowledge-intense solutions. The late Jean Ribout, an investment banker and chief executive officer of Schlumberger, said, "This technical revolution—artificial intelligence—is as important to our future as the surge in oil exploration. It will force us to design new tools, it will change the capabilities of our services, it will multiply the effectiveness of our instruments. It will change the order of magnitude ... of our business."[3]

Figure 11–1 Two-Level Strategy of Network Operators

DEREGULATED

VALUE ADDED

1. DIFFERENTIATION SERVICES
   - HEALTH SERVICES
   - ELECTRONIC PUBLISHING
   - FREQUENT FLYER
   - FREQUENT SHOPPER
2. INTELLIGENT DATABASES
3. SUSTENANCE

REGULATED

BASIC NETWORK

1. AI USAGE IN
   - DESIGN
   - CONTROL
   - DIAGNOSTICS
   - MAINTENANCE
   - SUPPORT
2. 99.99 % RELIABILITY
3. BROADBAND
4. EFFICIENT PROTOCOLS

3. Solutions for the 1990s

If new networking technologies are to be implemented and validated, developers of the new structures will need to be aware of the ways in which telecommunications can be applied to both process transformation and business evolution. This entails understanding how the technology will affect business strategies and business processes.

By the mid-1990s, five key technologies—parallel computing (supercomputing), hypermedia and hypertext, compound electronic documents, new management tools based on artificial intelligence (including neural networks), and speech recognition/synthesis—will come into play in the workplace.

Computers and networks will serve not only as a medium for communication, but also as a means for processing text, data, image, graphics, and voice. Digitized multimedia information will increase network usage both by providing improved handling of electronic documents and by giving users access to audio tapes, pictures, text, and videos.

Through scanning, searching, and other techniques, networks will create compound electronic documents that give users ready access to thousands of documents based on computers and photonics (optical disks). The networks will be driven by solutions that mimic human intelligence (i.e., the nervous sytems and the sensors) and will use expert systems, neural networks, speech recognition, language translation, and speech synthesis as tools.

Speech recognition, which processes spoken words into typed text, will enable managers and professionals to do word processing even if they lack keyboard skills. Speech recognition can also be used (in a manner similar to that employed in videoconferencing technology) to reduce the amount of bandwidth needed to transmit a telephone call, thus transmitting only the information needed to change a video image, rather than continuously retransmitting the entire image.

In the First World, the impact of photonics (optical fibers) on communications is already being felt. By the end of the 1990s, photonics will eclipse electronics in transmission, radically altering financial products and services, even those which are market leaders today.

The rapid growth in requirements and the availability of advanced technologies can be seen either as a challenge to be met or as a sound barrier. If the challenge option is chosen, the best approach to take is that of following a steady virtuous spiral (see Figure 11–2). In the manner in which it moves from conception to specification, design implementation, maintenance, and back to conception, this software development spiral radically alters the old concept of a "waterfall" model in systems work. Every time the spiral moves outward, the sophistication of the solution and its complexity—and the hoped-for results—increase.

If the sound barrier approach is chosen, the process is one of falling behind and decaying. (Some financial companies may feel that they cannot afford the course of steady challenge, and they may be right under their prevailing conditions; the alternative, however, may be losing their market share.)

Macrotrends such as globalization of the economy, acceleration of deregulation, the restructuring of industry, and the shift to a service- and knowledge-based economy, are accelerating because of the evolving pluralism of technical solutions, an explosion in bandwidth, the hybrid use of public and private networks, increased facilities in network management, and the spread of open systems. Other factors in this acceleration are multimedia applications and the mass market penetration of mobile radio, satellite, and optical fiber communications services.

**Figure 11–2   A Steady Virtuous Spiral in
Software Development**

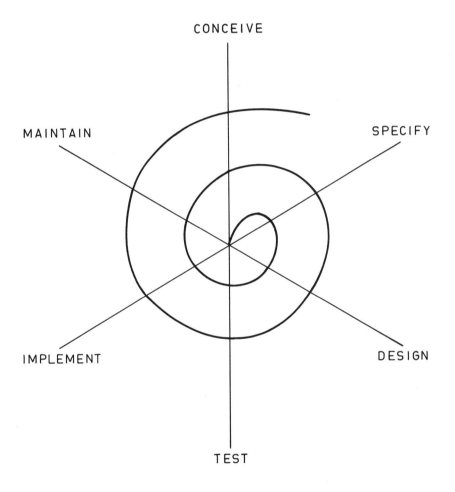

In the same way that electronic funds transfer created a global financial marketplace, network intelligence will have an impact in every business field. As companies begin to run their affairs with on-line computer and communications services, comparative advantage will depend almost entirely on the ability to leverage the available know-how.

At the microlevel, communications managers need to ensure that they can handle the increasingly powerful workstations that are coming, the intelligent databases that are needed and the complex networks that will interconnect them. Networking the workstations to a pair of file servers is the most efficient way to share the data. At the same time, the steadily evolving network should provide remote high-speed access to optical databases and supercomputers and assure wide broadband, high reliability, and easy fault isolation, in order to make it simpler to add capacity and to restructure. Optical fiber technology has set off a bandwidth revolution in First World telecommunications. Little more than a decade ago, design premises were based on one telephone call, which was carried on a twisted pair of copper wires. Today, single-mode optical fibers are available that have gigastream capacity.[4]

Already broadband switches are leaving the laboratory and entering the market. With the proliferation of wide-area broadband networks (or parts thereof) and fiber-based local area networks, as well as metropolitan area networks, it should be cost-effective to deploy broadband switches supporting niche applications. Doing this will aid in defining or restructuring the new financial market.

End-to-end broadband communications will soon become a vital tool for the business community. Commercial pressures are already forcing optical fiber into the local loop for business subscribers; large-scale investments are, however, necessary to create the basic infrastructure, which includes

1. system design and computer aided engineering equipment (software, hardware),

2. network management assisted through artificial intelligence,

3. diagnostics and maintenance enriched with expert systems,

4. multifunctional service development and a rich user applications pallet.

These investments are all inherently interlinked and, considering the development cycles of complex and extensive telecommunications systems, should soon be wide spread. The challenge will be fitting the system to future user requirements because design decisions made at an early stage of the process may determine the availability of options and facilities—and consequently, the network's commercial and economic success or failure.

4. The Intelligent Network

An intelligent network (IN) is designed to give the operators of a system the capacity to distribute switching intelligence, diagnostic capability, quality assurance, and a number of other AI-enriched facilities among system elements; it is designed to make it possible to interconnect large databases with remote access over telecommunication channels.

Today, there are a number of breakthroughs in diverse areas of telecommunications such as advanced signal processing, display-handling software, security, and automated diagnostics. Quality histories of network performance, as well as significant improvement of bit error rate and reliability, are also available.

One major objective of an IN is to identify key enabling technologies; another objective is to support a number of broad-based system trends and endow them with software techniques, such as customer profiles, that fit the IN concept.

Intelligent networks provide added value to telecommunications lines, swtiching centers, and their associated instrumentation. This value differentiation typically consists of

1. artificial intelligence constructs for switching, transmission, and maintenance;

2. high-quality networking with low bit error rate (BER);

3. high capacity (broadband);

4. non-blocking solutions;

5. on-line diagnostics and a quality database;

6. forecasting and load planning;

7. digitization in channel transmission and switching;

8. steady innovation, competitiveness, and corresponding investments;

INs are still under development. Current research focuses on the evaluating theoretical results via prototypes and business problems and specifying what is required for better functional performance and flawless implementation. Also, standardization of networks is an ongoing process. (When Bell Communications Research coined the term intelligent network in 1986, it did not define it precisely. As a result, many variants exist today, most of which are incompatible with each other.)

Because they combine the techniques of digital transmission, switching, data processing, and distributed database management, INs promise to be the integrating factor that will piece together analog and digital telecom lines, mobile personal communications, private networks and competitive value-added network services. They also signal the arrival of large computer and communications aggregates.

Networks can be made more efficient and economical by integrating CAD and AI. In turn, network intelligence makes it possible to introduce new services and capabilities more quickly and less expensively than in the past. With the cost of bit transport falling fast and voice telephone services increasing, the IN offers the operators of telephone services, or telcos, new revenue-generating options with reasonable incremental investments.

Nevertheless, the initial investment for an IN is large, and those telcos that cannot afford a steadily growing implementation of network intelligence will be reduced to the role of bandwidth suppliers and distributors of services to more advanced telecommunications firms or PTT[5] administrations.

Figure 11–3 shows an implementation target for an intelligent network. The ISO/OSI model describes how network lines and switches should interconnect. Intelligence resides at the nodes. The outer layers are private and public databases. They interconnect through the public network, which itself may be an intelligent structure.

Ideally, these public databases would belong to information providers such as Dow Jones, Reuters, or many others. While a telco could own a public database company, the transport and warehousing services for text and data would need to be fully unbundled in order to avoid the scenario of a monopoly. (Databases could also be operated by independent service providers or, even better, by user organizations themselves.)

The typical components—intelligent nodes and lines, quality databases, analytical tools (both algorithlic and heuristic), simulators and optimizers, and service schedulers—of

**Figure 11–3   Database-to-Database Using the ISO/
                 OSI Model for Interconnection**

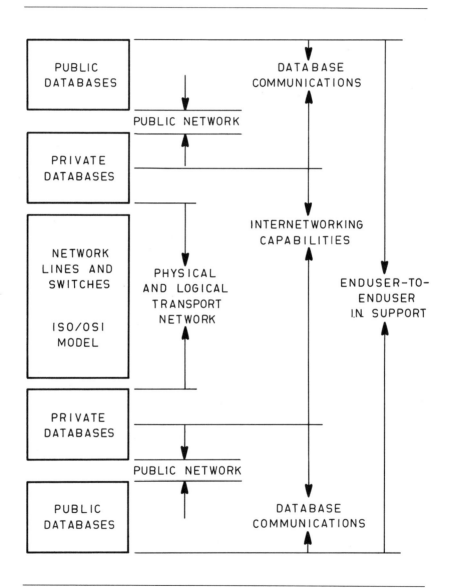

an IN, if used efficiently, can reduce costs while increasing the quality of service. The better-managed telcos appreciate this point and integrate it into their strategic plans. A financial institution, in figuring the cost of telecommunications services, can divide its budget into three major classes: personnel, capital investments at sites, and money paid to the carrier.

Investment banks and brokers sometimes complain that they pay too much for the services offered by telcos. In fact, their largest single expenditure is personnel, which often accounts for 60 percent to 65 percent of the telecommunications budget. Financial institutions that realize this are trying to control personnel costs through investments in software and hardware.

Even if they don't own intelligent networks, investment banks and securities houses have vested interest in decisions that may seem to be part of the internal affairs of telcos. The effort should be to optimize the total cost equation rather than only "this" or "that" of the cost chapters.

Other factors should also be given the attention they deserve. Because personal information can be stored in an IN, banks must deal with the issue of privacy protection. Another concern is who will have access to and control over online databases, which will carry extremely sensitive and commercially valuable data. How can such information be shared among competitive service providers?

These issues will become one of the major preoccupations of regulators in this decade; and with the conflicting goals of various pressure groups, solutions will not come easy.

5. Fiber Optics and Satellites

In a knowledge-based society, progress depends on the means by which information is captured, transmitted, stored, retrieved, manipulated, and used. Three-quarters of the world lacks adequate communications facilities; in the First World (America, Japan, and Western Europe), however, the exploration of communications frontiers is moving fast.

One of the major breakthroughs, fiber optics, makes it possible to communicate over long distances at gigastreams (gigabits per second, on GBPS), thus allowing a continuous stream of information to flow between businesses as well as between businesses and their clients.

In 1989 and 1990, an international optical fiber network, TAT-8, was installed in a phone cable line that links the United States to England and France.[6] This four-thousand-mile network can carry tens of thousands of telephone calls simultaneously in a cable less than an inch thick, reducing the cost of long-distance calling and increasing the services available.

Four months after the installation of TAT-8, a fiber line was run under the Pacific, connecting the United States and Japan; this was followed in the summer of 1990 by a second trans-Atlantic optical fiber line.

With discussions under way for a fiber cable that will tie Europe and East Asia directly together, fiber may soon girdle the world in an unbroken loop that transmits digital information in capacities unthinkable with conventional analog systems. This is the concept of a global digital superway.

The increased use of fiber optics in telecommunications is likely to lead to a decline in the market for public telephone exchanges. This is because the relationship between the cost of switching and that of transmission facilities has been radically altered by fiber optics; this will eventually lead to a steep reduction in the cost of transmission.

With optical transmission systems that can operate at several GBPS just about to hit the market, nothing else will be able to touch fiber optics for cheap wideband transmission. As a result, solutions for the 1990s will move away from the present complex hierarchy of local and regional switching centers.

Furthermore, where optical fiber is laid, it makes backhauling (the switching of circuits over apparently irrational routes; for example, going from Washington, D.C., to New York via San Francisco) increasingly economic. Already tariffs are being established based on the time of holding the connection, not on distance.

Thus, the economics of fiber-optic communications are redefining the rules for high-speed networking. The combination of network growth, in conjunction with increased requirements for bandwidth and high-speed interconnection of network devices, has led to the steady renovation of communications systems. The early 1990s will witness an explosion in fiber optic-based communications as the advantages of large bandwidth and low cost are applied to local- and metropolitan-area networks.

While some observers worry about a possible capacity glut, most of the communications industry sees the cables' capability and the competition that they foster as positive. This is true for both public communications networks and the in-house ones that corporations and governments are setting up in increasing numbers.

Fiber's appearance in the long-haul international market has caused some headaches for the 118-nation consortium Intelsat which, through the communications satellites it operates, has held a virtual monopoly on most sectors of the long-haul business since the mid-sixties. Today, this consortium is scrambling to cut prices and offer improved services in response to the newly competitive environment.

But there is still potential in satellites; recent political developments are opening the skies to commercial opportunity, impacting on a whole range of communications systems, such as high speed data transmission, facsimile, voice channels, videoconferencing, and computer communications that are already fast changing under their own technological momentum. Also, the considerable potential of new applications, such as mobile systems for land, sea and air, is also being assessed.

Companies such as Daimler-Benz are gearing up to operate two-way satellite communications networks that will use very-small aperture terminals (VSATs). These are designed for company use; but should they prove viable, they will most likely be marketed to other users.

The Daimler-Benz move represents the first attempt to have such a network in Europe, where heavy national regulations have stunted two-way VSAT ventures. Therefore, the automaker will set up the experimental network in cooperation with the firm Deutsche Bundespost Telekom, which is expected to secure the necessary regulatory approvals from other European telecom administrations.

Financial institutions can also benefit from VSAT approaches. With the advent of twenty-four hour trading, it will be in the best interest of securities and other markets to investigate not only how they can link on-line among themselves, but also with their markets and clients.

6. Teleports and Intelligent Buildings

It is good business strategy to consider buildings a part of information technology. Ever-increasing numbers of phone sets, terminals, workstations, printers, and teleconferencing practices are straining conventional solutions. Teleports offer an advanced telecommunications infrastructure in the form of a bypass mechanism that makes it possible for a business to interconnect its different operating centers (headquarters, branches, and so on) without passing through the city office of the telco.

Figure 11–4   The Common Area between
Telecommunications, Building Automation
and Office Automation Is Artificial
Intelligence.

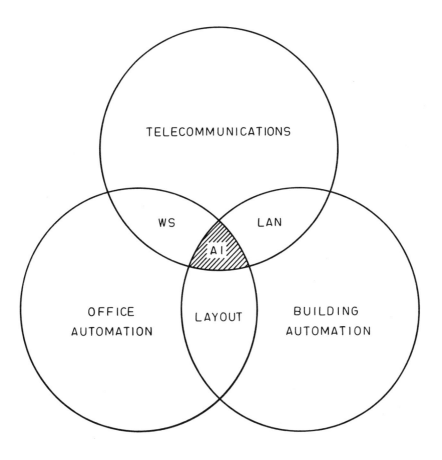

Teleports are a useful tool for any business seeking to reach a wider market, as they facilitate reaching a large area with sophisticated communications services, at a reasonable cost. They can also be used to transmit information and value-added services, thus expanding the field of financial products that a business can offer.

Teleports are necessary to help keep "intelligent" buildings, that is, those that are fully integrated and provided with sophisticated communications networks as well as environmental control systems, cost-efficient.[7] Teleports sustain an economy of scale by providing in-house services supported through an integrative approach.

The new generation of in-house services requires an infrastructure (see Figure 11–4), the development of which focuses on the areas of telecommunications, and office, and building automation.

In-house telecommunications systems use advanced digital switching (voice, data and message) in order to transfer information efficiently. Office automation provides state-of-the-art equipment and software; building automation encompasses areas such as integrated control, fire prevention, security, water consumption, energy management, diagnostics, and maintenance.

The overlap of these three main areas creates shared entities. These include workstations, whose proper functioning depends as much upon telecommunications as on office automation; local area networks, which interconnect workstations, servers and all other devices necessary for functioning of the intelligent building; and an optimal layout, which conserves resources while providing ideal office spaces.

If the neurons of the intelligent building are optical fibers running throughout the floors, the heart of all subsystems is artificial intelligence. In state-of-the-art implementations, AI constructs have a wide variety of functions. These include from assisting in executive decision-making, to performing quality control, monitoring energy and water resources, and providing security through computer-controlled remote surveillance.

Servers, workstations, and LAN[8] store, access, and transfer information (whether logical or physical subjects); electronic voucher processing has replaced paperwork in the areas of procurement, reception, and confirmation. Expense accounts are screened by expert systems and transferred to a host computer for processing.

Workstations are designed as electronic desks. Assisted by expert systems that handle multiwindows, bit map displays, and icons, and Hypertext, the workstation operator can use multimedia and Hypertext to create, edit, and transfer documents, including synthesized graphics and animation visuals.

An important function of the intelligent building and teleports will be to support multimedia teleconferencing. This technique will be a key element of many financial applications in the future, as it can be usefully employed whenever differently located individuals are involved in a cooperative activity. Requirements for telecommunications bandwidth, terminal facilities, and session control will vary according to the implementation; but, it will frequently be necessary to reserve the required network services in advance of the conference session.

Also, international teleconferencing will require not only user-friendly interfaces, but also translation facilities. One research firm, the Japanese Advanced Telecommunications Research Institute, is actively working on a method for translating language in real time.

The level of security and integrity associated with an intelligent building and its network will dictate the level of confidence that users have in it. Thus, the system must be capable of transfering multimedia communications safely, making reliable personal identification techniques available, and protecting the privacy of users.

Endnotes

1. Through mathematical models run on supercomputers and fed with instantaneous information through networks.

2. See also D.N. Chorafas and H. Steinmann, *Implementing Networks in Banking and Financial Services* (London: Macmillan, 1988).

3. Ken Auletta, *The Art of Corporate Success—The Story of Schlumberger* (New York: Penguin Books, 1985).

4. Billions of bits per second (GBPS).

5. State-owned post, telephone and telegraph operations.

6. The first trans-Atlantic communications cable was laid in 1866 to carry telegrams.

7. According to NTT, making a building "intelligent" costs only 6 to 7 percent more than installing traditional communications equipment; this investment can be recovered in five years from energy savings alone.

8. Local Area Network.

Chapter 12

Databases

Chapter 12

Databases

1. Introduction

A database (DB) is a model of the real world, but its information elements should be clearly projected and defined, available for diverse applications, and accessible to users through communications media. As well, they should be calibrated, updated, and supported by housekeeping services such as recovery, restart, journaling, and security.

Databases are an important source of support for trading and fund management. A collection of storage devices, however, does not constitute a database. In order to provide a working environment for end users, both private and public databases must be constructed.

The database administrator (DBA) and his or her assistants typically run a database with the help of a knowledge bank management system (KBMS), which creates a virtually homogeneous database out of a number of heterogenous distributed databases and the database management systems (DBMS) that reside in each machine.

Typically, a number of end-user workstations will communicate among themselves and with their database server on a local area network (see Figure 12-1) and will reach other databases through gateways. Each of these workstations contains a microfile that has applications programs, including both artificial intelligence and data processing.

Securities traders and investment advisors want an easy, efficient, and transparent database access; they also like doing text and data handling on their own. With networked workstations, they can receive and process information, maintain their microfiles, and solve problems single-handedly, all with a minimal amount of training.

2. Distributed Multimedia Databases

Communicating databases form a global database structure that requires polyvalent, AI-enriched capabilities in order to function properly. Knowledge-bank management systems can respond to this requirement by forming an upper layer with intensional capabilities over the extensional layer of the database management systems.

The efficiency of distributed databases is currently evaluated by examining the concepts of intentional databases and extensional databases and their applications. This subject will not concern us in this book.[1] On the other end, the issue of multimedia databases is quite relevant to the securities analyst, investment advisor, and trader.

The securities industry now focuses on distributed databases that may span continents (or even the globe) and on support multimedia capabilities. In a physical sense, a multimedia database is defined as traditional data plus voice (audio, sound), image, icons, and vector graphics, all in digital form. In a logical sense, a multimedia database is object[2] oriented, supports both data structures and text structures,

Figure 12–1   Networked Work Stations and File Servers

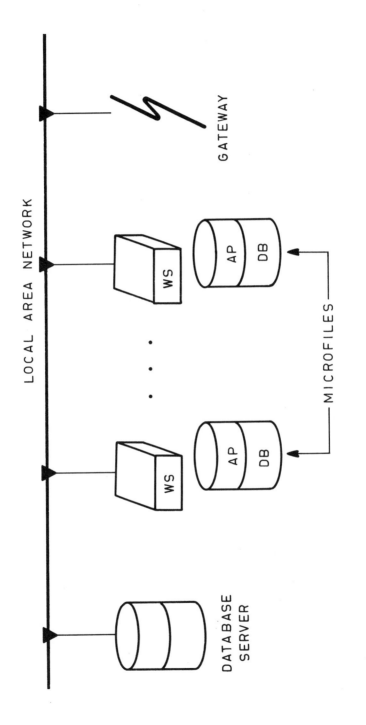

and integrates electronic documents for storage, retrieval, presentation, and exchange.

Multimedia databases are open-ended and extensible architectures. They are managed through relational principles at the base, but as discussed, require a KBMS at the upper layer.

The integrated use of multimedia is quite recent. It focuses more on document-type applications, which require order of magnitude advancements, than on the art of data handling; hence, there is a need for a system architecture that deals with all applications and their interconnections.

A multimedia architecture involves database management as well as intelligent user interfaces and uses recent advances in computer hardware and software (and in artificial intelligence) to handle increasingly sophisticated implementations.

Many areas of business—from engineering design to securities and foreign exchange operations, (which are the most complex, risky and rewarding in a banking environment, and therefore attract the largest high-technology investment), as well as management—now require sophisticated database systems. Distributed databases must be able to incorporate text-and-graphics-oriented information, sometimes with different data structures, and nearly always stored in diverse supports. In contrast with classical data, multimedia is often non-formatted text, figures, images, and voice messages.

Compound electronic documents require not only wideband communications and high resolution in presentation devices, but also new methods of information storage, including a means to account for uncertainty in retrieval. Solutions typically focus on the successfully exploring large volumes of information elements stored in distributed databases, and distributed multimedia databases could be a significant factor in enhancing the competitiveness of a securities firm.

Currently, there are few truly multimedia database systems in the investment banking community, and they are mostly in the experimental stage; nevertheless, their appearance in securities markets is guaranteed by technical breakthroughs that have been achieved in fields such as electronic publishing and engineering design.

Since the database is a model of the real world, an aggregate of information elements, algorithmns and heuristics see to it that this real world is transformed into a conceptual model. This is done in two steps: cognition and conceptual modeling.

The cognitive model centers on how acceptors can recognize the real world. A logical representation[3] follows, leading into model construction.

The conceptual model represents how the database designer recognizes the structures (in this case, the text and data structures) of the real world.

To represent the real world as a conceptual model, one must describe perceptions through a system of symbols. These could be alphanumeric characters or figures, including graphs, line drawings, plain and solid geometry, and icons.

An icon is a familiar object that is used to aid in representation and understanding. Other symbols, some of whose usage has become second nature, are images, including paintings, carvings, photographs, films, and video frames as well as audio, such as voices and other sounds. A combination of these helps to express a multimedia structure.

One of the challenges of the cognition process is that the knowledge and intelligence of the acceptor(s) may differ, leading to diverse interpretations. Multimedia structures will look the same only in terms of digitization (i.e. a series of bits that may represent either of the media and can be stored in a computer system).

The breadth of information that can be handled by computer has tremendously increased because of advances in the representation of real world objects. In the past, an object such as a map or a voice recording could not be stored in a computer database because of the inadequacy of input, output, and storage hardware/software. Today, it can not only be stored as a compound document (see Figure 12-2), but also manipulated.

Securities trading, investment advising, Forex operations, and other financial business lines benefit from advances in the areas of computer-aided design (CAD), word processing (WP), and new support media such as optical disks and digital recording.

In the area of handling multimedia information, however, the goal is not only to store a real-world object and allow a user to make changes to it, but also to understand the function of that object and to use the computer system to execute that function effectively.

3. The Concept of a Global Database

To turn themselves into an international trading network, several financial companies are now attempting to create after-hours solutions supporting twenty-four hour trading. In response, CHIPS (in New York) and CHAPS (in London) are planning to repackage and provide value-added services in fields such as portfolio management and analytical advice for money managers and corporate treasurers.

What these efforts have in common is that the thrust toward globalization is causing companies to attempt to link their databases into a worldwide network. For example, the three essential sections of the databases on Forex and securities prices—volume on trades and effective prices, perceived prices by other institutions and information providers, and a bank's own price estimates (corporate assets, liquidity risk, other risks, currencies, debt, equities, and commodities markets)—all need to be global.

Figure 12–2   A Multimedia Presentation

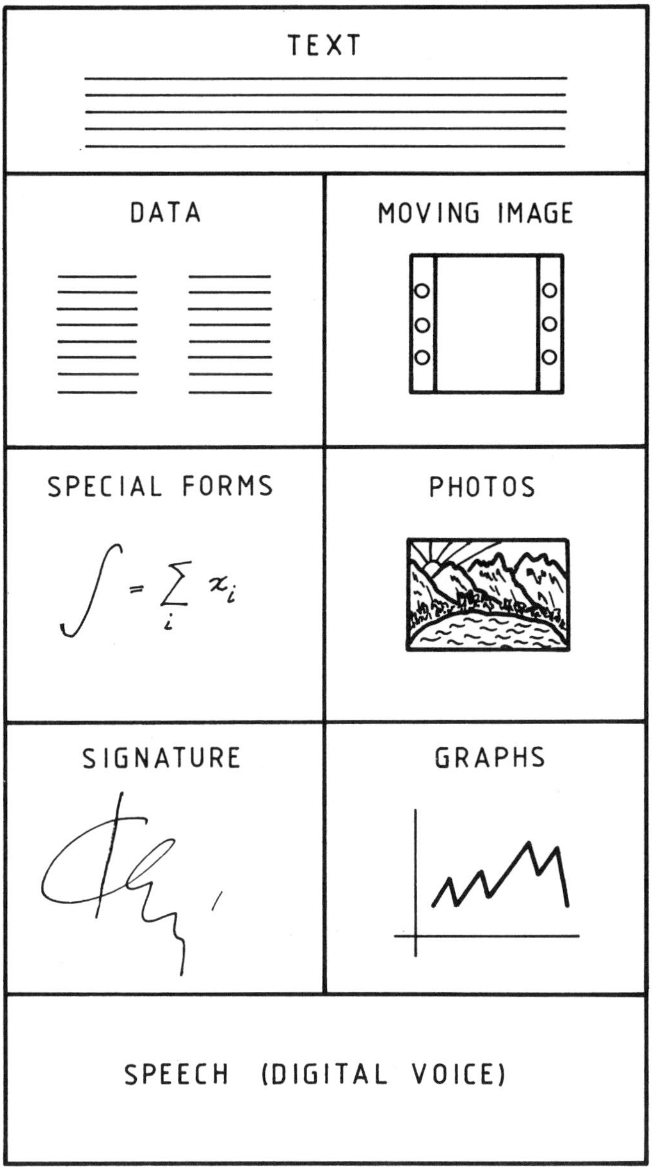

These information elements must be available in the database for ad hoc retrieval as well as manipulation in real space. As already explained, real space means real time on a networked worldwide basis, as if the broadly distributed databases were initially concentrated at the very point the ad hoc query was made.

Real space gives an investment bank a competitive edge, and for good reason. In its implementation, a global database is an aggregate of databases containing objects and, therefore, both information elements and commands. As discussed, all objects, from the microfile distributed file servers to the central text and data warehouse(s), are encapsulated callable entities pertinent to the global database structure.

The text and database, which should be a shared resource, will typically be a collection of interrelated information elements. Its structure must permit it to meet the needs of many kinds of users; also, access, authorization, journaling, insertion, modification, and deletion must be under control in a global sense. Significant service will be contributed by both the distributed and the centrally located data dictionaries— that is, repositories of information about text and data (metadata) regarding the financial institution's information environment.

Global databases cannot be successfully implemented (if at all) without a strategic plan for end-user computing and for administrating central resources. This plan should be made a priori, not when a firm discovers that it cannot support or maintain the diverse and incompatible databases throughout its organization.

The establishment of a system integration plan is also important; if a database system lacks global view, or is incomplete or inaccurate, if its tools are weak or hard to use, or if it lacks of common user interfaces, and contains applications that are hard to develop and maintain, the overall result will be multiple, overlapping but partial structures that stay as diverse islands and become expensive and ineffective.

A financial institution's global database should also contain sunset clauses, which tell the computer when and where to delete part of its contents.

Information elements that are no longer important should be weeded out of the system; those that are important but no longer useful should be archived in ways other than live storage, for example, on optical disks. Otherwise, valuable on-line database space will be consumed by old data. Archives, however, should be kept on-line as system backup (a much easier process than dumping to tape and then attempting to manage the thousands of tapes in the library).

At the global level, agile end-user interfaces are indispensable for dealing with multimedia entities such as images, voice and other sound recordings, complex graphics structures in vector form, text, classical data, and compound electronic documents. Companies should also support graphic and other objects which are linked to database utilization, including dynamic update and should explore the problems of synchronizing different media, for example, sound and images in the context of animated graphics.

For effective global multimedia management, a firm should have general-purpose enduser-oriented document supervisors operating at the database level. It is also important to have solutions to cognitive issues involved in presentation and manipulation. Supports include

1. enabling modalities, such as voice annotation of graphics and text;

2. speech command augmentation of menus or icon selection by mouse;

3. touch and speech command in a put-that-there mode;

4. hypertext, or non-sequential document handling.

Hypertext is an approach to information management in which data is stored in a network of nodes connected by links. These nodes may contain classical data, text, source code, graphics, audio, video, and other forms, all of which are meant to be viewed and manipulated interactively.

Hypertext solutions can involve the cognitive aspects of using and designing hypertext systems, supporting collaborative work, the management of complexity in large information networks, and strategies for effective use of hypertext, as well as copyrights, royalties, and social issues. The information technologist also has to pay attention to creating a homogeneous and fairly compatible database out of numerous heterogenous and incompatible databases developed over the years.

This is the crux of system integration at the database level, and it has to be achieved in a distributed sense. But without the enabling technology of AI—from taxonomical classification to pattern recognition and the attainment of a virtually consistent database image—a technologist can neither organize nor manage even single media databases.

As far as a financial institution's global database is concerned, paper, whether produced by typewriters and paper filing or by word processors, is a liability. It involves high costs and inhibits universal access. The preferred mode is imaging, or optical disk storage and retrieval.[4] Multimedia supports such as this must be networked among themselves, computer resources, and workstations. And they should be administered through knowledge-bank management systems (KBMS).

4. An Office-Document Architecture

In the real-time retrieval of information elements, particularly from a distributed multimedia database, two approaches to text retrieval—full inversion, and a serial search of the entire database—have traditionally been used. Serial searches take considerable time. Full text-inversion approaches, on the other hand, involve index structures that may become as large or even larger than the originally stored text and data. Time is also required in order to update the indexes when new information elements are added or deleted.

What is often forgotten is that both serial search and full inversion are methods that originated with small databases. As the size of databases grew, they became increasingly inefficient; serial searches, for example, are done through keys. The use of a key is a process of elimination; at each step, there is a choice of two or more items, and the machine must choose the description that best fits the searcher's objectives. With the exploding text and databases, serial search time has becomes extremely long, even if some level of parallelism is included.

Newer database-handling solutions provide users with the ability to implement multiple keys, define files, and access structures of encapsulated information elements. They provide for synonyms but also require new conceptual approaches to database design as well as truly powerful machines.

Coupled with very fast and reasonably low-cost computers such as the Connection Machine (which features 2,500 to 10,000 MIPS and costs about $3 million), adaptable database heuristics make it possible to exploit the advantages of episodic memory. Memory Based Reasoning[5] is event-oriented and leads to a different type of reasoning than do other solutions, including relational databases. Its main thrust is the intensive use of storage to recall specific episodes, which contrasts with the traditional assumption in AI that most expert knowledge is encoded in the form of rules.

Such tools are very important: they ensure that all the end-user needs to know is how to ask ad hoc queries and exploit personal views as they develop during daily work. The computer should help frame the user views into conceptual text and data structures. Figure 12–3 shows what an intelligent front end as opposed to a DBMS rear end should provide.

The knowledge-bank management system supervises network-wide and on a global basis the operation of an episodic memory structure, ensuring that multimedia IE are stored at point of origin, downloaded to their destination, received by the latter, and retrieved ad hoc on the basis of queries. It would be easier to do this job if data structures (read: text structures) were normalized throughout the system when the different distributed databases were created; generally speaking, however, this has not been done. Furthermore, today, network-wide normalization cannot be done system-wide without disrupting ongoing operations, which means it cannot be done at all. There are solutions, however.

State-of-the-art financial institutions ensure that the retrieval mechanism follows heuristic approaches, which provide better results than deterministic or even stochastic ones. Heuristic solutions involve AI, which leads to the concept of idea databases.

The term idea databases is very recent, and though its implementation may not be that easy, concept itself can be expressed as a simple query: "I need sales statistics for Treasury; which Treasuries will give me representative statistics for market liquidity?"

This is a fuzzy query and, as such, can only get a non-crisp answer. It is also a complex query that involves a concept, rather than memory locations, and set of operations that require the retrieval of many IE in addition to sorting, com-

Figure 12-3   Man–Machine Interface through an Intelligent Front End

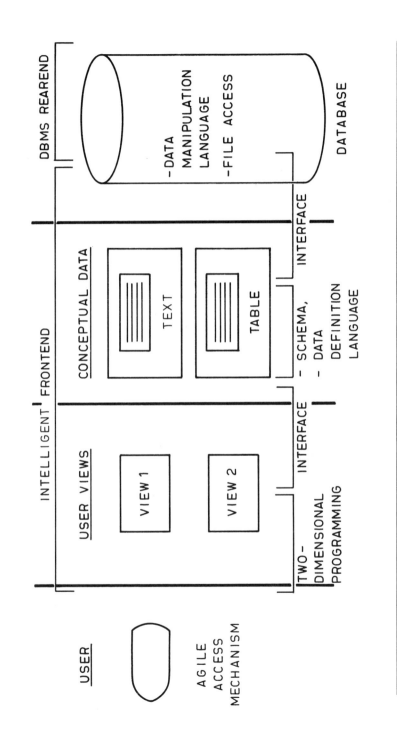

paring, and developing a pattern that might answer the query.

The search for a new, AI-enriched methodology to assist database usage is motivated by growing end user requirements and the fact that queries are ad hoc, as well as expressed in a fuzzy way. But, it is made possible by technological advances. With classical computers, efficiency is based 98 percent on database design, and 2 percent on the means by which the query is generated. Idea databases change this ratio. Query generation is done through AI and has a much larger effect than design on the execution of database operations.

This procedure is closely related to electronic document searches, and, far from classical office automation. Emphasis is now increasingly placed on an intelligent office document architecture. The developing document retrieval theory for *ad hoc* and other queries outlines the properties for query language in office environments:[6]

The incomplete specification of assertions allow the query to be framed in a sense:

< Report, Text >

Flexible specification assertions make it possible to exploit a range of queries, as well as retrieving look-alike IE, which will be further screened in a more focused manner. Interrelating assertions about different views of documents calls for a manipulation language associated with text/data models. In all cases, query specification must ensure that there is a mechanism for the generation of query predicates able to capture and represent the uncertainty associated with many queries.

Uncertainty is a very important part of retrieval, and idea database approaches account for this fact. The efficient handling of uncertainty will, in the future, become not only a fundamental part of office studies, but also a basic component of managerial and professional productivity.

The hypothesis that a database search that is fuzzy (vague, uncertain, heuristic) gives much better results than a crisp and precise search was part of the conclusions reached at the April 1987 NBS Symposium on Office Automation. Further developments have shown that with certainty, only very limited goals can be satisfied. Partial match is a richer approach than full match; it is always possible to reach a given information element by applying successive filters.

Finally, another contribution of intelligent databases is text animation. In order to drive a computer-based consultation, animation distills the knowledge and information contained in text residing in the knowledge bank. The Microelectronics and Computer Technology Corporation (in Austin, Texas) is actively working on a program-animation project, the information from which can be transferred to the financial industry.

5. A Text-and-Data Warehouse

While up until now most data processing installations have performed mainly procedural tasks, in the future they will need to be broad in scope and coverage, as well as integrated with the control of the systems they monitor. The argument for integrative solutions is strengthened by the fact that practically all computer users find that much of their hardware, as well as their software, is incompatible. Heterogeneity is the norm for operating systems, database management systems, data structures, and applications programs.

Maintaining applications programs today often absorbs between 70 and 80 percent of the human resources in an organization. Also, because their applications often overlap, many of the current programs are quite inefficient.

There are similar problems with supported databases; financial institutions with experience in system management understand integrative goals cannot be attained with a traditional approach.

There is an urgent need for solutions that will make possible the network-wide warehousing of applications programs and information elements, as well as tools necessary for extracting objects (commands, data) in an ad hoc manner under uncertainty. As discussed in this book, the solutions to these problems would be embodied in a Corporate Memory Facility.[7]

GTE's Intelligent Database Assistant (IDA) and its implementation in California (CALIDA) represents focused efforts to solve text and data warehouse problems within one organization, in spite of heterogeneous supports.

For data and for programs, metadata (data about data) and metaprograms (programs about programs) are needed. Metaprogramming is a prerequisite for the program transformation technique known as *partial evaluation*. Some research groups, for example, ICOT (Japan's New Generation Computer Project), use partial evaluation metainterpreters to compile very high-level nonprocedural knowledge representations into a lower level. This seems to be the most solid approach so far devised for reverse engineering.[8]

The process is called partial evaluation because, in broad terms, the *metainterpreter* runs a high-level code until the code becomes input-dependent. This approach will likely be a basis for the new generation of languages employed in the 1990s; but, it will not work on old programs, as IBM's mainframe Repository aims to do.

Since the failure of IBM's UNCOL (Universal Computer Language) in 1959, no company has yet fond a solution able to reverse-engineer computer programs for anything other than trivial tasks. Text and data, however, are much easier to manipulate, even to reverse-engineer, than programs.

Using knowledge engineering approaches, it is possible to work through metadata, collecting in one logical location (which may be a hundred or a thousand physical locations) all the pieces of information elements that are necessary to manage corporate text/data/image requirements and associated processes. Though it may not in itself contain detailed corporate data, an AI-enriched repository will

1. know where all multimedia data is located;

2. understand how to get this data;

3. contain data attributes (i.e., definitions, size, type, and other characteristics);

4. include all necessary rules about data;

5. provide needed security measures;

6. incorporate a procedural code to be executed on appropriate information elements.

In other words, if managed through a distributed KBMS, the repository will behave in a knowledge-intense manner. (Figure 12–4 shows the functions supported by a KBMS and those supported by a DBMS.)

A couple of distinctions should be made between a knowledge bank and a database. A coarse-grain difference is that a database uses implementation-oriented structures to organize information elements in a way that facilitates efficient computer processing, and a knowledge bank uses AI techniques (i.e., it operates in a manner that reflects a real-world situation and allows for intelligent IE handling).

At fine-grain level, the DBMS deals with implementation, concentrating on how the machine sees and processes the IE, while the KBMS addresses itself to users, focusing on the way each particular user looks at text and data models of the real world, hence, the notion of the intensional database.

Figure 12–4   A Layered Approach to Data Resources

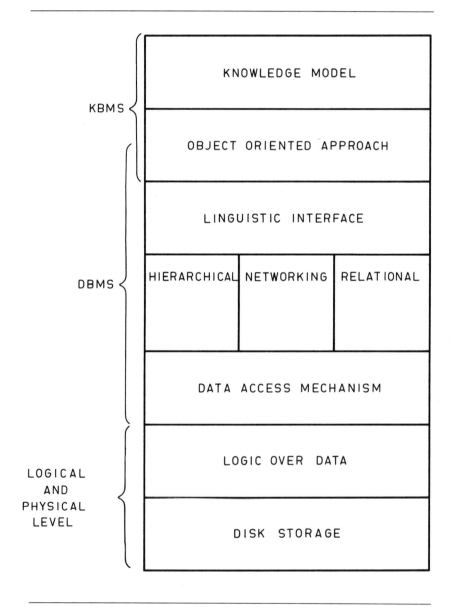

The KBMS solution could replace the heterogenous collection of various proprietary dictionaries, catalogs, libraries, methods, and processes with a set of coherent, manageable, and standardized objects. Each development tool, operating system, data access method, processor, user window, and so on, would have an active part in the corporate computer and communications network.

This is more a concept than a solution. The method is too ambitious to work one hundred percent, even within one organization. But it might work partially, with a focus on only its most vital elements. Another major goal, that of creating one logical homogeneous database out of many physical heterogenous databases, has been approached by IDA. The architectural concept behind it, known as federated databases, has already been implemented.

Metadata approaches are hard work. If this work is properly done, however, a corporate text and data warehouse is a good solution for those financial companies that are investing money and resources in sprawling databases and in the communications systems needed to interconnect them.

Databases are booming. One organization, the Lawrence Livermore National Laboratory, has reached ten terabytes (a billion bytes of computer memory) of on-line storage; and the largest American banks have exceeded one terabyte with a couple having two terabytes or more.

In coming years, Fortune 1000 organizations will be hard-pressed to develop solutions able to handle the tremendous recent increases in on-line storage. And with many computer vendors seemingly incapable of assisting with the job, user organizations may have to do it alone.

Fortunately, user institutions seem to have ideas about how to integrate their sprawling databases and implement image systems. The aim is to handle plain text messages and images, as well as coded messages that may not be governed by prior probability distributions, across databases and networks in a multimedia sense.

6. Modeling and Filtering Different End-User Views

Managing financial databases usually involves handling text and data; but, there are also growing requirements for graphics and image handling. With graphics, (as with data) heterogeneity is the norm; software and hardware are available from a number of suppliers; and the state of integration leaves much to be desired. Were higher and lower functions consistently presented and file structures standardized, it would be easy to transport files among networked databases and between successive levels; but, file structures vary, and the input data for different modules are quite often in different formats.

Another key problem is that of differing views. A view is a specific semantic representation of an object. Different trading modules may be seen as different views of the same object. Each trader, financial analyst, or investment advisor, when working on a model, expresses an independent view. The challenge is to keep consistency between different views and still provide for a valid working aggregate. This can be difficult because traders and account managers work on a variety of components and subsystems. They often use home-made semantics, handle text and data in different formats, develop and/or receive non-compatible views, and do experimentation and simulation that require consistent database access without the benefit of an integration routine.

One solution is view modeling, in which each user's requirements are analyzed and represented in some common form. Associated with each view is a set of entities, attributes, and interrelationships among entities, describing objects and events in the actual system being modeled. This leads to the concept of view integration.

As the end user's requirements (specified in a standard form) consolidate into a single global view, inconsistencies and redundancies must be recognized and resolved. If the eventual target system provides a subschema mechanism, the individual results of view modeling may be used to design the subschema. After further processing, the result of view integration becomes the schema.

A trader or investment advisor will interactively build a microfile, design its contents, access portions of the global database, and support a variety of customer- and market-oriented activities. Because the design of a financial database is interdisciplinary, there will also be communications needs to be addressed.

Solutions should go beyond text, data, and image to respond to the end user's domain knowledge and to incorporate the user's level of expertise. There are many valid arguments against a simple bipolar view of the end user as either novice or expert in favor of one that recognizes varying levels of expertise. It takes knowledge-engineering skills to account for varied individual preferences in interactive computer usage, but this is the way of the 1990s.[9]

As discussed in this chapter, it is important use object-oriented approaches. Elaborated within the context of a financial database, objects are intended to be used repeatedly. In a dynamic financial environment, they may contain an arbitrary mixture of image, graphics, data, and text created at any position on a viewing surface.

Alterations may be applied to a selected object occurrence or to all occurrences; the same is true of filtering. Any instance of a repeated object can be edited in an ad hoc form, given a new version number, manipulated for focal requirements, and integrated into a larger object. Objects may also be filtered by each user according to the needs of the moment.

Filtering should take place interactively and embrace all of the distributed database if applications requirements demand it. A query, for example, may indicate vague comparators, such as, more than . . . or less than . . ., or may involve a range of values. A filter can be built mathematically that will represent vague and even imprecise queries.

A financial institution made a real-life application with vague comparators. It addresses itself to a database containing data from companies quoted at NYSE, and involves the following three data filters:

1. Filter I represents greater than x return on investment (ROI) on a suggested portfolio.

2. Filter II represents the maximum risk acceptable.

3. Filter III represents degrees of freedom in regard to factor y as per investment manager's advice.

This investment portfolio data filter was implemented using possibility theory.[10] Figure 12–5 shows one of the filters, return on investment. The possibility curve expresses a subjective likelihood.

For example, of the companies in the sample under examination (taken from the database), none is likely to have less than 5 percent ROI; there is an increasing possibility that ROI will be between 5 percent and 15 percent; the possibility is roughly the same of finding companies with ROI between 15 percent and 20 percent (virtually a cutoff point). There is a small possibility of locating up to 25 percent ROI and none of locating a greater percentage.

The notion of relative importance is implemented through weights, which tell the expert system that the investment advisor is not interested in companies with less than 10 percent ROI. There is a growing interest for ROI up to 18 percent while the highest interest lies in the 18- to 25-percent range.

Figure 12–5 Notion of Vague Weights in Fuzzy Engineering

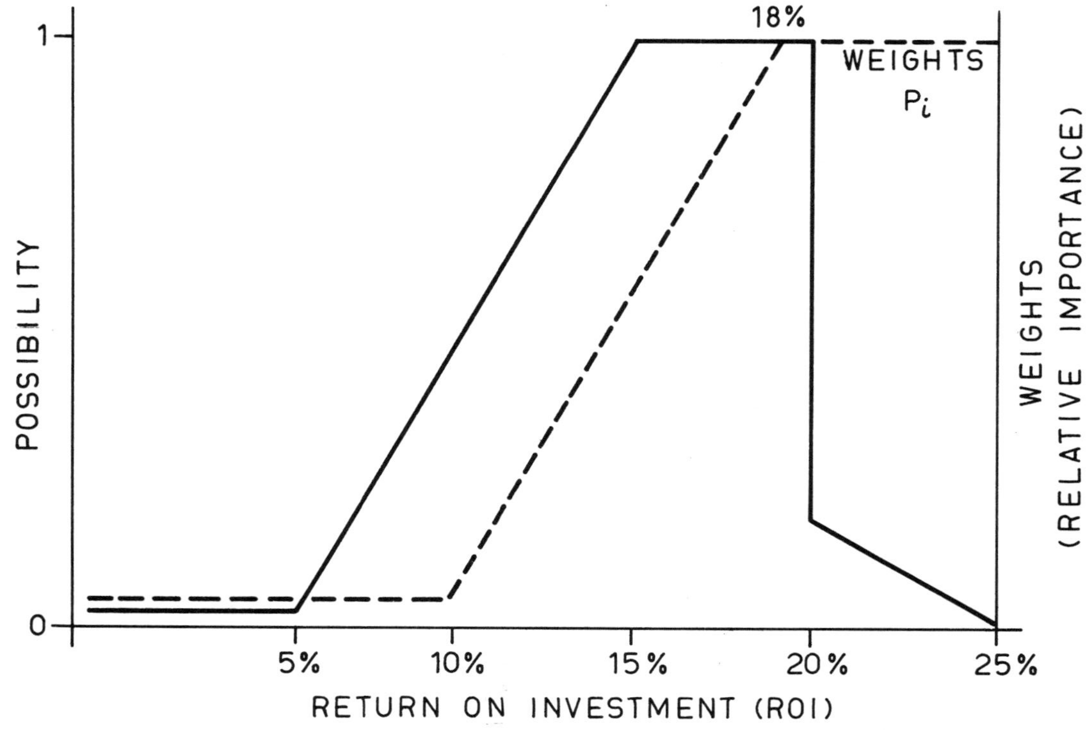

Mathematical and AI-based solutions are needed in order to define the notion of filtering, which involves classification, choice, and optimization. For other financial applications, technicians have been developing filters that combine the evidence from two independent variables using Bayes' rule. The method of these specialists is to select from a large number of alternatives through multi-variable filtering and reduce polyvalent real-life situations with certain implicit assumptions (a technique beyond that of simulation).

These considerations may seem somewhat technical; nevertheless, because of the large monetary investments in high technology made by securities houses and other financial institutions, management often finds it wise to ask technical assistants to make thorough evaluations and then follow-up on the results.

Endnotes

1. See D.N. Chorafas and H. Steinmann, *Supercomputers* (New York; McGraw-Hill, 1990).

2. An object is an abstract data structure (extensional) or data and command (intensional); it is an entity that is callable by end users, workstations, programs, and other objects, and can be located anywhere in the distributed database.

3. The equivalent of the conceptual schema in ANSI/X3/SPARC.

4. See also D. N. Chorafas, *The New Technologies* (Manchester, England: Sigma Press, and London: John Wiley, 1990).

5. Developed by Dr. David Waltz, of Brandeis University and of Thinking Machines, Inc., Cambridge, MA.

6. Exemplified by ISO's Office Document Architecture.

7. See D.N. Chorafas, *Risk Management* (London: Butterworths, 1990).

8. How successful reverse engineering can be is a big, open question. So far results have been trivial.

9. See also D. N. Chorafas, *System Architecture and System Design* (New York: McGraw-Hill, 1989).

10. See D.N. Chorafas, *Knowledge Engineering* (New York: D. Van Nostrand Reinhold, 1990).

Chapter 13

Supercomputers

Chapter 13

Supercomputers

1. Introduction

Since the end of the 1980s, leading financial services have been using number-crunching processors that bringing a high multiple of the power of room-size, mainframe computers to units not much bigger than a desk. These new masters of the technological domain, supercomputers, have two to three orders of magnitude more power than classical machines. Their performance is measured not in millions of instructions per second (MIPS), but in giga instructions per second (GIPS).

Several scientific contributions have gone into the development of supercomputers. One of these, the very high density memory chip, is an essential part of modern computer technology. A million-bit chip was first mass-produced in 1985; today 4-megabit chips are a standard part of mainframes, maxis, and personal computers.

To give an idea of what this means, a 4-million-bit memory chip can store nearly four hundred pages of double-spaced typewritten text and read them in one-quarter of a second; and its memory cells are so small that forty-eight thousand of them would fit in an area the size of the period at the end of this sentence.

Even this 4-million-bit chip will be superseded soon, by a *16-million-bit* chip. Selected portions of this chip have already been fabricated and are being tested; in the meantime, research laboratories are now experimenting with chips that will store 64-million-bits of information, and even examining prototypes for a 256-million-bit chip, whose circuit lines will be only a few hundred atoms wide.

The use of memory chips is not the only feature of supercomputers; another is number-crunching power (see Section 2); yet another is logical processing capabilities. Supercomputers are thus capable of handling hybrid systems that include sophisticated AI constructs and simulators together with more classical DP parts; they also contain advanced software tools. Another major reason to use supercomputers is that they are cost effective. One benchmark showed that, for doing a certain job, the cost of using a mainframe with vector processing was 47.5 times higher than the cost of using a hypercube solution.

The military, universities, and the atomic energy and petroleum industries were the first to use supercomputers. Now Wall Street has joined the user population. Major investments banks and securities houses are installing the number-crunchers in order to maintain a competitive edge.

2. What Makes a Supercomputer?

Some faulty concepts of supercomputers advanced by certain mainframe vendors define them as machines that cost more than $10 million, or that only Los Alamos can afford; machines that do not yet exist; and machines that can run an infinite loop in less than two seconds.

While these are false definitions, they have a common thread; they seem to suggest that mainframes have still a long way to go—even if the most advanced applications (i.e., the exploitation of very large databases) have reached the limits of the von Neumann architecture of current computers. For a number of years, software costs have far exceeded hardware investments; hence, new architectural concepts are needed to provide solutions for the 1990s. Today's response to these needs is known as a fifth-generation computer (5GC).[1]

Over the years, the term supercomputer has been used to refer to machines that were substantially faster than whatever were currently the fastest commercially available computers. In the late sixties and early seventies these supercomputers were experimental models. Some models, such as RP3 and GF11 at IBM's Watson Research Labs, are still experimental.

The first commodity machine to be designated a supercomputer was Cray 1 (designed by Seymour Cray and marketed by Cray Research). It was followed by Cray 2, in XMP and YMP versions.

By the mid-eighties a number of array processors, called minisupercomputers and patterned after the Cray machine, were commercially available; some of them were much lower in cost than the Crays (and a little slower). One of them, an Allient machine, was first installed in the investment banking community by Morgan Stanley.

In the mid-eighties, the cosmic cube, a truly parallel architecture for closely coupled multiprocessing applications, was designed by the California Institute of Technology. This computer, which is also known as a hypercube, has since been successfully marketed by Thinking Machines, as the Connection Machine, by Intel Scientific as the Intel Personal Supercomputer (iPSC), and also by NCube.

The direct binary hypercube network consists of $N = 2n$ nodes, which are interconnected by using point-to-point links according to a simple rule; two nodes whose binary addresses differ in exactly one-bit position are connected by a link. Each of these bit positions corresponds to a dimension in the network. Figure 13–1 shows a binary 4-cube with 16 nodes.

Figure 13–1   A Hypercube Computer Architecture

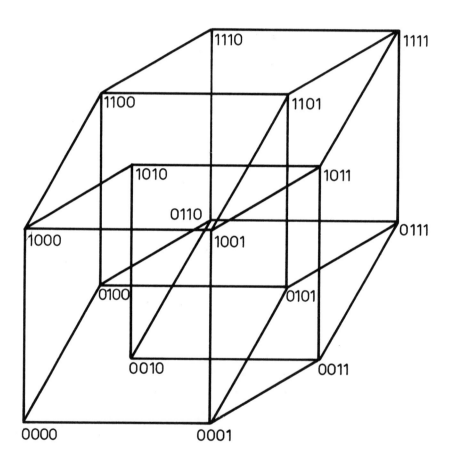

A node in the hypercube structure has a processing element, local memory, and enough capability to communicate with its neighbors by the transmission of messages. Each node "talks" to others by routing incoming messages. This routing can be done with the use of software, by the processing element itself; or, the node may incorporate a switching module that will perform this function.

This description seems to suggest that a supercomputer architecture such as the hypercube is non-von Neumann.[2] In other words, it constitutes a departure architecturally from the computer structure—now known as the von Neumann bottleneck—that has dominated designs from the late forties until today.

A supercomputer can thus be defined as having the following characteristics (keeping in mind that not all of them should or could be present at the same time in the same machine):

1. Its computing power is greater than 1,000 MIPS.

The Connection Machine (CM-2) delivers 10,000 million instructions per second peak power (10 GIPS), and 2,500 MIPS steady power (2.5 GIPS). As discussed, MIPS is no longer a preferred unit of measurement; with supercomputers, it is better to speak in terms of billions of instructions per second (GIPS).[3]

2. It has a new design architecture.

Supercomputers include array processors, which are older models, and hypercubes and mesh types, both of which are new architectures.

3. It features a high degree of parallelism.

Supercomputers can be fine-grain such as the Connection Machine, a massively parallel hypercube that contains up to 65,536 nodes, or coarse-grain, such as iPSC. This hypercube has up to 128 nodes, but each of them is much more powerful than any of the CM-2's nodes.

4.   It has the ability to turn a CPU-bound job into an I/O-bound job.

The central processing unit (CPU), a von Neumann design, is a limiting factor in computing complex problems that demand large amounts of power. Supercomputers reduce this time by more than two orders of magnitude; in some cases the bottleneck becomes the Input/Output (I/O).

5.   It incorporates advanced networking capabilities.

The hypercube itself is a network, and its many processors are interconnected by links that work at two to three megabits per second (MBPS). If incorporated into a communications network, the hypercube can be shared by many workstations, each of which will assign its work to a certain group of processors or virtual processors.

6.   It exploits very large databases.

As discussed in the preceding chapter, the exploitation of very large databases is an enormous challenge. The example of Dow Jones shows the effectiveness of massively parallel supercomputers in handling complex database jobs (see Sec. 5).

7.   It uses new types of software.

Supercomputers use various types of artificial intelligence, from expert systems to pattern recognition, and also provide environments in which to analyze and experiment with simulation.

8.   It ensures a significant cost effectiveness.

As discussed, supercomputers' operating cost is considerably less than that of mainframes; supercomputers are faster, more versatile, and more dependable over a large range of applications.

To recapitulate, supercomputers were once reserved for military, nuclear, and oil-exploration projects. Today their applications range from airline crew scheduling to mapping the financial market into the computer. With their ability to analyze developing business opportunities in real space, supercomputers will add a new dimension, both qualitative and quantitative, to the financial industry.

3. Newer and Newer, Faster and Faster

Of 600 readers polled in a 1988 study by Datamation, 12 percent used supercomputers, and 30 percent employed some type of high-performance computing solutions, whether minisupercomputers, mainframes with attached vector processors, or supercomputer timesharing services. These percentages have increased significantly over the last three years; today, of firms without supercomputers, a significant number plan to purchase one or to time-share in a Service Bureau.

Nevertheless, the development of supercomputers is best thought of not as a revolution, but as an evolution. Networks of processors were first used in the Solomon project of the 1950s, and later in ILIAC machines. These were followed by vector processors, pipeline organization, and many other efforts in hardware and software; each step along the way had many antecedents, in the form of both successes and failures.

Today's supercomputers were developed with the help of very-large-scale-integration (VLSI) technology. Other breakthroughs were also significant; for example, researchers involved in the CLIP project, among others, developed parallel pixel processing, which led to visualization—that is, the turning of numbers into images. Nobel Laureate Kenneth G. Wilson compared the development of visualization to that of the microscope and telescope. He said that while the art is not yet perfected, its breakthrough nature will accelerate the discovery process and reduce time spent in problem conception and data analysis.

Not only in finance and economics, but also in scientific exploration, multimedia visualization is the eyepiece of the computer. The best advice to computer vendors and their researchers is to develop faster, larger supercomputers that can effectively model and predict complex dynamic systems.

In the financial industries, particularly in financial research, graphics is the new frontier. Dynamic graphics and image animation require parallel computers, and parallel processing goals are at the heart of research regarding the design and marketing of new financial instruments.

Parallel processing offers superior performance at much lower prices by simplifying software effort; inference processors and memory devices are networked and the whole engine works as a unification entity whose architecture separates processing proper from I/O, but automatically integrates the results.

The advent of massive parallelism promises significant increases in computational speed; it clears the way for teramips (one million MIPS) performance. As discussed, a GIPS means a billion instructions and a GFLOPS a billion floating point operations per second; a teraflop is one trillion floating point operations per second. Figure 13–2 shows megaflop

**Figure 13–2   32-Bit Floating Point Operations per
Second per Processor—
A Supercomputer Evolution**

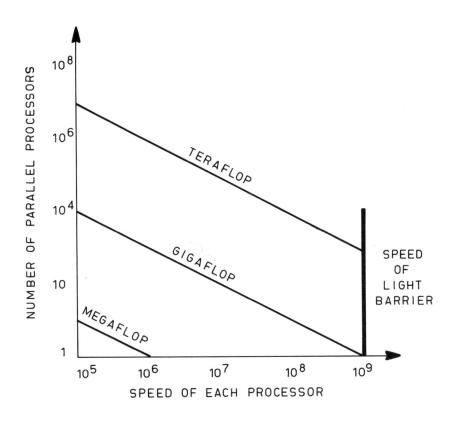

LOG–LOG PLOT OF A PARAMETER SPACE FOR
COMPUTER POWER

(not MIPS, but floating operations), gigaflop, and teraflop computing speeds positioned against constraints due to communications limits and the speed of light.[4]

The graph in Figure 13–2 is a logarithmic-logarithmic (log-log) plot of a parameter space. In a massively parallel machine; the speed of each processor is plotted along the abscissa, and the number of processors are plotted along the ordinate. The peak processing power of the computer is the product of these two factors; therefore, the limit of constant peak processing power appears as straight lines with a slope of –1 on the log-log graph.

The Defense Advanced Research Projects Agency (DARPA) is currently sponsoring two new computing projects, contracted by Thinking Machines and Intel, that will use machines three orders of magnitude faster than the fastest current supercomputers. Also, in January 1990, AT&T announced its optical switching computer prototype, which also works three orders of magnitude faster than the best machine available today.

In exploiting fine-grain parallelism and high-speed power, it is necessary to use radically new software designs and significant architectural simplifications. One basic software principle incorporated into fine-grain massively parallel computers is a programming paradigm calling for the association of processors with data. For instance, an application might associate one processor (node) per walker in a Monte Carlo calculation.

Mapping complex applications into the computer is made possible through the notion of interprocessor connectivity. As previously discussed, processors can communicate point-to-point with anything from a near neighbor to a remote node in the hypercube.

In a financial environment, a supercomputer model of operations may involve, for example, the real-life mapping of the topology of financial markets (e.g., New York, London,

Zurich, and Tokyo). Hypercube infrastructures will permit the admission of more financial markets as requirements develop. Within each of these markets, it is possible to map other factors, such as, currencies to be handled at the selected constellation of financial markets and customer profiles based on past business and on AI-assisted models.

Each of the business factors selected can be analyzed at a finer level. There may be, for example, a need for at least three customer profiles—corporate client, institutional investor, and wealthy individual.

Other projects are using supercomputers in applications such as message-based, massively-parallel processing environments with multiple data streams; still others are using parallel engines for conventional computer applications, such as transaction processing and relational database systems, by implementing redundancy techniques to support continuous availability of data.

In many supercomputer projects, a primary thrust of the software effort has been the development of algorithms to distribute data across every node in the system. Databases are being designed both to provide for parallel access to data in a single file distributed across several nodes and to ensure continuous availability of all data in the system through the use of redundancy.

Algorithms and heuristics are being developed to minimize the overhead required to achieve greater reliability of databases. Additional research is done to develop low overhead communication solutions, thereby taking advantage of the performance of distributed processors and memory devices.

4. Using Supercomputers in Forex and Securities

Morgan Stanley, Bear Stearns, Prudential Bache, and other brokerage houses all now use supercomputers in their operations. Why? To obtain results. By using supercomputers in Forex, for example, firms can perform massive currency transactions, thus taking advantage of transient currency exchange rate inequalities throughout the financial market. A supercomputer's subsecond response time makes it possible to benefit from market anomalies.

Software is, as always, vital. Petri-nets can help by representing various currencies as nodes in a complete directed graph. According to a study done by Professor David Waltz, chief scientist of Thinking Machines, a critical factor is the logarithm of the exchange rate between the two currencies represented by the two vertices of hypercube edges. According to this approach, the shortest path between two nodes or, between a node and itself, is the most profitable sequence of currency transactions. Whenever the shortest path is less than 1, money is made purely on the transaction itself.

A fine-grain parallel supercomputer is ideally suited for this type of application. Regardless of the number of exchange rates fed into the machine, the time required to plan a transaction is nearly constant (polylog time on the Connection Machine). Such an application, however, is compute-intensive, requiring minimal data storage but fast network transfer.

A similar approach can characterize stockmarket futures trading. The method described in the preceding paragraphs is also valid for stocks and bonds. The model to be built will require a knowledge acquisition phase that focuses on how the securities expert perceives a business opportunity and makes decisions. Such a model should emphasize a dynamic transaction environment and the ability to match trades.

Projects like these have been done with serial computers, from mainframes to PCs; nevertheless, parallel computing takes the process into another dimension, as its advantages go well beyond greater power (which in itself is significant). Figure 13-3 shows an impressive speed factor: for twelve

Figure 13-3   Parallel Execution Speedup Ratios vs. Processors

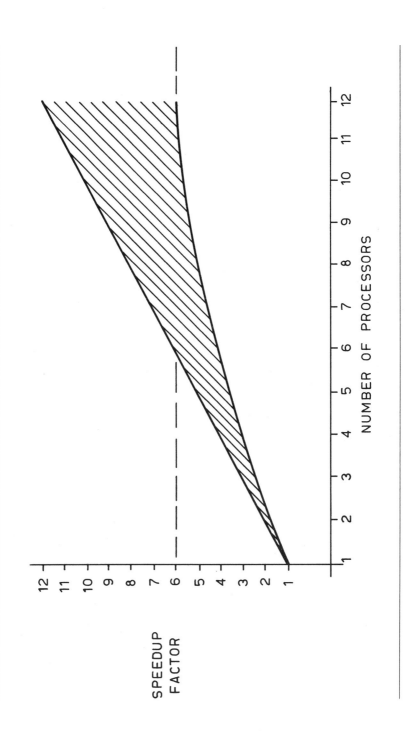

parallel processors, the speedup goes from six to twelve, depending on which application is running on the system.

Computing power is very important in estimation, prediction, and hypothesis testing, which are all part of securities and Forex applications. Furthermore, optimization requires factorization and inversion of very large matrices, which calls for high speed computation; hence, the impact of the the speed factor in parallelization.

In trading, it is also helpful to use software that is able to emulate customer-generated demand for transactions (Forex or securities) as well as the responses of corresponding banks and brokerage houses, all the way to acceptance (i.e., to the conclusion of the deal). Along this line of thinking, an artificial intelligence application by Manufacturers Hanover Trust supplies dealers not only with business opportunity advice for Forex transactions, but also with the base price at which such transactions will be profitable to MHTC.

While the dealer will still do the actual trade, he or she will perform a currency switch while fully informed in real time of opportunities, risks, and limits. By enriching the MHTC approach with the services to be provided by a global network, it is possible to do a real-space implementation that integrates networks and supercomputers.

Advanced implementations also require agile, yet consistent, end user interfaces; consistency refers to the quality of the consultation shell. The end user has to rely on a consistent set of visual conventions that the system always respects. This is one of the cardinal principles in man-machine interface (MMI) design.

The same is true of presentation forms and escape mechanisms. If locked into a special mode, such as dialogue boxes, a user must be able to quit by a single standard command and be able to proceed with easily executed analytical ad hoc queries—a goal helped through greater computer power. These principles are important because supercomputers, even if made available to dealers in Forex and securities, will be of little use if their interfaces are jammed.

Software must ensure that an end user sees normal interfaces; the system should handle output routines incorporating receive, send, and presentation parameters. There should also be control aspects for parametrizing layer behavior, and user processes should, if possible, have protocol-independent access.

Ultimately, any high technology-based solution, from its human window to its central resources, is designed for the benefit of end users. Therefore, responsiveness, user-friendliness, and consistency should be guidelines for designing and implementing open systems.

It is also important to be able to ensure continuous system operation even if one component fails. Reliability and security should be given high priority in system design. Other subjects that should be addressed are those of protecting the integrity of the database and periodically pruning the database so that it holds only information pertinent to traders.

To sustain analytical queries, an approach should include the use of possibility theory. As previously discussed, a possibilistic user's query is interpreted as a set of assertions about desired objects. It then becomes the supercomputer's task to determine whether the query assertions are true. If they are, the document is retrieved and presented to the user in real time.

Assertions can deal with many aspects of a document, including type, contents, structure, and layout. In most cases, the contents of a document alone are not sufficient to determine the truth of query assertions.

To further support ad hoc situations facing a securities dealer, the system must make use of a knowledge bank of facts and rules, some of which may be uncertain. Uncertainty may also occur in the description of documents and queries.

Therefore, the supercomputer-supported retrieval process should be regarded as a type of plausible inference, the plausibility being quantified by some form of possibilistic measure.

5. Supercomputers and Intelligent Databases at Dow Jones

Dow Jones maintains a business wire service and other information retrieval products, all of which it keeps connected to its public databases. Since the firm began public database operations, data from hundreds of sources have been fed daily into company mainframes. For many years, the accompanying text search software has been STAIRS (from IBM). This inverted lists approach, which is based on Boolean concepts, became rather cumbersome in shaping queries.[5]

As Dow Jones' databases have become richer and its clients' queries more polyvalent, the process of searching for and retrieving data has become increasingly complex, particularly in the area of wire service offerings. The company's information scientists began to see the approach being used as inefficient for themselves, the corporation, and its clients.

After searching for an optimal solution to its text and data retrieval problems, Dow Jones installed two Connection Machines. This architecture offered a solution that was radically different from what the company was accustomed to; it also had some unknown variables. Nevertheless, Dow Jones took a chance on it.

A senior Dow Jones executive at the time of the decision said, "We decided that there was nothing in the current architecture that would give us an answer. . . . Nothing that IBM had could come close to this [in performance]. IBM told us that we were heading in the wrong direction by going with a radical architecture and a new company. That is when we knew we were doing the right thing. We want to be on the leading edge and are willing to take risks."[6]

Dow Jones' supercomputer application, called DowQuest, is now up and running. It permits Dow Jones' clients to gather quickly current information on market-related topics from a wide variety of business publications.[7]

DowQuest works in two phases. First, the user enters words that describe the subject he or she is interested in. In response, DowQuest displays a starter list of articles for the user's review. These cover different aspects of the subject, and while not all articles will be relevant, he or she can use those articles that are relevant to improve the search or quest.

Second, the user tells DowQuest which articles or paragraphs are good examples of the subject in question. Based on these examples, DowQuest will retrieve a new list of articles that should match the user's subject more closely. To fine-tune the quest, the user may repeat this process.[8]

Not only does DowQuest produce interesting and unexpected information that would never turn up by using classical database retrieval procedures, but it also allows users to state their interests in conversational English. There are no complicated commands to memorize or search techniques to learn.

The more descriptive words a user enters, of course, the better the chance that he or she will find close examples of the topic in the first search. But if the user has no specific question in mind, or does not know exactly how to phrase a query, DowQuest provides for database search based on concepts and general topics.

Thus, this solution is a powerful research tool because it allows a user to look at a subject from different perspectives, including some he or she may not have previously considered. (The contents of this list are ranked according to how closely they match the words the user entered.) This flexibility is designed for users who are not sure what they want, what is available, or how to search.

By using a process called relevance feedback, DowQuest can perform a second, third, fourth, or fifth search using all the words in up to three selected articles as search words. Thus, the content the first relevant article to be located becomes an excellent source of synonyms and keywords, which are then picked up by the computer in order to look for more articles of a similar nature.

The concept of relevance feedback is so simple that no special training or instructions are necessary to perform searches. The system prompts its user to enter as many relevant words as possible, to employ full names but avoid numbers, and to take advantage of the relevance-feedback facility by searching articles and paragraphs.

6. Opportunities and Risks in Using Supercomputers

When used for opportunity-and-risk applications, super-computers have three main advantages over classical main-frames—raw speed, a relevance-feedback function, and the ability to weight terms.

Dow Jones' Connection Machine has ultrafast responses. The user types in "Search" and presses a key, and the answer appears on the screen with subsecond speed. Each transaction (search) is handled in about seventy-four milliseconds.

As explained, relevance feedback finds documents that a Boolean or keyword search would miss. (It has been known for some time that a conceptual search with interactive feed-back is a powerful tool; but, prior to the CM-2, this technique was not used because it is so computationally intensive.)

The disadvantage of a Boolean search is that it uses word connectors like AND, OR, and NOT. If during a classical query the computer misses a term or end, then it misses the article. By employing a concept-based search using relevance feedback, the machine still finds the article because the terms that might have been missed will almost certainly be included as synonyms in one of the articles.

For example, the user might on the first pass choose two or three articles as relevant, then ask the computer to search again. The second search employs those articles, which might have one thousand searchable words in them, as a thesaurus.

The parallel computer software ranks those words according to weight, taking those that are the rarest and giving them the most weight. Then the computer truncates that list of one thousand words to the top one hundred.

Dow Jones and Thinking Machines researchers have determined that the results of this search differ insignificantly from those obtained by using the top two hundred or four hundred search words. Also, using the top one hundred is a faster process, which makes this solution ideal for text search and retrieval.

Among improvements planned to the current solution is a graphical interface to display search results. If a user searches for a particular corporate merger, the articles will show up as a cluster of points representing that merger. Points mapping mergers by other companies will be in nearby areas; farther out on the graph will be points representing other types of buy-outs and takeovers.

Two Connection Machines have been installed by Dow Jones, with the second designated as a research engine to develop and test new products. It also acts as a hot backup for the first; if there is a failure in the first machine, the second can take over in ten to fifteen seconds.

The software of the Connection Machine provides for elaborate safeguards to save transactions, so that the backup engine can pick up without losing anyone's search. Hot backups have been tried for nearly twenty years with mainframes, but it takes a new type of hardware and software to make them effective.

What makes DowQuest a powerful tool for finding information is that its multiple processors allow users to quickly focus on the object of their search then zoom in on the details. This will become the standard for database access in years to come.

In other words, securities houses and investment banks must realize that the most sophisticated current applications simply cannot be done on mainframes (see Figure 13–4); nor is it possible to obtain acceptable response times from networked workstations without having a supercomputer on the network. Companies should thus weigh the advantages of having this access against some of the changes that they will have to make to accommodate it.

For example, until commodity software becomes available on supercomputers and improvements in compiler technology languages are developed, customers will have to restructure applications.

At Dow Jones, software had to be rewritten in order to move the job from an IBM environment to the VAX/Connection Machine configuration, as well as to make necessary improvements (e.g., relevance feedback) to the process.

Dow Jones deemed the cost of rewriting software and the risk of acquiring a nontraditional machine from a new company worth the gamble, as the result enabled it to improve dramatically the efficiency of a crucial income-making service. "We are unique in our computing requirements and we have always dealt with small companies," said a cognizant Dow Jones executive. "We have to consider the risk, but we were comfortable with its level."

Companies must also train their personnel to think in parallel rather than in terms of the nearly obsolete images of classical data processing. Computer people trained to work on serial processors are not capable of utilizing the full potential of parallel-processing.

Figure 13–4   A Solution for Mortgage-Backed Finance Computations

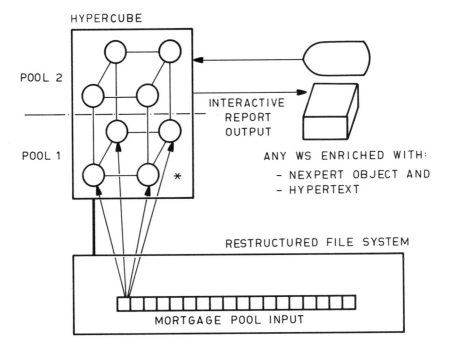

HYPERCUBE

POOL 2

POOL 1

INTERACTIVE
REPORT
OUTPUT

ANY WS ENRICHED WITH:
- NEXPERT OBJECT AND
- HYPERTEXT

RESTRUCTURED FILE SYSTEM

MORTGAGE POOL INPUT

* EACH OF THE FOUR NODES IS DEDICATED TO ONE
KEY FACTOR OR TIME INTERVAL.

Yet, large-computer users have made massive investments in sequential code, and the staff needed to write it, rather than accepting the inevitability of converting to parallel processing; they have made unsatisfactory compromises. For example, early attempts at resolving the software problem centered around providing concurrent extensions to existing languages. This placed the burden of parallelization of the software on programmers, who had to control the execution of code on several processors at once.

Supercomputer vendors could have a role to play, by developing parallel-programming software that is easily accessible as well as standardized. Today, vendors tend to market software that is specific to one machine's architecture. Portability between different parallel computer architectures is almost nonexistent.

In conclusion, what we have learned from nearly 40 years of computer and communications experience in banking can be phrased in these terms:

1. The able application of information systems is a matter of culture—not of machines.

2. We get little from our investment unless we have clear goals and effectively use technology to reach them.

3. Without the proper know-how, results will be minimal—but know-how should be applied to the job, it should not be left as a theory.

This places emphasis on the need for supercomputer literacy, but it also emphasizes the importance of getting out of old structures which limit our ability to obtain results and cost too much for the service they provide.

As business and industry has entered the last decade of these hundred years—decisions taken at the present time will propel our organization into the 21st century. For any practical purpose, the battle of the 21st century has started—and the domain of this battle is high technology.

Endnotes

1. See also D.N. Chorafas and H. Steinmann, *Supercomputers* (New York: McGraw-Hill, 1990).

2. Nevertheless, the idea of neural automata originated from Neumann; therefore, it is not quite appropriate to speak of a non-von Neumann machine.

3. Another measure of machine power, particularly for scientific applications, is billions of floating-point operations per second (GFLOPS). MIPS, GIPS, MFLOPS, and GFLOPS are theoretical peak execution speeds. Typical programs achieve these speeds for only a fraction of a second, if ever.

4. There is no exact relation between GIPS and GFLOPS; the two are units of measurement more or less applicable in different environments.

5. See the discussion of the inefficiency of inverted lists in Chapter 10.

6. *Datamation*, 1 May 1988.

7. Information in the database comes from recent issues of *The Wall Street Journal, Barron's, Fortune, Forbes, Business Week, Money, The Washington Post,* and other national and regional publications. There are selected articles from more than 140 city, state, regional, and national journals; as well as articles from specialized publications such as *Financial World, American Demographics,* and trade publications.

8. Each processor on the fine-grain Connection Machine (32K of them in each unit) is responsible for searching only

eight or nine articles, which is why DowQuest responds so
quickly.

Index